# BEARING WITNESS

Essays on Anglo-Irish Literature

AUGUSTINE MARTIN was Professor of Anglo-Irish Literature and Drama at University College Dublin until his death in October 1995. Born in Ballinamore, Co. Leitrim, in 1935, he was educated at Cistercian College, Roscrea, and University College Dublin. His books include a critical study of James Stephens, a biography of W.B. Yeats and a history of Anglo-Irish Literature. At the time of his death he was engaged on the biography of Patrick Kavanagh and was general editor of the collected works of James Clarence Mangan. A well-known broadcaster, he devised and presented programmes for Telefís Scoile (Schools Television) and edited and contributed to several series of Thomas Davis Lectures for Radio Éireann. He was a member of the Senate, representing the National University of Ireland; a member of the Governing Body of UCD from 1969; Chairman of the Board of the Abbey Theatre, Dublin; Director of the Yeats International Summer School (Sligo); and Founder and Director of the Baileys James Joyce Annual Summer School (UCD).

ANTHONY ROCHE was born in Dublin in 1951 and is a lecturer in Anglo-Irish Literature and Drama at University College Dublin. He was educated at St Conleth's College, Trinity College, Dublin, and the University of California at Santa Barbara. He is the author of *Contemporary Irish Drama: From Beckett to McGuinness* (Gill & Macmillan, 1994) and has written and broadcast extensively. He has been Chair of the Irish Writers' Union, Associate Director of the Yeats International Summer School, and is on the Executive Board of the *Irish University Review*.

# BEARING WITNESS

## Essays on Anglo-Irish Literature

AUGUSTINE MARTIN

*edited by* Anthony Roche

University College Dublin Press

*Preas Choláiste Ollscoile Bhaile Átha Cliath*

First published 1996 by University College Dublin Press,
Newman House, St Stephen's Green, Dublin 2, Ireland

ISBN  1 900621  01 0 (hardback)
1 900621 02 9 (paperback)

Cataloguing in Publication data available from the British Library

Typeset in Ireland by Seton Music Graphics, Bantry
Printed in Ireland by Colour Books, Dublin

# Contents

# *Acknowledgments*

The editor wishes to thank the following for their advice, assistance and encouragement: Claire and Aengus Martin; Katy Hayes; Richard Pine; Barbara Mennell and UCD Press

The editor and publisher wish to thank the following for permission to use copyright material. Every effort has been made to trace all the copyright holders, but if any have been inadvertently overlooked, the publisher will rectify the omission in any subsequent reprint.

*Studies* for 'Apocalyptic Structure in Yeats's *Secret Rose*' (Spring 1975); 'Inherited Dissent: The Dilemma of the Irish Writer' (Spring 1965); 'A Skeleton Key to the Stories of Mary Lavin' (Winter 1963); 'The Rediscovery of Austin Clarke' (Winter 1965) and the review of Seamus Heaney, *Death of a Naturalist* (Winter 1966)

Colin Smythe Ltd for 'Hound Voices Were They All' from *Yeats, Sligo and Ireland*, edited by A. Norman Jeffares, 1980; 'Christy Mahon and the Apotheosis of Loneliness' from *Sunshine and the Moon's Delight: A Centenary Tribute to John Millington Synge 1871–1909*, edited by S.B. Bushrui, 1972; 'Sin and Secrecy in Joyce's Fiction' from *James Joyce: An International Perspective*, edited by S.B. Bushrui and Bernard Benstock, 1982; 'Novelist and City: The Technical Challenge' from *The Irish Writer and the City*, edited by Maurice Harmon, 1984.

Alpha Academic for 'Priest and Artist in Joyce's Fiction' from *Anglo-Irish Studies*, edited by P.J. Drudy, Vol. II, 1976.

Allen Figgis for 'Anglo-Irish Literature: The Protestant Legacy' from *Irish Anglicanism*, edited by Michael Hurley, 1970.

Gill & Macmillan for 'James Stephens's, *The Crock of Gold*' from Augustine Martin, *James Stephens: A Critical Study*, 1977.

The Mercier Press for 'Fable and Fantasy' from *The Genius of Irish Prose*, edited by Augustine Martin, 1985.

*Irish University Review* for 'That Country Childhood: Extracts from a Biography of Patrick Kavanagh', Vol. 22, No. 1, Spring/Summer 1992; 'Quest and Vision: Eavan Boland's *The Journey*', Vol. 23, No. 1, Spring/Summer 1993.

Bloodaxe Books Ltd. for 'Technique and Territory in Brendan Kennelly's Early Work' from *Dark Fathers into Light: Brendan Kennelly*, edited by Richard Pine, 1994.

*The Irish Times* for the review of Francis Stuart, *The Pillar of Cloud* and *Redemption*.

*Irish Literary Supplement* for 'Yeats Remembered', Spring 1989, and for reviews of Edna O'Brien, *Time and Tide*, John Montague, *The Dead Kingdom*, Aidan Matthews, *Lipstick on the Host*.

# Introduction

Thomas Augustine Martin (1935–1995), known to one and all as Gus Martin, committed the prodigious energies of a lifetime to the development of Anglo-Irish Literature. That same enthusiasm found its expression in a staggering diversity of platforms. As Professor of Anglo-Irish Literature' and Drama at University College Dublin from 1979 until his untimely death in October 1995, Gus Martin lectured to all three undergraduate years on his favourite Anglo-Irish writers: Jonathan Swift, Thomas Moore, Samuel Ferguson, James Clarence Mangan, George Moore, W.B. Yeats, James Joyce, James Stephens, Patrick Kavanagh, Edna O'Brien and many others.

Through thirty years of UCD lecturing, Gus Martin would have come into contact with thousands of undergraduate students, young, mostly Irish and bewildered by their first experience of university life. The reassurance he offered was a combination of natural authority and unpretentious ease, a friendly, avuncular presence. His lectures challenged his listeners to trust in their own instincts (rather than retreating behind a protective screen of secondary sources), urging them not to grow complacent by showing them that there were further reaches of a text to be sounded. A lecture by Gus Martin on Joyce's 'The Dead' in 1969 was my first encounter with Joyce and proved exhilarating; as a direct result, I spent that summer reading *Ulysses*. I know this experience was shared by many undergraduates before and since.

1969 also saw the appearance of the Leaving Certificate poetry textbook, *Soundings* edited by Augustine Martin, which would provide for an even greater number of young Irish people their first (and it might be only) encounter with poetry. The anthology was the fruit of Martin's endeavours, as a schoolteacher at his *alma mater* Cistercian College Roscrea and through his co-founding of the Association of Teachers of English, to modernize the Leaving Certificate curriculum and, in particular, to find room for Anglo-Irish poets as well as the standard English canon. Some were drawn to the austerities of Clarke and Kinsella; but the lion's share of the selection and of the students' affections was won by Yeats and Kavanagh. The shift in perception of Kavanagh, in particular, from someone to avoid on the streets of Dublin to a gifted poet illuminated by a sense of wonder, owes much to Martin's sensitive questioning of the tone and themes of his poems.

If many Irish people first encountered Gus Martin while secondary school students reading *Soundings* or as university students attending one of his packed lectures, he also garnered an international audience during his sixteen years as Professor of Anglo-Irish Literature and Drama. There was the development of the MA in the subject and the wide number of international students it attracted. Professor Martin was always concerned that a certain balance be struck in the makeup of the group, so that an American coming in would be mixing with Irish students as well as fellow Americans, so that the Irish students in turn would be exposed to a truly international group. There were also the PhDs he directed. He was one of the best close readers in the academy, encouraging the enterprise while remaining alert to the slipshod phrase or scholarly flaw. Gus Martin also lectured widely in other countries throughout his career, anxious to visit fresh fields and pastures new rather than just treading the well-worn academic circuit. One of his last visits was to Korea, a country he had never previously visited; and David Norris of Trinity College, Dublin, recalls how he and Gus Martin were virtually the only Irish academics to take up an invitation to lecture at Beirut in 1982. Norris attests that Martin's ecumenism was no less evident on the home front, his love of University College Dublin no barrier to drawing on the expertise of a Trinity College lecturer in organizing various Dublin-centred Joycean events.

But one did not have to be in a university to meet Gus Martin. With his love of Latin phrases, he would have known better than most that the root of 'education' lay in '*educare*—to lead (out) from'; and as an educator to the bone, he reached out through the various media to address a wider audience, those who resembled Leopold Bloom (more than Stephen Dedalus) as members of the 'university of life'. He was a regular and valued reviewer for all three daily Irish national newspapers and the Sundays, assessing novels and poetry from home and abroad, but demonstrating also a flair for reviewing biographies. When the new national television station opened, Martin was poised by virtue of personal and cultural circumstances to contribute to the burgeoning national confidence it represented, through the many programmes he devised and presented for Telefís Scoile (Schools Television) and special programmes on individual writers. Throughout his career, Martin was a lucid and eloquent contributor to RTÉ radio also, organizing and contributing to more than one Thomas Davis Lecture series on Irish writing and a frequent guest on arts and books programmes. When Mary Lavin died in March 1996, the archive broadcasts testified to how central he had been in advancing her cause over the years. RTÉ producer Michael Littleton spoke to me of how diminished the celebrations of Austin Clarke's centenary in 1996 would be without Augustine Martin's contribution, his own inestimable witness.

There remains more to be said, even in this Introduction, of the various media and platforms from which he spoke to a wider world. There were the Summer Schools, the Yeats in Sligo, to which he was such a central, mobilizing and inspirational force as lecturer, Associate Director and Director, and the James Joyce Summer School, which he founded in 1988 and which was run annually in association with UCD and Bailey's Irish Cream, drawing together a spectrum of interests from the most advanced students and experts to the interested lay person. He also ran a series of Bailey's Lectures with a range of distinguished novelists as lecturers—including Umberto Eco, Marilyn French, Anthony Burgess, Edna O'Brien, David Lodge, William Kennedy and many others—held (to honour Joyce) in the Physics Theatre in the old Earlsfort Terrace Dublin location of UCD. These lectures were, as he used to say, 'for the town and not for the gown'. In all of these endeavours he drew on and was supported by his wife Claire and their children Breffni, Gráinne, Niamh and Aengus; their home a gathering place.

I have chosen to approach this edited collection of Gus Martin's writings by showing the relevant contexts from which these writings emerged and to which they in turn contributed. His gifts as a passionate communicator, honed by his lecturing in UCD and at the various Summer Schools over the years, meant that he illuminated every subject about which he wrote. In particular, he sought to keep the literary object at the centre of his critical activity, paying close attention to individual lines and passages while elucidating in graphic strokes the overall shape, structure and purpose of the work. His criticism reveals his erudition, whether discussing the metrical innovations of Austin Clarke or invoking the various novelistic traditions with which Joyce's *Ulysses* might stand comparison. But this information was never intended to stand between the reader and the text. His reading more often expressed itself in the weight of experience one sensed behind and between the lines, matching apt quotation and illuminating commentary in the act of literary judgement. Throughout his writings Gus Martin displayed a respect for the reader's intelligence and the same care and love for the English language that he valued in his subjects. As a result, he was regularly sought out as a contributor to learned journals and books; their editors knew that they would receive a scholarly, authoritative essay which would also prove stylish, witty, generous and readable.

In addition to his contributions to Irish education, there seem to me to be three stages in Gus Martin's writing career. The first was in the early to mid-sixties when the Roscrea schoolteacher contributed a series of brilliant essays of literary criticism (four of them reprinted in this collection) to the Jesuit journal, *Studies*. In reading these issues of the 1960s one can sense the greater intellectual freedom inaugurated by the reforms of Vatican Two and the greater wave of economic buoyancy of the Lemass era, as a range of young Irish academics made their contributions in the various disciplines (economics, philosophy, catechetics, literature). Striking amongst the literary articles in *Studies* is the innovative, confident attention to Anglo-Irish literature repeatedly displayed by the young Gus Martin, the sense of reclaiming Yeats and Joyce from non-native critics and of contributing directly to the development of contemporary Irish writing.

The second phase of Gus Martin's critical career is represented by the books he published around the time of his professorial appointment. His full-length and original study of the writings of James Stephens was published by Gill and Macmillan in 1977, dealing not just with the acclaimed prose works, *The Charwoman's Daughter* and *The Crock of Gold* but with Stephens's undervalued achievement as a poet (the subject of his UCD MA). In 1980, he produced a brief, incisive and authoritative survey of the field of Anglo-Irish Literature for a series of publications from the Department of Foreign Affairs. And in 1983 he supplied a major need for an interim biography of W.B. Yeats in his contribution to Gill's Irish Lives. The Yeats which emerged from his book was the poet not as arrogantly isolated figure but as someone profoundly connected to family, friends and colleagues; it culminated in what Thomas Kilroy's review in *The Irish Times* described as 'a splendid essay on the poet's "close companions", his great capacity for friendship and for converting the experience into poetry.' This period, and on through the 1980s, was also marked by a series of contributions to the 'Irish Literary Studies' series produced by Colin Smythe, either the printing of papers originally delivered at conferences or original articles commissioned for publication (three of these are included in the present volume).

The last decade of Gus Martin's life saw him engaged on a number of ambitious, long-term projects. Having secured the archive of the poet Patrick Kavanagh for Ireland and UCD, he was writing the biography of the poet; a twenty-page extract, covering Kavanagh's education and teenage years in Inishkeen, is included here to give some sense of what might have been. He was also General Editor of the Collected Writings of James Clarence Mangan and had worked hard to complete his own contribution on the prose; the project will be seen through under the General Editorship of Peter van de Kamp. It was during this involvement with longer-term projects that Martin, it seemed to me, found a renewed energy and interest in contributing essays to scholarly journals and books. Where he had been the rising star in the *Studies* era, in the 1990s he was sought out as contributor by a number of younger scholars and writers in the field—including Richard Pine, Theo Dorgan, myself—who wished to have his acumen and style represented in their volume. If he was now the mature expert showing these young ones how it was done, he also very much respected the distinct roles of contributor and editor, encouraging dialogue and revision of his piece to make sure it was as good as it could be. These contributions to volumes on Eavan Boland and Brendan Kennelly were singled out for praise when they appeared. He also relished the opportunity to review, taking on (in every sense) the latest theory-driven monographs on Yeats and Joyce in the scholarly journals while honouring a new generation of Irish writers (Dermot Bolger, Aidan Carl Mathews, Micheal O Siadhail among them) in the reviews he continued to contribute to Irish newspapers.

As in all of the areas to which he contributed, Gus Martin's writing output was prodigious. This collection aims to provide a representative and generous selection of his articles together with a brief sampling of his many reviews. In the second half of this introduction I will discuss the rationale for the selection and arrangement of the essays. *Bearing Witness* is divided into five sections. The first highlights Yeats and Joyce, the two great figures of the field Professor Martin did so much to develop and with whose works he had a lifetime's involvement. The second contains two major essays with a wide discursive and historical sweep: 'Inherited Dissent', his ground-breaking challenge of the 1960s for contemporary Irish writers to break with prevailing stereotypes; and 'The Protestant Legacy', which examines the contribution made by writers from both the nineteenth and twentieth centuries. The remaining sections centre on Irish fiction after Joyce and Irish poetry after Yeats, with a section of reviews designed to fill out the picture of both. The entire selection is undertaken in the belief that these humane, engaged essays by Augustine Martin continue to stand as a passionate encounter with the literary matter of Ireland.

The book begins by celebrating the achievement of Yeats and Joyce in six essays which reveal Martin's intimate, ongoing concern with certain key elements in their work: the apocalyptic violence in Yeats and the Catholicism that remained crucial to Joyce's habits of thought and composition. 'Apocalyptic Structure in Yeats's *Secret Rose*' is one of several essays in which he considered the apocalyptic strain evident not just in such key later works as 'The Second Coming' but throughout Yeats's career. In 'The Yeatsean Apocalypse', Gus Martin gives his own succinct definition of the term in its various applications:

In the Christian Dispensation the word 'apocalypse' denotes the revelation granted to John the Evangelist on the Isle of Patmos, foretelling the end of the world and the signs and wonders accompanying it. That last book of the New Testament which Catholics call The Apocalypse of St John is usually referred to as the Book of Revelations in the Protestant tradition. The term 'apocalypse' has otherwise largely been used to mean any kind of revelation involving the end of the world, or at least the end to some decisive phase in the world's history marked by signs and portents. [1]

Martin's imagination was drawn to those larger historic movements in Yeats's emerging schema by which a momentous shift occurred from one predominant mode of being to its opposite, a period of violent and terrifying irruption of the supernatural into the world of human affairs. The seeds of those prophetic intimations are sown in what were for him among the greatest achievements of Yeats's career, the critically neglected prose stories of the 1890s. His careful analysis makes a claim for Yeats as a writer of fiction by describing *The Secret Rose* in terms which could apply equally well to Joyce's *Dubliners*: 'a fictional structure repeating itself—with significant variations—in the individual stories' in which a 'moment of revelation marks the climax of the action'.[2] Criticism subsequent to this 1975 essay has done much to elucidate the extent to which Joyce's short stories are indebted to Yeats's prose fiction of the 1890s;[3] but Martin's intuitions brought him there early, guided by the remark he quotes from Joyce's *Stephen Hero*: 'He [Stephen Dedalus] repeated often the story of "The Tables of the Law" and the story of "The Adoration of the Magi".' Martin described to Seamus Hosey in a radio interview how he found common ground between Yeats and Joyce:

What people often do not realize is the extraordinary correspondence between these two writers, because they worked in the same town, grew up in the same culture and, in a sense, they divided it between them. There is a hell of a lot more of Yeats in Joyce and Joyce in Yeats than appears to the naked eye. One feeds off the other in the reading of them.[4]

The second Yeats essay 'Hound Voices Were They All' brings the apocalptic theme from the 'reverent expectation' of the 1890s stories through the middle phase where 'these prophecies were coming true before his eyes . . . in the Easter Rising, the Russian Revolution, the Black and Tan War and the later Civil War in Ireland' to the 'more excited and desperate' and, to many Yeats critics, the most disturbing late phase of his career.

Certainly, Martin's conclusion about the poem 'Hound Voice', that it instances a rare 'exultant participation' in the violence it contemplates, is disturbing. The third Yeats piece was originally written in 1989 to celebrate the fiftieth anniversary of the poet's death. It warns against our taking any single one of Yeats's poems, 'Hound Voice' included, to represent a definitive stance and statement on Yeats's part; not only were his views continuing to develop but they were doing so in a dialectical fashion. Martin's article is a considered and mature response to the charge of Yeats's fascism, taking its final stand on the range and quality of the poet's contribution to an emergent Ireland. As well as having all the poems by heart, Martin emulated Yeats in contributing to the moulding of a country's institutions: both served terms as Senators; in the 1980s he was a member of the Board and Chairman of the theatre Yeats had founded. And he served as a long-standing member of the Governing Body of UCD.

If Yeats provided the model for multi-levelled participation in building a politically and imaginatively independent Ireland, Joyce was for him quintessentially the Dubliner, the finest flower of the 'rich humus' (Martin's own phrase) of Ireland's capital city. Where non-Irish critics had downplayed Joyce's lived relationship with the city he grew up in, Gus Martin celebrated it, reserving the greatest measure of his affection for the short stories of *Dubliners*. In viewing how the once-neglected early Joyce was now attracting theory, he was frequently 'tempted to exclaim as Joyce did: "O my poor fledglings, poor Corley, poor Ignatius Gallagher!"'[5] He read *A Portrait of the Artist as a Young Man* as a 'radical *Bildungsroman* [which] presented the traumata of a wilful, sensitive Catholic boy'[6]. All three essays display Martin's unparalleled ability to draw on his experience as an Irish Catholic in reading Joyce. In *Ulysses* his sympathies and interests are evenly divided between the scholarly Stephen Dedalus, with whom he shares an interest in occult writers, and Leopold Bloom, as husband and father (the experiences that Joyce believed equipped Bloom to be the hero of *Ulysses)* and *l'homme moyen sensuel,* savouring the day with gustatory relish.

The essay on Synge's *The Playboy of the Western World* finds its place in this first section, as an assessment of another major figure in the Irish Literary Revival, and as a rare but successful venture into drama criticism. Though most of Martin's writing was on poetry and prose, this did not prevent him from being an inveterate playgoer, always keen to compare notes about the latest play at the Abbey or the Peacock, the Gaiety or the Gate. He counted as a personal highpoint making the pilgrimage to New York to attend the opening night of Brian Friel's *Dancing at Lughnasa* on Broadway. That visit was also the climax of his distinguished period as Chairman of the Board of the Abbey Theatre. With Synge's *Playboy,* he had presumably seen many productions over the years; but 'The Apotheosis of Loneliness' is fresh and original in its reading. It singles out Christy's loneliness as the emotional and dramatic core of the play, and draws a crucial distinction between the settled men, the householders, and the poetry people, that can be applied to all of Synge's plays. The playwright Marina Carr, a student of Martin's at both BA and MA level, referred to his interpretation in her programme note for the Abbey's 1995 production of *The Playboy*; and if her 1996 play *Portia Coughlan* bears traces of Synge, she has already acknowledged her debt to her academic mentor in that graceful reference.

Probably no single piece by Gus Martin has had the seismic impact of his 20-page essay which kicked off the Spring 1965 *Studies*. 'Inherited Dissent: The Dilemma of the Irish Writer' called for a revolution in attitude by contemporary Irish writers which he saw as deriving in knee-jerk fashion from the inherited, unexamined influence of Yeats and Joyce. According to this prescription, Ireland was still the old sow that ate its farrow, drove her writers into exile, etc., etc. Martin's essay is concerned to contrast the prevailing stereotype of a stultifying, backward country with the real social conditions of Ireland in the 1960s, noting the relaxation of censorship, improvements in education, working conditions, diminished anti-intellectualism, etc. He calls on younger writers to engage, whether in criticism or celebration, with a socially dynamic and credible Ireland and to push themselves beyond 'literary palesmanship' into (in critical terms) wholly neglected areas of the country. The critic John Wilson Foster cites 'Inherited Dissent' in his Introduction to 'Irish Fiction 1965–1990' in Volume Three of *The Field Day Anthology of Irish Writing* and points out:

Martin's accusation had a measure of justification and it was not shoneenism that stimulated him to contrast the contemporaneity in 1965 of British writers like Angus Wilson, Graham Greene, C.P. Snow, John Wain, Kingsley Amis and Muriel Spark with the inward look of their Irish peers. (Frank O'Connor had already drawn the contrast, citing C.P. Snow as an example.) The repetitive subjectivity of Irish fiction needed in the 1960s to be qualified or balanced by a larger social canvas, a more normative viewpoint, a greater objectivity.[7]

This essay, which remains groundbreaking and relevant, is paired here with another major discursive piece, a Catholic appreciation of the Protestant background of many of the Literary Revival's leading writers. The main thrust of 'Anglo-Irish Literature: The Protestant Legacy' is to contrast the ease with which writers like Yeats, Synge and Elizabeth Bowen shed their Protestantism, with the traumas that continued to afflict Catholic writers like Joyce and Austin Clarke.

But the earlier noting of Yeats's preoccupation with apocalypse suggests the persistence of certain religious perturbations into the imaginative realm and may lie behind the concern with fantasy and fable that certain writers of the Revival like James Stephens enjoy. As Vivian Mercier noted in praising Martin's book on James Stephens in a *Times Literary Supplement* review, 'Augustine Martin has traced . . . the fluctuating influence of theosophy upon Stephens's poetry with accuracy and skill, showing that the poet's total acceptance of its teachings from about 1927 "presents Stephens with an almost insoluble problem: the supreme object of his poetry is no longer amenable to language. His deity has no attributes and is therefore inexpressible."' Mercier concludes his review: 'Augustine Martin deserves our thanks for his sympathetic yet judicial assessment of an artist who has long eluded or defied the critics.'[8]

I have included a chapter from this study on Stephens's best known and loved work, *The Crock of Gold,* where the apocalyptic note shared with Yeats now mutates into a comic vein anticipating Flann O'Brien. 'Fable and Fantasy' extends this line of descent to Samuel Beckett's *Murphy* and Mervyn Wall's Fursey books. Martin speculates that the demise of fantasy in Irish writing may have to do with the retreat of religion itself. Certainly, the emergence of the Irish short story in the 1930s may be seen to sponsor a certain kind of social realism, in its post-romantic disillusionment. Gus Martin does not demur from the view which sees Sean O'Faolain, Frank O'Connor and Liam O'Flaherty as masters of the short story, the form on which he had written his PhD. But he wishes to expand the canon to include Mary Lavin and, in noting that 'no body of criticism has grown up around her writings', may be shrewdly underscoring the extent to which O'Faolain and O'Connor produced criticism on the short story which justified their own practices. He takes issue with Frank O'Connor's churlish treatment of Lavin ('a brief and somewhat rambling commentary on three or four of her stories'), subsequently reproduced as the final chapter of O'Connor's *The Lonely Voice,*[9] and blazes a critical trail by relating Mary Lavin's short stories to a European rather than an Irish tradition and by identifying her chosen fictional ground: 'against the background and amid the milieu of Irish middle-class existence—the small town with its shopkeepers, priests and farmers from the surrounding countryside.' No inherited dissent here.

The next section features a number of Gus Martin's reviews to give the flavour and personality of that aspect of his writing, the verve he brought to balancing sympathetic reading with critical assessment in a brief space. And these reviews make possible the inclusion of a wider range of writers: the reassessment of a neglected figure like Francis Stuart, with Martin offering widely divergent responses to two of Stuart's novels where most readers tend to line up on one side or the other; the ongoing critical championing of Edna O'Brien in his review of 1992's *Time and Tide* where a perhaps overgenerous assessment of this novel is preceded by a brilliant formulation of the critical double bind by which O'Brien's novels are unjustly dismissed; and a dizzy Joycean engagement with the ludic fictions of Aidan Carl Mathews, which sees through to the compassion at their core.

The review section also inaugurates this volume's final engagement— with Irish poetry after Yeats. It is fascinating to read with hindsight Martin's review of Seamus Heaney's first volume, *Death of a Naturalist*, from 1966. How right he got it, down to quoting the last three lines from 'Digging' as he reflects how for Heaney 'poetry is a task like farming, a task that must be faced with the puritan virtues of courage, industry and skill. The business of living and making is, for Seamus Heaney, rather a craft than an art.' These lines apply with prophetic force to much that Heaney has written since. There's a poignancy in the fact that Gus Martin was taken ill and admitted to hospital on 5 October, 1995, the same day that Seamus Heaney was awarded the Nobel Prize for Literature; he was interviewed over the phone by RTÉ just before going in and spoke of the delight he felt, both personally and in terms of the subject he professed, in the award going to Heaney. The other poetry review is of a volume by John Montague, one of his three important sequences, 1984's *The Dead Kingdom*. In that same interview with Seamus Hosey, Martin revealed:

John Montague is the Irish poet I think I read most often, next to Patrick Kavanagh, because of his extraordinary accessibility. He manages the heart's affections with great honesty and is supremely good on sexual relations and marriage.[10]

The next two essays honour his joint fidelity to Austin Clarke and Patrick Kavanagh, those poets who came after and had to struggle with the shadow of Yeats. His loyalties were in turn engaged by their poetry, Kavanagh with his intimate experience of the reality of Irish rural life, Clarke with his vision of the Celtic Romanesque. Gus Martin was born and raised in Ballinamore, Co. Leitrim, and so shared a similar background with Kavanagh, an understanding evident in his sympathetic discussion of the poet's education and youth in a small rural town. In Martin's 1965 essay 'The Rediscovery of Austin Clarke', the reader can sense the critic's excitement at that rediscovery, of staking out the claims and the territory for an obscure but demanding *oeuvre*. The critical pioneer he invokes is Donald Davie, who was teaching at Trinity College in the 1950s. In his 1982 volume of recollections, *These the Companions*, Davie writes of a later critical encounter with Gus Martin:

In 1969, I published in *The Irish Times* a poem called 'Ireland of the Bombers', in which I had shaken the dust of Ireland from my feet because of IRA atrocities against the innocent ('Blackbird of Derrycairn/ Sing no more for me . . .'). . . .

Some years later (it must have been 1975), when Augustine Martin, a Senator of the Republic, wrote asking me to resume my connections with the Yeats Summer School, he took note of my poem: 'Despite what you have written . . .' Is there another country in the English-speaking world where the publication of a poem in a periodical is taken so seriously, taken such note of . . .? If not, small wonder that we poets and enthusiasts for poetry nurse for this country, Ireland, a love not at odds with our several patriotisms, but enriching those and complicating them, sometimes painfully.[11]

As Mrs Georgina Wynne of the Yeats Summer School in Sligo informed me when we spoke at Christmas 1995 about Gus Martin, Donald Davie, another friend, had died that same winter.

Davie had noted that Martin termed Austin Clarke 'a deeply religious man'.[12] The same was true for Kavanagh. Both were for him deeply religious poets whose struggles with language and subject matter were in the end a testing of the spirit. *Bearing Witness* concludes with two of the last and best essays Gus Martin ever wrote, on the poetry of Brendan Kennelly and Eavan Boland. These essays draw on a lifelong acquaintance with their work (which he had frequently reviewed) and show how, in their very different but comparable journeys, both poets had to learn through experiment and fortitude to abandon the poem they could all too readily write (or that could write them) and go a painful stylistic and personal journey to write the poetry they had to write. Kennelly's rollicking exuberance covered in Martin's view 'an apprehension of existential terror, not unmixed with a sense of self-loathing' which the poet came to confront most fully in his great epic poems, *Cromwell* and *The Book of Judas*. For Eavan Boland too there is a momentous transit which Martin has tracked volume by volume 'into that crucial *terra incognita* where ancestry and feminism could be discovered and possessed.'

When speaking of Irish poets in particular, Augustine Martin frequently said that they should 'bear witness', be a living example of their commitment to a craft and a vocation. For him, as for so many Irish writers, in the beginning was the word and that commitment to language bore with it a range of imperatives, an obligation to standards of literary excellence. But these were never solely technical matters, however exciting the linguistic struggle, for the writer's choice of, and attitudes towards, their subject were no less loaded when it came to the matter of Ireland. *Utile*, then, but *dulce* too, for the business of the poet, as Yeats puts it in 'Adam's Curse', is 'to articulate sweet sounds together';[13] and, as Gus Martin (citing James Stephens) himself stressed at the close of his Introduction to *Soundings*, 'unless delight is behind' the act of literary criticism, 'behind the frustration, reflection and effort that is a necessary part of that teaching and learning, the entire exercise is in vain'.[14] Let delight, then, have the last word.

ANTHONY ROCHE

# NOTES

1  Augustine Martin, 'The Yeatsean Apocalypse', in *Studies in W.B. Yeats*, edited by Jacqueline Genet (Groupe de Recherches d'Etudes anglo-irlandaises du C.N.R.S., 1989), p. 223; revised and expanded as 'Politics and the Yeatsian Apocalypse', in *Tumult of Images: Essays on W.B. Yeats and Politics*, edited by Peter Liebregts and Peter van de Kamp; *The Literature of Politics, The Politics of Literature*, Vol. 3 (Amsterdam; Atlanta, Ga.: Rodopi, 1995), p. 27.
2  All references are to essays in *Bearing Witness*, unless otherwise indicated.
3  See John Paul Riquelme, *Teller and Tale in Joyce's Fiction: Oscillating Perspectives* (Baltimore and London: The Johns Hopkins University Press, 1983), pp. 128–9.
4  Seamus Hosey, *Speaking Volumes* (Dublin: Blackwater Press, in association with RTÉ, 1995), p. 207.
5  In a review of recent Joyce criticism for the *Irish University Review*, Vol. 18, No. 1, Spring 1988, p. 145.
6  Augustine Martin, *Anglo-Irish Literature* (Dublin: Department of Foreign Affairs, 1980), p. 40.
7  John Wilson Foster, 'Irish Fiction 1965–1990: Introduction', *Field Day Anthology of Irish Writing*, Vol. 3 (Derry: Field Day, 1991), p. 941.
8  *Times Literary Supplement* December 23 1977, p. 1509.
9  See Chapter 11, 'The Girl at the Gaol Gate', Frank O'Connor, *The Lonely Voice: A Study of the Short Story* (London: Macmillan, 1963), pp. 202–13.
10  *Speaking Volumes*, p. 209.
11  Donald Davie, *These the Companions: Recollections* (Cambridge: Cambridge University Press, 1982), pp. 106–7.
12  Donald Davie, *Under Briggflatts: A History of Poetry in Great Britain 1960–1988* (Manchester: Carcanet, 1989), p. 37.
13  W.B. Yeats, *Collected Poems*, edited and with an introduction by Augustine Martin (London: Arena/Arrow Books, 1990), p. 76.
14  Augustine Martin, 'Introduction', in *Soundings: Leaving Certificate Poetry* (Dublin: Gill and Macmillan, 1969), p. xx.

# Section One

## Yeats, Synge and Joyce

# – 1 –

## *Apocalyptic Structure in Yeats's* Secret Rose

Critics of the short story seem to agree on at least one distinction that can be made about the form. Some stories, the theory goes, end with a discord, others with a concord. In the former type the reader receives a terminal shock which throws the previous action into ironic relief. The pressure of the story's action seemed set for one kind of resolution only to suffer a reversal at the end. The invariable effect of the discord ending is to throw the mind backwards over the events; and in a good short story these events appear in a new light, exhibiting a new unsuspected consistency.

The concord ending depends neither on surprise nor reversal. It is a culmination of what has gone before, it strikes the keynote of the experience. It gathers and suspends the mood in a final emphasis, a moment of stasis from which the mind can move forwards as well as backwards. The future as well as the past is seen as implicit in the story's action. One has only to think of Maupassant's 'The Necklace' on the one hand and 'Boule de Suif' on the other to see the distinction exemplified.

Neither formula fits Yeats's stories of the 1890s in *The Secret Rose* where a persistent method of closure gives a key to the book's themes, structure and technique. Here the stories end neither in reversal nor synopsis. Instead they step beyond the logic of human cause and effect into revelation. Even in the few stories that are not overtly apocalyptic, which do not involve supernatural revelation or prophecy, the action resolves itself in a moment of visionary insight such as Hanrahan's song to Kathleen the daughter of Houlihan, or his prayer to the 'Blessed Queen of Heaven' to preserve him against the emissaries of old age.

In all of these stories the hero is forced by ecstasy or suffering to the frontiers of the natural world where, in a moment of collision with the world beyond, he is granted a transnatural insight. The human situation, in other words, resolves itself in terms of transhuman vision, if not in actual prophecy or apocalypse. The human situation builds itself to a point of intensity that can be answered only by a final, upward thrust into the numinous. It is a frequent structural resource of Yeats's middle poetry: in poems like 'The Second Coming' and 'Nineteen Hundred and Nineteen' the human, historical crisis enacted in the body of the poem resolves itself in a vision that takes it beyond time and history, an apocalypse of rough beasts and unicorns. In the stories, the moment of revelation marks the climax of the action, when the hero encounters the unseen world. What we find, therefore, in *The Secret Rose* is a fictional structure repeating itself—with significant variations—in the individual stories. It is organized around a moment of visionary climax, and is expressly calculated to embody, in a great variety of situations, an over-riding theme which Yeats announces in his dedication of the volume— 'the war of spiritual with natural order'.[1] The liabilities of such a uniform fictional method are obvious. The lesser stories tend to be monotonous and predictable, to give the sense of a formula mechanically imposed on the experience. More than once Yeats is forced as he approaches the moment of revelation to coerce his language into extravagant liturgical metaphors and cadences in order to produce a sense of the supernatural. Such faults have, however, obscured the excellence of certain individual stories, the technical sophistication which Yeats develops as he proceeds from his first story to his last, and above all the elaborate unity of the book as a whole. Because in *The Secret Rose,* more than in any other collection of stories that I know, the individual pieces are arranged into such a complex design that it is difficult to consider any of them in isolation. It is better, therefore, to begin by sketching the outlines of this over-arching pattern before dealing with individual stories.

## Patterns of Unity

The first obvious pattern is historical. The book opens with two stories set in pagan Ireland, 'The Binding of the Hair' and 'The Wisdom of the King'. The second two stories, 'Where There is Nothing, There is God' and 'The Crucifixion of the Outcast', are set in Ireland's monastic age. The fifth story, 'Out of the Rose', with its crusading knight, belongs to the late Middle Ages. The sixth story, 'The Curse of the Fires and of the Shadows', takes us into the period of the religious wars, specifically Cromwell's invasion of Ireland. The two stories that follow, 'The Heart of the Spring' and 'Of Costello the Proud, of Oona the Daughter of Dermott and of the Bitter Tongue' are also located in the seventeenth century. The suite of Hanrahan stories that follows and 'The Old Men of the Twilight' are of the eighteenth century. 'Rosa Alchemica', with which the book ends, is clearly late nineteenth century in its background. Indeed if the publisher had agreed to the inclusion of the two remaining 'apocalyptic' stories, 'The Tables of the Law' and 'The Adoration of the Magi', the important *fin de siècle* culmination to the book would have been stronger and the overriding thematic unity of the book more explicit.[2] In terms of historical perspective, therefore, the book takes us progressively from pagan times to the end of the nineteenth century.

The span of the book's time-scale is about two thousand years. The book begins in violence, in a decisive war over the 'People of the Bag'. The apocalyptic nature of that struggle is stressed in the narration. A messenger announces to the young queen that 'nations with ignoble bodies and ragged beards have driven us from the fires and have killed many'. It is a conflict between civilization and rampaging barbarism. When the battle is over it is noted that in it 'the nations of the People of the Bag had fought desperately for the last time before they were scattered'. The young queen finds the severed head of her bard on a bush and listens to the song that issues from its lips. The closing sentence is heavy with the omens of apocalypse:

And then a troop of crows, heavy like fragments of that sleep older than the world, swept out of the darkness, and, as they passed, smote those ecstatic lips with the points of their wings; and the head fell from the bush and rolled over at the feet of the queen.[3]

As far as the story itself is concerned the action has reached its visionary climax: time has collided with eternity, the spiritual principle represented by the queen and the bard has made its stand against the world of shapeless violence and insisted on its own demands. As far as the book is concerned the moment initiates a fictional sequence which is to span 'twenty centuries of stony sleep'[4] which will also end in apocalypse—the dance of Michael Robartes and his followers on the face of Christ in 'Rosa Alchemica'. In the intervening stories the struggle between the spiritual and the material goes on fitfully, conducted by the poets, mystics, gleemen, anchorites, crusaders and magicians, the opponents of 'external order and outer fixity'. It is clear, therefore, that, running hand in hand with the historical scheme of the volume, there is a thematic pattern of apocalypse framed by the opening and concluding stories.

The third sense of unity is geographical. Michael J. Sidnell has pointed out that the Hanrahan stories are so organized as to form 'a ring round Sligo'.[5] Similarly, throughout the volume Ireland goes beyond being a mere setting and becomes an active entity in the stories' theme and atmosphere. The Dedication announces:

So far, however, as this book is visionary it is Irish; for Ireland, which is still predominantly Celtic, has preserved with some less excellent things a gift of vision, which has died out among more hurried and more successful nations. . . .

Consequently, the war between the spiritual and material proceeds more urgently there than in other nations. The old Knight in 'Out of the Rose' comes to Ireland 'hearing at last how this western isle was fuller of wars and rapine than any other land'. It is in the west, at the furthest remove from the modern world, that the spiritual vision is most alive. Hanrahan, cast out by priests and people, 'resolved to be gone westward, for Gaelic Ireland was still alive', and 'as he wandered slowly and aimlessly he passed deeper and deeper into that Celtic twilight, in which heaven and earth so mingle that each seems to have taken upon itself some shadow of the other's beauty'. In 'Rose Alchemica' Robartes leads his companion across Ireland to the Atlantic seaboard where the temple of the Alchemical Rose is situated; as they proceed he brings his vision of apocalypse—which is Rosicrucian, cosmopolitan, esoteric—into synthesis with Irish mytho-logical and popular tradition when he speaks of the old gods returning, of the Dagda, Lu[gh] and Angus:

Their reign has never ceased, but only waned in power a little, for the Shee still pass in every wind, and dance and play at hurley, and fight their sudden battles in every hollow and on every hill; but they cannot build their temples again till there have been martyrdoms and victories, and perhaps even that long-foretold battle in the Valley of the Black Pig.

When Robartes returns with his message of a new dispensation he chooses three old Gaelic sages who live in an island off the west coast and whose minds, never having 'endured the body and pressure of our time, but only distant times, found nothing unlikely in anything he told them, but accepted all simply and were happy'. Ireland, therefore, either overtly or by implication, is more than a setting for the stories; it is knit into their theme, integral to their atmosphere. The harlot in 'The Adoration of the Magi', whom the old men go to see in Paris, is an Irishwoman. The apocalypse, especially in the earlier versions of the stories, is an assertively Irish affair.

The fourth unifying element in the volume is related to the third, and central to the structural technique of the individual stories. It is the symbolism of the rose and the cross; the elements of this symbolism working separately or together frequently mark the moment wherein the hero encounters his crisis of vision. The rosy cross, as readers of Yeats's poetry know, represents spiritual beauty suffering on the cross of earthly time. Also in the poetry the rose is a symbol for 'old Éire and the ancient ways'.[6] In these stories it carries both these connotations; but here they are subsumed into a third, that of apocalypse. The wind that blows the rose petals asunder is the wind of the new dispensation. The prefatory poem, 'To the Secret Rose' ends:

Surely thine hour has come, thy great wind blows,
Far off, most secret, and inviolate Rose?[7]

The book ends with a story in which the climax is an orgiastic dance which brings 'the petals of the great rose . . . falling slowly through the incense-heavy air'. After twenty centuries the hour of the great Rose is at hand, Robartes its high priest, prophet and martyr. The gleemen, saints, knights, bards and outcasts who have been granted partial visions and revelations in the preceding stories can be seen as his precursors. The book, therefore, exhibits a densely-wrought unity of structure based on history, locale, theme and symbolism.

## Moments of Vision

The word 'apocalyptic' therefore applies to the book in two related senses: the individual stories reach their climax in a moment of vision; the stories are so arranged that these moments of vision mark stages in the progress of history between one apocalyptic change and the next. The opening story we have glanced at. The second, 'The Wisdom of the King', still set in the pagan world which has been secured by the victory of the Tuatha de Danaan, dramatizes a moment when the people of Ireland have betrayed the ancient vision and have settled for the values of law and administration. The heroine rejects the wisdom of the young king and his allegiance to the inspirations of the Dagda, of Lir and of Angus, and he departs into the air. The next two stories, 'Where there is Nothing there is God' and 'The Crucifixion of the Outcast', present two phases of Ireland's monastic age. In the former a wanderer is given sanctuary in a monastery, probably Tallaght of the eighth century, and is revealed to be Angus, 'the lover of God', in a characteristic moment of vision. The monastic community is seen as benign, mystical and spiritual, combining in its contemplative life Christian piety with ancient astrological wisdom. It is a characteristic Yeatsean synthesis exemplified in the saint's name: Angus the 'culdee', *céile Dé*, 'lover of God' is, I believe, meant to echo the pagan Angus, 'God of Love', and to suggest that medieval Ireland has recovered spiritual vision. 'The Crucifixion of the Outcast', clearly intended as a companion piece, is a radical adaptation of an existing Irish tale, 'The Vision of MacConglinne'. Set three centuries later, it exhibits an Ireland where the ancient wisdom has been suppressed, where the monks have become rigid upholders of 'external order and outer fixity'. Yeats's handling of the goliardic tale leaves no doubt as to his intention. In the old tale a wandering scholar arrives at a Cork monastery, overcomes the inhospitality of the monks by his energy, satire and inventiveness, cures the local king of a hunger demon and achieves a triumph for the spirit of freedom, poetry and exuberance. In Yeats's story he is also harshly treated, but it is the monks who triumph. He is seen as their enemy because his race is 'always longing after the Son of Lir, and Angus, and Bridget, and the Dagda, and Dana the Mother, and all the false gods of the old days'. In a manner that echoes Christ's passion he is made carry a cross to the hilltop where he is crucified. In 'Out of the Rose' Yeats expands the scope of his vision—in a manner that anticipates the global Rosicrucianism of Michael Robartes in the final stories—by taking as his hero a medieval knight of the Order of the 'Divine Rose of Intellectual Flame' who comes to Ireland to fight against 'the Powers of Corruption'. He dies passing on his message to an uncomprehending peasant, representative of the people he had tried to save.

In 'The Curse of the Fires and of the Shadows' the representatives of materialism are the Cromwellian troopers—a foreshadowing of his late poem, 'The Curse of Cromwell'—who violate the Friary at Sligo. Here they are destroyed by the agency of a fairy piper, and ride to their death over Lugnagall. The pattern of 'Where there is Nothing there is God' is re-echoed here in the implied spiritual alliance between the Friars and the Shee. It is more overtly recapitulated in the next story, 'The Heart of the Spring', also set in the seventeenth century, where the hero is an old hermit called Angus, a student of astrology, who is seeking for the moment 'after the Sun has entered the Ram and before he has passed the Lion' so that he can become one with 'the Immortal Powers'. He gains his ambition and in gaining it dies. It is surely significant in the scheme of the book that this appearance of Angus occurs a millennium after his manifestation in the earlier story.

The story of 'Costello the Proud' marks the moment in the volume where Yeats begins to personalize his characters more elaborately as he moves closer in history to his own time. He found the original story as an extended gloss to 'Úna Bhán' in Douglas Hyde's *Love Songs of Connacht* and his adaptation of it is as significant as his re-writing of MacConglinne. Half-way through the story Costello, having been refused by Oona's parents, rides off towards his mysterious destiny as yet another doomed follower of the mystical rose. At Oona's death he sees a vision of the Shee 'rushing together in the shape of a great silvery rose'; he is found dead on the island where she is buried 'with his arms flung out as though he lay upon a rood'. The bluff clansman of Hyde's anecdote has been recast as a martyr to spiritual beauty, crucified in the service of the rose. Taken all in all he is an uneasy conscript to the Rosicrucianism that becomes more explicit as the stories succeed one another, just as his story is an uneasy blend of realism and symbolism.

Red Hanrahan, the most fully developed character in the book, is the hero of the next six stories. From the outset he is portrayed as a man apart, moving on the fringes of settled society. In the original version of the first story he is led by the Shee to the devil's book, the Book of the Great Dhoul, and by means of it he calls down a fairy woman, Cleena of the Wave, and subsequently rejects her. He is cursed by the spiritual powers and cast out by priest and people. The five remaining stories relate his wanderings and visions until the visionary moment of his death. Hanrahan is at once a descendant of the Gaelic poets and of the ancient druids; in the scheme of the book he comes a thousand years after the crucified gleeman of whom he is an eighteenth-century counterpart. In his gloomy and tormented psyche the battle between social order and spiritual vision proceeds with especial drama and intensity. Yeats's handling of his fictional character is most clearly seen in 'The Twisting of the Rope' which is again adapted from a folktale which Hyde appends as a gloss to a Gaelic poem, 'An Súisín Bán', in *The Love Songs of Connacht*. In Hyde's story—as in Hyde's subsequent play, *Casadh an tSúgáin*— the action and its culmination are comic. The wandering poet enters the cottage as preparations for a marriage are at their height. The poet's flatteries beguile the young bride from her betrothed. Her mother contrives to get him out of the house by inviting him to twist a straw rope while he moves backwards through the open door. She then throws the rope after him and locks him out. The story ends in a triumph for the cottagers who continue with their celebrations. Yeats, however, adds an incident which radically changes the significance of the action. The defeated Hanrahan goes down to the sea where he hears the voices of the Shee calling out:

Sorrow be upon him who rejects the love of the daughters of Dana, for he shall find no comfort in the love of the daughters of Eve. The fire has taken hold upon his heart. Cast him out, cast him out, cast him out.

The comic structure of the folktale which had contained and completed the action within the social pattern of the daily world has been opened at the end to reveal a tragic tension between the hero and eternity. Like the medieval outcast, Hanrahan is crucified on the cross where the temporal and the eternal intersect and conflict.

As *The Secret Rose* nears its end the sense of magic and miracle becomes more overt, as if in expectation of the apocalyptic dissolution of its close. In 'The Rose of Shadow' a peasant girl, against her parents' wishes, insists on singing one of Hanrahan's songs to bring back the memory of her savage lover who has died. It ends in a climax of apocalyptic terror:

Suddenly the thatch at one end of the roof rolled up, and the rushing clouds and a single star flickered before her eyes for a moment, and then seemed to be lost in a formless mass of flame which roared but gave no heat, and had in the midst of it the shape of a man crouching on the storm. His heavy and brutal face and his partly naked limbs were scarred with many wounds, and his eyes were full of white fire under his knitted brows.

In 'The Old Men of the Twilight' the old voteen, Michael Bruen, shoots a heron and finds that it has turned into an ancient bard who has been wandering the skies since St Patrick's time. Because he had clung to his craft in defiance of the new religion the saint had turned him into a heron. The bard now begs Bruen to let him touch his rosary beads so that he may die reconciled. He is refused and dies. The blind superstition of the old voteen suggests that Patrick's era may be coming to an end, a hint that is picked up and reinforced by a similar figure on the seashore at the end of 'Rosa Alchemica'. Similarly the image of the heron man coasting the skies for almost twenty centuries throws our mind back over the book's time-span—'twenty centuries of stony sleep'—now that it is approaching its momentous conclusion.

## Towards Final Revelation

The three stories with which the book as first planned was meant to end, 'Rosa Alchemica', 'The Tables of the Law' and 'The Adoration of the Magi', are usually referred to as the 'apocalyptic stories' and for understandable reasons. In them the theme of apocalypse is overt and salient. They deal with the fate of fictional characters who are intellectually conscious of an impending change in the world: Robartes, Aherne and the unnamed narrator who links the stories into unity. They are typical figures of *fin de siècle* literature, obsessed with magic, alchemy, Rosicrucianism and Symbolist art. Yet they are linked with the book's earlier personages in several significant ways. The veiled discussion of the Platonic year in 'Where there is Nothing there is God' prepares us for the millennial preoccupation that looms so large in their meditations and actions. Hanrahan, like Aherne, was undone by the study of a forbidden book. The old Knight with the rose of ruby in his helmet foreshadows the 'three old men, in armour studded with rubies' who appear in the earlier version of 'The Adoration of the Magi'.[8] The theme of poetic martyrdom which recurs in the earlier stories is central to the destinies of Robartes and Aherne. Like the earlier heroes, Robartes and Aherne are outcasts from the quotidian world, its social conventions and religious orthodoxies.

   'Rosa Alchemica', the only story of the three included in the volume on its first publication, relates how the narrator had shut himself off from eveyday life behind his peacock curtain until he is visited by his former Rosicrucian mentor, Michael Robartes. Robartes tries to re-convert him to the service of esoteric mystery. Together they journey west to the Temple of the Alchemical Rose on the Atlantic's edge. They are abused by an old voteen with a rosary beads who calls them idolators who have driven the herrings from the bay; he is symbolic of the old dispensation which Robartes is determined to destroy. The narrator is initiated into a ritual dance which he performs together with the other initiates. As the dance proceeds he perceives

that the floor was of a green stone, and that a pale Christ on a pale cross was wrought in the midst. I asked Robartes the meaning of this, and was told that they desired 'To trouble His unity with their multitudinous feet.'

As the dance reaches its climax he realizes that he is surrendering his soul to the Immortals, and faints. On awakening he escapes from the temple just as the fanatical fisher-folk are about to attack and destroy it. In the final sentence the narrator affirms his return to orthodoxy and his reliance on the rosary which he carries round his neck as a defence against him 'whose name is Legion'. The recurrence of the rosary in these stories is probably doubly significant. Not only is it an obvious symbol of traditional Christian piety, it also recalls the rose as symbol of the Blessed Virgin, the official rose of the Church, the antithesis of the occult, forbidden rose of Rosicrucianism.

'The Tables of the Law' reveals the narrator in full possession of his renewed orthodoxy twice encountering his former colleague, Owen Aherne, who has gone the way of forbidden knowledge. In the second encounter Aherne is disclosed as a man hounded by the guilt of his occult adventures:

I am not one of those for whom Christ died, and this is why I must be hidden. I have a leprosy that even eternity cannot cure. I have lost my soul because I have looked out of the eyes of angels.

As Aherne delivers himself of these remarks the story reaches its visionary climax. The room darkens and spectral figures bearing torches appear and call upon the narrator to surrender his being to their spiritual ministry. Again he realizes that 'the order of the Alchemical Rose was not of this earth, and that it was still seeking over this earth for whatever souls it could gather into its glittering net'. He escapes and in the story's last sentence expresses himself terrified at Aherne's disclosures and his fear that the 'spirits whose name is Legion' are driving the unhappy heretic before them round the world.

'The Adoration of the Magi' brings the entire sequence to its culmination. The narrator is visited by the three old Irish sages who tell him of their visitation by the spirit of Robartes and his charge to them to travel to Paris to witness what is to be the new incarnation. The dying woman they are to seek is to be the vehicle of the new dispensation, mother of the savage god:

. . . this woman has been driven out of time and has lain upon the bosom of Eternity. After you have bowed down the old things shall be again and another Argo will carry heroes over the deep, and another Achilles beleaguer Troy.

They find her in a Parisian garret and when they tell her of their quest 'a look of great joy came into her face'. She proceeds to tell them in Gaelic of 'many secret powerful names' and especially of the Sidhe of Ireland and 'of their love for the Cauldron, and the Whetstone, and the Sword, and the Spear'. Having delivered herself of her message she dies. Her death is followed by the apparition of a man who is clearly Robartes. He dismembers a rose whose petals become 'beautiful people who began to dance slowly'. When the vision passes one of the three old men, attempting to find a meaning for the experience, suggests that 'Perhaps Christianity was good and the world liked it, so it is going away and the Immortals are beginning to awake.' The narrator concludes his tale by affirming again his return to Irish Catholicism as a defence 'against the demons' who are threatening the order of Christian civilization. So the sequence ends.

It has not been possible in the space of this essay to analyse the individual stories of *The Secret Rose* in any depth of detail, to examine such matters as characterization, language, narrative technique, to discuss their historical authenticity, or to deal with their various revisions through the years. Such an analysis would reveal, I believe, a range of technical skill and stylistic resource so far unsuspected in Yeats the fictionist. What must be clear, however, even from this swift summary of the book's overarching design, its persistent themes and symbols, and the manner in which the individual stories support and complement one another, is that *The Secret Rose* was conceived as a unified work of art, and that it reflects in depth and extension a central preoccupation of the poet's thought at a crucial stage in his development. When this concern with apocalypse surfaces again in the great visionary poems of the 1920s, 'The Second Coming', 'Nineteen Hundred and Nineteen' and 'Meditations in Time of Civil War', the technique of apocalyptic closure returns with a new force and eloquence. It is, I think, clear that the groundwork for that later achievement, both its theme and method, had been laid in this early and neglected volume of short stories.

# NOTES

Augustine Martin's annotations throughout this book have been checked and augmented by Anthony Roche. 'Inherited Dissent' (pp. 81–99) remains unannotated.

'Apocalyptic Structure in Yeats's Secret Rose' was first published in *Studies*, Vol. LXIV, Spring 1975.

1  Yeats's dedication of 1897 was to fellow Irish poet and mystic, A.E. [George Russell]: 'they [the stories] have but one subject, the war of spiritual with natural order; and how can I dedicate such a book to anyone but to you, the one poet of modern Ireland who has moulded a spiritual ecstasy into verse?' *The Secret Rose, Stories by W.B. Yeats: A Variorum Edition*, edited by Phillip L. Marcus, Warwick Gould and Michael J. Sidnell (Ithaca and London: Cornell University Press, 1981), p. 233.

2  '"The Tables of the Law" and "The Adoration of the Magi" were intended to be part of *The Secret Rose*, but the publisher, A.H. Bullen, took a distaste to them and asked me to leave them out, and then after the book was published liked them and put them into a little volume by themselves.' W.B. Yeats, *Mythologies* (London: Macmillan, 1959), p. 1.

3  W.B. Yeats, *The Secret Rose* (Dublin: Maunsel & Co., 1905), p. 10. This edition of the book is textually identical with the original English edition by Laurence & Bullen (London, 1907) and unless otherwise indicated all references are to it. [Editor's note. Given its unavailability, no further page references are made to this edition. The reader is referred to W.B. Yeats, *Mythologies*, where 14 of the original 17 stories appear, along with 'The Tables of the Law' and 'The Adoration of the Magi', and a story added in 1905, 'Red Hanrahan'. The three omitted stories from 1905, 'The Binding of the Hair', 'The Book of the Great Dhoul and Hanrahan the Red' and 'The Rose of Shadow', may be found in *The Secret Rose, Stories by W.B. Yeats: A Variorum Edition*, ed. Marcus, Gould and Sidnell.]

4  'The Second Coming', *The Variorum Edition of the Poems of W.B. Yeats*, edited by Peter Allt and Russell K. Alspach (New York: Macmillan, 1957), p. 402.

5  Michael J. Sidnell, 'Versions of the *Stories of Red Hanrahan*', in *Yeats Studies* Vol. 1, No. 1, May 1971 (Shannon: Irish University Press), p. 119.

6  'To the Rose upon the Rood of Time', *The Variorum Edition of the Poems of W.B. Yeats*, ed. Allt and Alspach, p. 100.

7  'The Secret Rose', ibid., p. 170.

8  See *The Secret Rose, Stories by W.B. Yeats: A Variorum Edition*, ed. Marcus, Gould and Sidnell, p. 169. The line became 'three old men in chain armour' after 1914 and is thus reprinted in Yeats, *Mythologies*, p. 313.

# Hound Voices were they all:
# An Experiment in Yeats Criticism

This essay is experimental. It is based on a conviction that the best commentary on Yeats's poems is provided by his other poems. No source outside Yeats is therefore used in the commentary and there are only two significant appeals to his prose.

> Because we love bare hills and stunted trees
> And were the last to choose the settled ground,
> Its boredom of the desk or of the spade, because
> So many years companioned by a hound,
> Our voices carry; and though slumber-bound,
> Some few half wake and half renew their choice,
> Give tongue, proclaim their hidden name—'Hound Voice'.
>
> The women that I picked spoke sweet and low
> And yet gave tongue. 'Hound Voices' were they all.
> We picked each other from afar and knew
> What hour of terror comes to test the soul,
> And in that terror's name obeyed the call,
> And understood, what none have understood,
> Those images that waken in the blood.
>
> Some day we shall get up before the dawn
> And find our ancient hounds before the door,
> And wide awake know that the hunt is on;
> Stumbling upon the blood-dark track once more,
> And stumbling to the kill beside the shore;
> Then cleaning out and bandaging of wounds,
> And chants of victory amid the encircling hounds.
>
> 'Hound Voice' (1938)

This most neglected of Yeats's last poems can yield one of his most explicit statements on history and individual conviction in the poetry of these final years. Its neglect may be due to its apparent simplicity or, ironically, to its apparent vagueness, or perhaps even to A. Norman Jeffares's only remark on it in his *Commentary*[1] that it was written 'in a spirit of mockery'. For my own part I have always been appalled by its sanguinary images and the poet's endorsement of some bloody and triumphant personal consummation. Unlike all his other 'apocalyptic poems' the 'I' says yes, and with obvious relish, to the bloodshed. But this is to anticipate; 'Hound Voice' is not normally numbered with his apocalyptic poems, and the blood that is shed, at least at first glance, is that of the huntsmen's normal quarry, fox, deer or hare. Indeed the main images of landscape, sleep, hound and blood—that most complex of all Yeats's words—are so familiar from the poet's earliest work that our first task is to establish their connotations for this particular lyric. All of them wait on our sense of 'We', because by a curious sleight of hand the poet and his elected company are at once the hounds' masters and their voices.

The *hound* as companion appears in his earliest work, notably in 'The Ballad of the Foxhunter' and 'The Wanderings of Oisin'. In the former the dying foxhunter calls for his hounds and asks his huntsman Rody to sound the horn before he expires. It would hardly strain the simple pathos of the ballad—adapted from an incident in Kickham's *Knocknagow*—to note that it is redolent of the aristocratic and traditional, and that it may even symbolize the decay of those values in the Ireland of 1889. But while the hounds in this ballad are 'human' in a metaphorical sense, in 'The Wanderings of Oisin' they are literally so: Finn's aunt, Uirne, had turned into a hound when pregnant and had given birth to the hounds Bran and Sceolan. Apart from this detail—which admittedly plays no part in the long narrative—hunting with hounds is used by Oisin to typify the warrior, and therefore aristocratic life as he reveals it to his opposite, the 'primary' Christian, St Patrick:

> Caoilte, and Conan, and Finn were there,
> When we followed a deer with our baying hounds,
> With Bran, Sceolan, and Lomair.[2]

A further connotation of the hound image occurs towards the end of the first Book of the poem when the lovers, Oisin and Niamh, pass by a 'hornless deer . . . chased by a phantom hound'(11) with one red ear. This image for human desire is later personalized to express the poet's love for Maud Gonne in 'He mourns for the Change that has come upon him and his Beloved, and longs for the End of the World':

> Do you not hear me calling, white deer with no horns?
> I have been changed to a hound with one red ear;

The poet has not only become a 'hound voice', but the occasion is, in the early Yeats style, overtly apocalyptic:

> I would that the Boar without bristles had come from the West
> And had rooted the sun and moon and stars out of the sky
> And lay in the darkness, grunting, and turning to his rest.(153)

Equally significant, of course, is the fact that the name of his favourite hero, his 'double' and his 'anti-self', Cuchulain, means in Irish 'the Hound of Culan', a name which the boy Setanta assumes by symbolically assimilating himself to the character of the animal which he slays in one of the prefatory tales to the *Táin*. Finally one may mention Yeats's wry use of the tongue hound as metaphor in expressing his aristocratic hauteur for 'certain Bad Poets', his imitators:

> You say, as I have often given tongue
> In praise of what another's said and sung,
> 'Twere politic to do the like by these;
> But was there ever dog that praised his fleas?(262)

The hound imagery in Yeats is consistent from his earliest writings: apart from its specialized sense of erotic desire and pursuit,[3] it connotes courage, nobility, the aristocratic life-style and its historical obverse of warrior culture.

Turning to the 'women that I picked' one comes upon difficulties. The most obvious candidates are Maud Gonne and Constance Markiewicz, and in each case one must assume a revisionary impulse in the poet. Constance had certainly spent an aristocratic youth 'companioned by a hound' but that was before her 'voice grew shrill':

> What voice more sweet than hers
> When, young and beautiful,
> She rode to harriers?[4]

Maud, in 'A Prayer for my Daughter' had bartered the horn of plenty to become an 'old bellows full of angry wind'(405). Mabel Beardsley, his ideal of the female 'sprezzatura' in 'Upon a Dying Lady', could hardly in any vocal sense have 'given tongue' though her identification with 'Grania's shade,/All but the terrors of the woodland flight forgot'(366) would indicate her heroic mettle. Iseult Gonne in 'The Death of the Hare' is the quarry not the hound. Though Olivia Shakespear certainly 'spoke sweet and low' it is hard to determine a sense in which she gave tongue.[5] Provisionally I suggest that it is Maud and the Gore-Booth sisters that he has in mind: all three turned from 'dispensing round/Their magnanimities of sound'(404) to revolutionary action. He turns to the sisters for help in burning time in 'In Memory of Eva Gore-Booth and

Con Markiewicz' and he comes to recognize a pre-ordained destiny in Maud's fanaticism in the last poems, notably 'A Bronze Head'.

There Maud is imagined as a bird, a goddess and a thoroughbred horse, all consistent with the pride and mettle—'wildness' is his preferred word here—of a higher race looking down upon 'this foul world in its decline and fall'(619). But she is also described emphatically as 'a most gentle woman'(618). Certainly 'that terror's name' in 'Hound Voice' finds a plausible echo in the vivid characterization of Maud in the third stanza of 'A Bronze Head':

> But even at the starting-post, all sleek and new,
> I saw the wildness in her and I thought
> A vision of terror that it must live through
> Had shattered her soul.(619)

The terror of the imploding gyre, the 'irrational streams of blood',[6] the heart's fullness and the coming emptiness[7] register on the elect, those whose values are most obviously at risk. However, if my hunch as to the identity of the women is correct, there is also the implication that they have the capacity somehow to fight the terror. Thus we may see here Yeats's final reconcilement to their defection from the world of privilege to fight the battles of the time; his return to the mood and stance of 'No Second Troy' with the huntress image of the 'tightened bow' drawn against the ignobility of the age—'Why, what could she have done, being what she is?' (257).

The landscape images are at least initially daunting. The preference for 'bare hills and stunted trees' is altogether consistent with the hunt, and with the warrior culture out of which the aristocratic caste evolves, and the freebooting life implied is consonant with the antithetical values which are currently under threat from the twentieth century. But since *The Wild Swans at Coole*—from as far back as 'Upon a House Shaken by the Land Agitation'—Yeats has as his most persistent theme the celebration of ancestral houses by special virtue of their antiquity: 'Where passion and precision have been one/Time out of mind'(264). In 'The Tower', 'Meditations in Time of Civil War', 'A Prayer for my Daughter', the Coole Park elegies of 1929 and 1931, later in 'To Dorothy Wellesley' and in the play *Purgatory* (works contemporary with 'Hound Voice'), the values of stable, aristocratic life, of 'custom' and 'ceremony', of 'famous portraits of our ancestors'[8] and of 'gradual Time's last gift, a written speech'[9] are untiringly praised. How, therefore, do we identify the 'We', these reluctant converts to the settled life?

In answering one must invoke what might be called the 'tower' syndrome as distinct from the 'house' syndrome in Yeats's symbology. It is variously significant that Yeats, when he removed to Galway on his marriage in 1917, chose a tower to be his residence and his symbol. The juxtaposition of 'Ancestral Houses' with the tower 'My House' in the first two movements of 'Meditations in time of Civil War' is sharply schematic. The ancestral houses represent an autumnal flowering of the aristocratic lifestyle: having been conceived and designed in the first place by 'violent and bitter men' who longed for the 'sweetness' of a settled ease, of 'slippered Contemplation', they are seen as threatened from within by the decay of manliness in their inheritors

> And maybe the great-grandson of that house,
> For all its bronze and marble, 's but a mouse.[10]

This innate threat is reinforced by the menace of the times, the actual Civil War dramatized in section V, 'The Road at my Door' and VI, 'The Stare's Nest by My Window'; and by the apocalyptic finale where he envisions the collapse of civilization and the onset of a new barbarism— 'A glittering sword out of the east'(426). Indeed the innate threat to the 'stamina' of his caste seems to obsess Yeats through these years, not less in his Senate speeches than in a poem like this. The Tower is accordingly presented as chief among his 'Befitting emblems of adversity'(420). Before the manor house was built there had to be a fortress. Now that the house is doomed, its inheritors must fall back upon that ancestral resource; greatness can only be renewed out of bitterness.

Consequently the high ground and stunted trees of 'Hound Voice' are foreshadowed in the landscape of the tower:

> An acre of stony ground,
> Where the symbolic rose can break in flower,
> Old ragged elms, old thorns innumerable,
> The sound of the rain or sound
> Of every wind that blows:[11]

The 'man at arms' who first founded there with his 'dwindling score' of 'castaways' are plausible kindred for the mountainy freebooters we have sought to identify for the purposes of our explication. It becomes irresistible that 'Hound Voice' is deeply embedded in Yeats's idea of cyclical historic process, that it is 'apocalyptic' in its vision, and that it invokes an alternative sense of the aristocratic to the elegiac sense in which the great houses are lamented. Also that this alternative sense involves the warrior culture epitomized in Oisin and Cuchulain which has its later counterparts in the soldier ancestry of the Irish Ascendancy. Civilization, now at the stake, must rely on these warrior atavisms to survive through the contemporary violence and work towards a future renewal of their strength and value.

The possibility of such renewal is best exemplified in the great elegy 'In Memory of Major Robert Gregory'. Gregory had not only fought and died heroically in the Great War but he had embodied in his personality the Renaissance 'sprezzatura' which Yeats saw as the hallmark of high civilization. He was therefore our 'Sidney and our perfect man'(325), combining the gifts of 'Soldier, scholar, horseman'(327). More relevantly to our theme, however, Gregory rode superbly 'with the Galway foxhounds', he loved the symbolic landscape of 'Hound Voice', the 'old stormbroken trees / That cast their shadows upon road and bridge' and he was born, significantly,

> To cold Clare rock and Galway rock and thorn,
> To that stern colour and that delicate line
> That are our secret discipline
> Wherein the gazing heart doubles her might.(326)

Before dealing with the image of 'blood' it is useful at this point to sketch the historical time-scale which Yeats is assuming in all of these apocalyptic poems of his final period. His key period is five hundred years. The great moments of civilization have occurred when his subjective or antithetical gyre has reached its fullest extension. From the primary or objective climax of Christianity's founding it took five hundred years to reach a new subjective 'unity of culture' at Byzantium. It then declined while the objective gyre expanded to its fullness in the Middle Ages. From there the subjective gyre grew to its perfection in the Italian Renaissance on 'Urbino's windy hill'(288). Since then the primary gyre has grown to its fullness and is approaching its disintegration in Yeats's own time with the rise of democracy, socialism and communism the 'levelling spirit' of modern 'mechanical' civilization. The Christian era is at a close, the 'twenty centuries of stony sleep'[12] are ending and at the inner centre of the old gyre the 'rough beast' of a new antithetical civilization is beginning to stir. To adapt Synge's remark in the preface to his poems: before civilization can become human again it must first become brutal.[13] This process will take five hundred years and must endure a prefatory period of war and violence as the old dispensation gives way to the new. Looking out upon that violence in the late thirties and looking back at Ireland of 1913, 1916, at the Troubles and the Civil War, looking at Europe of the Great War and of the October Revolution, Yeats is inevitably concerned for those aristocratic values which he cherished and for their survival through this turbulent transition. He naturally harks back to the values, the resources, the virtues that sustained his forbears five hundred years before, in the early days of conquest. It is these virtues that 'Hound Voice' celebrates. But the full force of that celebration cannot be adequately felt before the final term 'blood' is briefly annotated.

There are two senses of 'blood' in the poem. The simpler is the quarry's blood, shed by hounds and hunters. The hunters are also wounded in the chase or its climax, hence the 'cleaning out and bandaging of wounds' as if after a battle. The hunt must stand for something complex and momentous in human terms. This first sense of blood, frightening enough in itself, is stressed and amplified by the second sense conveyed with that ominous vagueness I mentioned at the outset: 'Those images that waken in the blood.' The most immediate suggestion is that the hunters' blood is up, the hunt is on. But underlying this colloquial import of the word is the ancestral, the genetic, perhaps even the Lawrentian sense of the 'dark gods in the blood'. Yeats had been exulting in 'blood/That has not passed through any huckster's loin'(269) since the 'Introductory Rhymes' to *Responsibilities* (1914). In 'To a Shade' he had compared the efficacy of fine art to 'gentle blood'(292) passing from parent to child. The same sense of aristocratic blood, of thorough breeding, lurks behind the imagery of his Senate speech on divorce where he describes his Anglo-Irish as 'one of the great stocks of Europe'.[14] Therefore the blood of those who respond to 'those images'—a phrase still far from precise—is the blood of an elite, those with a shared racial memory, who can pick each other 'from afar' and feel within their veins a peculiar 'terror' incomprehensible to the many.

Which brings us to 'those images' themselves, sensed by the hunters in their sleep, leading them to a bloody consummation 'some day' when they rise before dawn. It would be careless to ignore the short poem entitled 'Those Images' published in March of the same year. The relevant gloss is found in the fourth stanza:

> Seek those images
> That constitute the wild,
> The lion and the virgin,
> The harlot and the child.(601)

Images such as these are not ostentatiously relevant to 'Hound Voice'— unless it is read as an apocalyptic poem. But if it is, if it is seen to enact a personal Armageddon, their relevance becomes not just patent but interesting. The most explicit of Yeats's early apocalyptic visions occurs in 'The Adoration of the Magi'. In that story three Irish Magi answer the command of Michael Robartes and travel to a brothel in Paris to kneel by the bed of a dying Irish harlot who gives birth to the avatar of a new savage dispensation.[15] Similarly the 'lion' prowls through Yeats's apocalyptic scenario in a wide range of postures, not only the 'shape with lion body'(402) in 'The Second Coming' or the 'lion and woman'(629) of 'The Circus Animals' Desertion', but even more significantly through

'The Wanderings of Oisin' where, in Book Three, it forms part of a recurrent motif and refrain:

> O flaming lion of the world, O when will you turn to your rest?(56)

If therefore we decide that 'Hound Voice' can hear an apocalyptic reading, if in other words we decide that a Yeatsean apocalypse is somehow possible without a single 'occult' emblem—no sphynx, incubus, fiend, unicorn, brazen hawk, or dragon of air—we are well advised to determine how this version of apocalypse differs from the others.

One can distinguish three phases in Yeats's antecedent sense of apocalyptic change. In the Nineties, notably in *The Wind Among the Reeds* and the *Secret Rose* stories, the sense of radical historic change was mediated almost exclusively through invented *personae,* or through the third person singular; the tone was mostly one of reverent expectation; the iconography was drawn from the alchemical process and from the allied formulae of Joachim of Flora which defined and foretold a new dispensation: 'the Kingdom of the Father was past, the Kingdom of the Son passing, the Kingdom of the Spirit yet to come.'[16] Thus the narrator of 'Rosa Alchemica' saw alchemy as 'a universal transmutation of all things into some divine and imperishable substance . . . the transmutation of life into art, and a cry of measureless desire for a world made wholly of essences.'[17] It was overwhelmingly the idiom of aspiration and prophecy, manifesting itself without explicit violence:

> Surely thine hour has come, thy great wind blows,
> Far-off, most secret, and inviolate Rose?[18]

The second phase arose out of the poet's horrified recognition that these prophecies were coming true before his eyes in the process of history, in the Easter Rising, the Russian Revolution, the Black and Tan war and later the Civil War in Ireland. This phase was marked by the threatening nature of the omens which no longer spoke of a fine transmutation but rather declared themselves as dragons, rough beasts, brazen hawks, insolent fiends. The relevant volumes are *Michael Robartes and the Dancer* and *The Tower.* In these apocalyptic visions the narrator, the Yeats figure, is dissociated and terrified: his wits are astray, his sight troubled, he restrains himself from crying vengeance on the murderers of Jacques Molay, absolves himself from involvement in 'something that all others understand or share',[19] climbs to his 'proper dark',[20] traffics in mockery.

The third phase is more excited and desperate, it announces itself most clearly in 'Parnell's Funeral' at the opening of *A Full Moon in March* (1935) where he sees the history of his own country yield ignobly to the 'contagion of the throng'(542). Later in the same volume in 'Meru' the poet acknowledges that civilization is maintained only by 'manifold illusion'(563). As the gyre staggers and the face of civilization cracks the poet is forced back upon his old concept of 'tragic joy' which he had first adumbrated as a dramatic theory in 1910:

> What matter? Out of cavern comes a voice,
> And all it knows is that one word 'Rejoice![21]

This attitude bespeaks a degree of collusion with the ugliness and the violence, but no involvement. The poet and his surrogates—as in 'Lapis Lazuli'—stare on 'all the tragic scene'(567), no longer horrified or afraid because, in the nature of that 'unfashionable gyre' the entire civilization can be built again. The times are ugly and the elite may have to brace their sensibilities as spectators to observe 'this age and the next age/Engender in the ditch.'[22] But they remain spectators; they do not bear a hand in the mayhem; the gross imagery of blood and carnage preclude participation on either side; the poetic self stands, however fearfully, aloof.

But in 'Hound Voice' the poetic self is almost drunk with excited participation in the chase and in the kill. Furthermore the apocalyptic images are no longer drawn from the underworld of black magic or the 'frog-spawn of a blind man's ditch';[23] there are no witches, incubi, no dubious hybrids or occult monsters. Instead there is the open-air exhilaration of the chase, the aristocratic verve and vitality, the triumph of the best. If we set this unique version of apocalypse against Yeats's political formulations of the time we find that it takes on an even more formidable implication.

In his last extended essay, *On the Boiler* (1939), Yeats reveals an obsession with breeding. In that section of it entitled 'Tomorrow's Revolution' he prefaces his observations on the contemporary scene with six pages of commentary on selective breeding drawn from Burton, Fernelius, Curtius, Shaw and Cattell and notes with dismay that since 'about 1900 the better stocks have not been replacing their numbers, while the stupider and less healthy have been more than replacing theirs.'[24] He goes on to note that the 'Fascist countries' who know that 'civilization has reached a crisis' are—to his disgust—offering bounties for large families, thus adding to the universal decline in human excellence. 'Sooner or later we must limit the families of the unintelligent classes.' In a passage that echoes much of what has already been said in theme and image he projects the possibility of an aristocratic future:

Yet we must hold to what we have that the next civilization may be born, not from a virgin's womb, nor a tomb without a body, not from a void, but of our own rich experience. These gifts must return, not in the mediumistic sleep, dreaming or dreamless, but when we are wide awake. Eugenical and psychical research are the revolutionary movements with that element of novelty and sensation which sooner or later stir men to action. It may be, or it must be, that the best bred from the best shall claim again their ancient omens.[25]

These prose sentences resemble 'Hound Voice' not only in language— 'sleep', 'wide awake', 'ancient omens'—but in the deliberate sense of mystery it creates through its rapt prophetic cadences. The argument of the essay presses forward to strange plans of practical action: 'The formation of military families should be encouraged' to confront 'the disciplined uneducated masses of the commercial nations.' A hundred such men would be the equal of 'a million of the lesser sort' because 'we have as good blood as there is in Europe.' This faith in noble blood and its long-term destiny for Ireland and Europe is reinforced in a frequently quoted passage from 'A General Introduction for my Work' (1937) where an ominous vagueness, reminiscent of 'Hound Voice', gives witness to the poet's apprehension of the years to come:

When I stand upon O'Connell Bridge in the half-light and notice that discordant architecture, all those electric signs, where modern heterogeneity has taken physical form, a vague hatred comes up out of my own dark and I am certain that wherever in Europe there are minds strong enough to lead others the same vague hatred rises; in four or five or in less generations this hatred will have issued in violence and imposed some rule of kindred. I cannot know the nature of that rule, for its opposite fills the light; all I can do to bring it nearer is to intensify my hatred.[26]

This brings our survey of the poem's background to an end. It remains to read it again in the light of these annotations—drawn exclusively from Yeats's work—and look for the source of its curious power, for the psychic realities which it communicates through its violent and victorious rhetoric.

Immediately it appears that its theme is the awakening of a 'rule of kindred' to encounter and defeat the spawning democracy of the age. This awakening will not occur immediately, may not occur even soon, but 'Someday' the challenge will be presented and the best blood will answer. For now the impulse is dormant, 'slumber bound.' But when it awakes it will marshal all its ancient, ancestral energies, and call upon its friends. The civilities of courtly life where the women 'spoke sweet and low' will reveal their old strength, the pass and violence which had achieved in the first place 'the sweetness that all longed for night and day.' Blood will cry out to blood and for blood; the crucial images that make and break civilization will beckon to the savage consummation. The seeds of a new high culture will be sown as aristocracy calls upon its warrior heritage to face the new Salamis, Thermopylae, Valley of the Black Pig:

> That civilization may not sink
> Its great battle lost.[27]

But what makes 'Hound Voice' unique among these poems is the poet's exultant participation. No longer does he merely look on in expectation, dismay or tragic joy. He is magisterially present, not with a 'gift to set a statesman right',[28] but with the poet's instinct to recognize the right cause, the true allies, the crucial moment of test for all his kind. That 'hour of terror' will, it seems, wipe out vacillation and remorse because the individual will now find its sanction in the universal imperative. Stephen Dedalus had spoken of history as a nightmare from which he hoped to awake. The Yeats voice here aspires to awake, as it were, *into* the nightmare of history as one of those choice and master spirits which he had spent his lifetime summoning in demonic rage—Oisin, Cuchulain, Pearse, Connolly, Robert Emmet and Wolfe Tone—'Aye, and Achilles, Timor, Babar, Barhaim, all/Who have lived in joy and laughed into the face of death.'[29] It was inevitable that at some stage the self would want to become the anti-self, casting off hesitation and scruple, that the anxious and sedentary poet should wish to assume the hero, 'violent and famous' like Cuchulain, or live momentarily, like Oisin among

> Companions long accurst and dead,
> And hounds for centuries dust and air.[30]

It is the one poem in which Yeats gives himself to the blood-dimmed stream of history and becomes personally 'fighting mad.'[31] That identification can be interpreted as an imaginative leap into vicarious violence which he had spent a lifetime contemplating through a whole range of personae and scenarios, fictional, mythical, historical. Or it can be seen as a dramatic presentiment of the moment when, in a not far future reincarnation, the poet would become the swordsman while Cuchulain sang and sewed in Hades among cowards. In either case it gives us Yeats, however obliquely, entertaining with relish a rare moment of violence and triumph on the shore of modern history.

# NOTES

First published in *Yeats, Sligo and Ireland*, edited by A. Norman Jeffares (Gerrards Cross, Bucks: Colin Smythe, 1980).

1   A. Norman Jeffares, *Commentary on Yeats's Poems* (London: Macmillan, 1968), p. 500. Professor Jeffares told me that when he asked the poet's widow about the poem, she replied that Yeats had given her this one cryptic comment on it.

2   *The Variorum Edition of the Poems of W.B. Yeats*, edited by Peter Allt and Russell K. Alspach (New York: Macmillan, 1957) p. 3. All future references to this edition will be incorporated in the text when the poem's title is specified there; otherwise, they will be footnoted.

3   See note in *Variorum*, pp. 806–7, in which Yeats explains that 'This hound and this deer seem plain images of the desire of the man "which is for the woman", and "the desire of the woman which is for the desire of the man".'

4   'Easter 1916', *Variorum*, p. 392.

5   Perhaps that spirited gentlewoman, Dorothy Wellesley, with her 'Great Dane that cannot bay the moon' being, perhaps ominously, 'sunk in sleep' (*Variorum* p. 579), is also sister of the company.

6   'The Gyres', *Ibid.*, p. 564.

7   'I See Phantoms of Hatred', *Ibid.*, pp. 426–7.

8   'Ancestral Houses', *Ibid.*, p. 418.

9   'Upon a House Shaken by the Land Agitation', *Ibid.*, p. 264.

10   'Ancestral Houses', *Ibid.*, p. 418.

11   'My House', *Ibid.*, p. 419.

12   'The Second Coming', *Ibid.*, p. 402.

13   'It may almost be said that before verse can be human again it must learn to be brutal.' J.M. Synge, *Collected Works Volume 1: Poems*, edited by Robin Skelton (London: Oxford University Press, 1962; Gerrards Cross, Bucks: Colin Smythe, 1982; Washington D.C.: Catholic University of America Press, 1982), xxxvi.

14   *The Senate Speeches of W.B. Yeats*, edited by Donald R. Pearce (London: Faber, 1960), p. 99.

15   It is perhaps useful, though not necessary, to note here that before Yeats had discovered the gyres, his symbolic 'sesame' to the recurrent cycles of history, he had derived from William Blake an antithetical concept of religious process:

> The Mother should an Harlot been,
> Just such a one as Magdalen  .  .  .  (Blake, 'The Everlasting Gospel')

16   'The Tables of the Law', W.B. Yeats, *Mythologies* (London: Macmillan, 1959), p. 296.

17   *Ibid.*, p. 267.

18   'The Secret Rose', *Variorum* p. 170.

19   'I See Phantoms of Hatred', *Ibid.*, p. 427.

20   'The Statues', *Ibid.*, p. 611.

21   'The Gyres', *Ibid.*, p. 564.

22   'The Old Stone Cross', *Ibid.*, p. 598.

23   'A Dialogue of Self and Soul', *Ibid.*, p. 479.

24   W.B. Yeats, *Explorations* (London: Macmillan, 1962), p. 423.

25   *Ibid.*, p. 437.

26   W.B. Yeats, *Essays and Introductions* (London: Macmillan, 1961), p. 526.

27   'Long-legged Fly', *Variorum*, p. 617.

28   'On being asked for a War Poem', *Ibid.*, p. 359.

29   'Her Courage', *Ibid.*, p. 366.

30   'The Wanderings of Oisin', *Ibid.*, p. 11.

31   'Under Ben Bulben', *Ibid.*, p. 638.

# – 3 –

# Yeats Remembered

When Yeats died in January 1939, W.H. Auden, perhaps the most excitable political intelligence among English poets, produced an elegy which appeared in the March *New Republic* and an article, 'The Public v. Mr William Butler Yeats,' which appeared in the Spring issue of the *Partisan Review* of that year. Both are sharply relevant to the poet's standing today, and to the political controversies that currently centre upon his work. Auden is torn between his admiration for Yeats's poetic accomplishment and alarm at his political attitudes. The poem is contorted with a desire to find excuses for Yeats: 'mad Ireland hurt you into poetry.' And in the long run 'time', that old reliable, having no political conscience, only an adoration of language, will in due course absolve him and his breed:

> Time that with this strange excuse
> Pardoned Kipling and his views,
> And will pardon Paul Claudel,
> Pardons him for writing well.[1]

Realizing, correctly, that time might not pardon him for writing thus Auden excluded these lines from subsequent editions of the poem. But other lines remain: to the effect that 'poetry makes nothing happen': 'Ireland,' after all, 'has her madness and her weather still.' And, in the article, the Defence Counsel concludes that 'art is a product of history, not a cause,' that the Prosecution is deluded in thinking that 'art ever makes anything happen.' It could be Haines, another troubled Englishman, telling Stephen Dedalus: 'It seems history is to blame'.[2] It goes without saying that this sort of absolution would have infuriated Yeats who in his youth would not give a penny for a song 'Did not the poet sing it with such airs/ That one believed he had a sword upstairs,'[3] and in his old age could lie awake wondering 'Did that play of mine send out/Certain men the English shot.'[4]

The decades that followed brought the New Criticism to dominate the academies, and for a long period there was little or no interrogation of Yeats's politics. Instead, extravagant energies were bent upon explication of the text, exploration of the weird and labyrinthine sources of the thought, exposure of the early drafts and their subsequent revisions, publication of the occasional prose and of the letters, biographical investigation of the Yeats family, and the perennial homage of the Summer School at Sligo. This could not and did not last.

The reaction set in with Cruise O'Brien's 1965 essay 'Passion and Cunning' in which he asserted that Yeats 'expected, and hoped, that Ireland "after the revolution" would be a sort of satellite of a Fascist-dominated Europe.'[5] Then came books, largely countervailing, by Elizabeth Cullingford and Grattan Freyer,[6] before the onset of the Freudian, Marxist, Feminist, Deconstructionist criticism of the 1980s. These criticisms found their chief Irish platform in the *Crane Bag* journal and continue among the Field Day pamphleteers, provoking a modicum of healthy controversy.

The Auden dilemma is, for instance, rehearsed but again left unresolved by Terry Eagleton when he dismisses 'All the values, in short, of the artistically admirable, politically revolting "Prayer for my Daughter".'[7] But 'writing well' does nothing to save the poet from sustained charges of 'phallocentric ideology', 'swaggering, anarchic, Byronic affirmation', and 'reactionary political ideology'. Tom Paulin is also disturbed by Yeats's 'phallocentric vision' and voices a recurrent contrast with Joyce (who is urban, pacifist, modern and 'socialist,' therefore favourite pupil of these schoolrooms): 'where Yeats often mobilizes some of the more rabid goblins of nationalist emotion, Joyce scorned consciously *völkisch* ideas.'[8] Such charges as these are rehearsed with various emphasis by Seamus Deane, Declan Kiberd, Fintan O'Toole and others who see Yeats as an irresistible challenge to a leftist, political —and largely polemical— criticism: his phony aristocracy and surrender to violence (Deane), his promotion of the phony pastoral at the expense of the authentic urban (Kiberd, O'Toole).

These charges, however rudely I summarize them, keep reminding me of my first lessons on literary criticism: that I should not rush to moral judgment; that the poem is first a poem and not a homily; that I should get rid of that schoolboy idea instilled by priests that a poem need be in any way 'uplifting'; that it is sharp practice to extract the conceptual meaning from a poet and judge the poem by judging it. On the other hand, 'writing well' is not enough. I don't understand how a poem can be 'politically revolting' while remaining a good poem, let alone a great one like 'Prayer for my Daughter'. (Does Terry Eagleton judge it a good poem in its totality? He declines to say.) In other words, I declare my prejudice against a criticism that asks the political or the moral questions first or which refuses to see a poem as an integral act.

Having said that, it is, it seems, necessary to say again that Yeats's attitude to any of these themes—sex, love, power, violence, class, history—cannot be established by recourse to any single poem. In the first place he was constantly developing, learning and unlearning. The same love poet wrote 'The Cloths of Heaven', 'The Travail of Passion', 'No Second Troy', 'Adam's Curse', 'Broken Dreams', 'The Mermaid', 'Solomon and Sheba', 'Crazy Jane Talks to the Bishop' and 'The Spur'. The same political animal wrote 'September 1913', corrected it with 'Easter 1916', reversed that with 'Nineteen Hundred and Nineteen', and cancelled all of them with 'The Great Day':

> Hurrah for revolution and more cannon shot!
> A beggar upon horseback lashes a beggar on foot,
> Hurrah for revolution and cannon come again!
> The beggars have changed places, but the lash goes on.[9]

So he kept changing, and changing his mind. He believed like every poet in history that poetry is a privileged mode of thought with the right to say, 'this might be how things are, or this, or again this.' His astonishing range, the endless variety of his forms, lyric, epic, elegiac, dramatic, reflective, and of his moods, is therefore an infallible hallmark of his genius. His elaborated response to every nuance of contemporary history, the dialogue between his public and private self, is another.

So he grew and changed. But furthermore his art is not syncretic but antinomial, dialectical. His method is to state a position with maximum intensity and draw from that utterance the energy to state its opposite. Neither statement is essentially 'true', far less so can it be held to represent the poet's settled conviction on the matter. One who knows his Yeats is therefore outraged to see another seize upon and isolate any single poem to trap the general conscience of the poet. Especially outraged to see a *section* of a long symphonic poem like 'Meditations in Time of Civil War' debated as if its status could be other than provisional in the poem's general economy. That opening movement, 'Ancestral Houses', has recently been a source of controversy between Seamus Deane and Denis Donoghue[10] where its statements on aristocracy, violence and greatness are treated as if the poem ended there and did not embody in its sixth movement, 'The Stare's Nest at My Window', one of the most piercing—and self-accusing—cries for compassion and peace in all modern literature:

We had fed the heart on fantasies,
The heart's grown brutal from the fare;
More substance in our enmities
Than in our love; O honey-bees,
Come build in the empty house of the stare.[11]

That poetic sequence, in fact, dramatizes in each of its seven parts a different apprehension of violence. The first asks, with resonant impersonality, whether man's greatness is somehow indivisible from his violence. The second records that the tower where he pursues his peaceful meditations, once built by men-at-arms as a fortress, has resumed for him its function as a 'befitting emblem of adversity'. The third contemplates Sato's sword, symbol of art and war, destruction and creation, and of apocalypse—'Juno's peacock screamed.' The fourth ponders whether his descendants, born between art and violence, will flourish or decline. The fifth finds the poet, a man of words, envying the men of action who appear at his door. The sixth, with mounting personal involvement, prays for peace—'the sweetness that all longed for night and day.' In the last, the poet, 'my wits astray', imagines himself in a vision of millennial panic without yielding to the fever of mob violence, before returning to the solitude of his sedentary craft.

The poem in Sidney's purest sense 'nothing affirmeth'; but no poet since Shakespeare has confronted the terrible urge to violence that human-kind has everywhere in common: our compulsion to murder and create. Nor has any poet, even Shakespeare, so dramatized the rage for order that accompanies our temptation to immerse in the destructive element. This is intrinsic to his greatness. It is easy to condemn violence, war, the lot. It takes special courage to confront it in oneself and give witness. That, I suspect, is why Yeats was so dismissive of Wilfred Owen and the war poets.[12] They had the comfort of being right. Yeats, on the other hand, takes the big risks, and goes all times over the top. But only the most perversely hostile reading would convict his poetry as a whole of sponsoring violence.

As for fascism: will this ever be got into perspective? He was a most conscientious senator of the fledgling state. With the exception of his speech on divorce—an altogether forgivable oratorical tour de force—his contributions to the House were sensible and balanced on education, censorship, public order, partition—which he suggested would be solved only by the Free State making its life-style attractive enough for Northern Unionists to want a share of it.

But the country was on the brink of anarchy with an unresolved civil war at home and the triumph of the Bolsheviks in Eastern Europe. Visiting Italy every summer in the mid-1920s and searching in his mind for a means of inserting in his Government's procedures the thought of Burke, Swift and Berkeley he found himself impressed by the manner in which Mussolini—whom he often mispronounced as Missolonghi—had surrounded himself with 'educated and able men'. He was particularly impressed with Gentile, the fascist minister for education, who had founded his thought on Berkeley. Like many of his Irish contemporaries Yeats believed in the possibilities of the corporate state whereby various interests—trades, crafts, unions, employers, professions—would be represented with a consequent alleviation of class divisions and resentments. The composition of the present Irish Senate is based on this principle. He made no secret of these activities and saw no more harm in them than did his contemporaries. He wanted to see his country reunited and the rule of law restored.

But his enthusiasm for fascist Italy receded with his withdrawal from active politics, and his sense of impending apocalypse. Letters of the last few years reveal that despite his dislike of communism he favoured the republicans in the Spanish Civil War, distrusting Franco's 'ignorant form of Catholicism'—having made long war on its Irish equivalent—and 'all through the Abyssinian war my sympathies were with the Abyssinians.' The suggestion that he would have collaborated with a foreign fascist regime in Ireland is not just unworthy but bizarre:

as a young man I belonged to the I.R.B. and was in many things O'Leary's pupil. Besides, why should I trouble about communism, fascism, liberalism, radicalism, when all, . . . are going down stream with the artificial unity which ends every civilization?[13]

He had despaired of conscripting the visions of Swift, Berkeley, or that of 'haughtier-headed Burke that proved the State a tree'[14] to the conditions of de Valera's Ireland. Only an implosion of the gyre would bring back the promise of an organized society, his constantly desired 'unity of being'. On leaving down A. Norman Jeffares' sparkling new biography of the poet[15] I found myself saying, 'What a marvellous life!' The greatest poet of his age, he had still founded and sustained one of the chief theatres of the century, written the great public poems of his country, served in its parliament, devised its coinage, contrived its second art gallery, founded its Academy of Letters, pioneered a radically new concept of total theatre in his verse plays, founded a family. His poetry is on the lips of every Irish schoolchild and at least one of his ballads is 'sung above the glass'. His Cuchulain will stalk through the theatre in this memorial year in all five manifestations under the direction of James Flannery; and his experiments with the Noh will be tested there by Masaru Sekine in a separate production. Let the deconstructionists rail and sweat. He'll not be begging anyone's pardon.

# NOTES

First published in *Irish Literary Supplement* Vol. 8, No. 1, Spring 1989, to commemorate the fiftieth anniversary of Yeats's death.

1  'In Memory of W.B. Yeats', *The English Auden: Poems, Essays and Dramatic Writings 1927–1939*, edited by Edward Mendelson (London: Faber, 1977), pp. 242–3.

2  James Joyce, *Ulysses* (London: The Bodley Head, 1960), p. 24.

3  'All Things Can Tempt Me', *The Variorum Edition of the Poems of W.B. Yeats*, edited by Peter Allt and Russell K. Allspach (New York: Macmillan, 1957), p. 267.

4  'The Man and the Echo', *Ibid.*, p. 632.

5  'Passion and Cunning: An Essay on the Politics of W.B. Yeats', *In Excited Reverie: A Centenary Tribute to William Butler Yeats 1865–1939*, edited by A. Norman Jeffares and K.G.W. Cross (London: Macmillan, 1965; New York: St Martin's Press, 1965), p. 272. The essay is reprinted and updated in Conor Cruise O'Brien, *Passion and Cunning and Other Essays* (London: Weidenfeld and Nicolson, 1988).

6  Elizabeth Cullingford, *Yeats, Ireland and Fascism* (London: Macmillan, 1981); Grattan Freyer, *W.B. Yeats and the Anti-Democratic Tradition* (Dublin: Gill and Macmillan, 1981).

7  Terry Eagleton 'Politics and Sexuality in W.B. Yeats', in *The Crane Bag* Volume 9, Number 2, 1985, p. 139. The essay is included in *The Crane Bag Book of Irish Studies Volume 2 (1982–1985)*, edited by Mark Patrick Hederman and Richard Kearney (Dublin: Wolfhound Press, 1987).

8  Tom Paulin, *Ireland and the English Crisis* (Newcastle-upon-Tyne: Bloodaxe Books, 1984), p. 144.

9  'The Great Day', *The Variorum Edition of the Poems of W.B. Yeats*, ed. Allt and Alspach, p. 590.

10  See Denis Donoghue, 'The Political Turn in Criticism', in *The Irish Review* 5 (Autumn 1988), pp. 56–67.

11  *The Variorum Edition of the Poems of W.B. Yeats*, ed. Allt and Alspach, p. 425.

12  In his Introduction to *The Oxford Book of Modern Verse 1892–1935* (Oxford: Oxford University Press, 1936).

13  *The Letters of W.B. Yeats*, edited by Allan Wade (London: Macmillan, 1954), p. 869.

14  'Blood and the Moon', *The Variorum Edition of the Poems of W.B. Yeats*, ed. Allt and Alspach, p. 481.

15  A. Norman Jeffares, *W.B. Yeats: A New Biography* (London: Hutchinson, 1988).

# – 4 –

# Christy Mahon and the Apotheosis of Loneliness

*I*

'It'll be a poor thing for the household man where you go sniffing for a female wife'.

Michael James
*The Playboy of the Western World*[1]

Agreement is general among critics that *The Playboy of the Western World* is a masterpiece. But there is still a curious diversity of opinion about the precise nature of its excellence. Those among its first audience who were not infuriated by the play were puzzled by it. Those who did not condemn it in sociological terms as a libel or a travesty of Irish life wondered what else it might be. Synge himself hastily called it an 'extravaganza'[2] and swiftly withdrew the label. Yeats, arguing with a judge in court, preferred to call it an 'exaggeration'.[3] Even when critics took the debate beyond the cockpit of affronted patriotism they could not reach agreement either on its dominating theme or on the allied problem of its dramatic category.

Una Ellis-Fermor called it a 'tragi-comedy' which took for its main theme 'the growth of fantasy in a mind or a group of minds.'[4] Ann Saddlemyer expands this insight when she suggests that 'in *The Playboy* we see the power of the myth to create a reality out of the dream or illusion itself.'[5] T.R. Henn in his Introduction to the Methuen edition of the *Plays and Poems* outlines seven possible readings of the play. He suggests that it might be seen as a 'semi-tragedy'; as a 'free comedy', in which moral issues are reversed, transcended or ignored in the desire for 'energy'; as a 'Dionysiac comedy'; as a 'satire' in which Christy becomes a 'comic Oedipus'; as 'mock-heroic' in which Christy becomes Odysseus; as 'a tragi-comic piece with the Widow Quin as Nausicaa'; and finally, a reading he seems to favour, as a tragedy with Pegeen as the 'heroine-

victim',[6] Norman Podhoretz in a persuasive essay suggests that the play
has 'the myth of rebellion against the father as its basis.'[7] P.L. Henry
sees Christy as the 'Playboy-Hero' and finds parallels to him in *Beowulf*
and the heroic Irish sagas.[8] Stanley Sultan finds in Christy's person 'a
pervasive, sincere and full-fledged analogue to Christ.'[9] Alan Price sees it
primarily as a play in which 'Christy's imagination transforms  the
dream into actuality.'[10] Ann Saddlemyer believes that '*The Playboy of
the Western World* deals with the actual creation of myth.'[11] Synge
himself has remarked that 'there are, it may be hinted, several sides to
*The Playboy*';[12] the critics continue to bear him out. Clearly the play is
capable of yielding a wide diversity of valid readings, depending what
'side' one approaches it from. But where is its centre? What basic myth
or fable does it enact? What theme is embodied in that fable? What kind
of play is it? These are still questions worth asking.

## II

More than one critic has complained that the end of *The Shadow of
the Glen* is unconvincing. The reconciliation between Daniel Burke and
Michael Dara—who after all had been planning to supplant him as Nora's
husband—has been seen as too sudden, too much of a *volte-face*. 'I was
thinking to strike you, Michael Dara,' Burke says, 'but you're a quiet
man, God help you, and I don't mind you at all.'[13] The point of course is
that they are two of a kind; they are settled men, householders. They
want a world in which they can have their drinks in peace. Michael Dara
is no longer a threat once Nora and the Tramp, the people of passion
and poetry, have been expelled. With their expulsion society has righted
itself and can get on with its quotidian business. The pattern is central to
Synge's comedies. As the curtain falls on *The Well of the Saints* the freebooters, Martin and Mary Doul, have departed, and the Saint leads in the
settled man Timmy the Smith and his bride Molly Byrne to be married.
In *The Tinker's Wedding* the Priest is left '*master of the situation*'[14] while
the tinkers retreat into their vagrant irresponsibility. The end of *The
Playboy* gives a richer, more complex, version of the same basic pattern.
Michael James remarks with relief that 'we'll have peace now for our
drinks'(173), while a disconsolate Pegeen laments, too late, the loss of
her only playboy. She realizes that Christy's visitation had presented her
with a vivid possibility of passion and poetry, and that she has failed to
grasp it. With the exit of Christy, launched on his 'romping lifetime', the
spirit of Dionysus has departed. She is back where we had found her at
the first curtain, in the world of Shawn Keogh and the papal dispensation
and the trousseau that must be ordered from Castlebar.

The two life-views offered by the play may usefully be called Dionysiac and Apollonian. Dionysiac is the more easily acceptable: Daniel Corkery was perhaps the first to apply it when he rejected the term 'extravaganza'— 'Dionysiac would have served him better, meaning by that word the serving of the irresponsible spirit of natural man.'[15] Northrop Frye, on the other hand, describes Apollonian comedy as 'the story of how a hero becomes accepted by a society of gods.'[16] If we take the definition at its 'low mimetic'[17] level we can see that *The Playboy,* for a good deal of its action, shapes like this kind of comedy, only to swerve into Dionysiac triumph in its final resolution.

It is clear from the early drafts[18] of the play that Synge considered and rejected many different kinds of ending: he contemplated a possible marriage between Christy and the Widow Quin, a *menage à trois* involving the two Mahons and the Widow Quin, even a wedding between Christy and Pegeen. But it became increasingly clear to him that his material demanded Christy refuse membership of the settled community, and also that Christy's discovery of his own nature involved the discovery and recognition of his real father and the rejection of the pseudo-Dionysian Michael James. For despite his recklessness at the wake, despite his willingness—at least while he is drunk—to have Christy as a son-in-law, Michael James ends up with a pathetic anxiety to protect our 'little cabins from the treachery of law'(173). On the other hand Old Mahon's final 'Is it me?' and 'I am crazy again' betoken his delighted recognition that Christy is really his son, instinct with the same savagery, energy and *braggadocio.*

Indeed one can discern three groups of characters in the play, and distinguish them in terms of the Dionysiac and Apollonian postures. Old Mahon from the beginning and Christy towards the end embody Dionysiac freedom, energy and excess. Shawn Keogh and the offstage but influential Father Reilly, at their low mimetic level, represent a version of the Apollonian—the rational, the settled, the well-ordered existence. The latter attitude finds expression not only in character and social pattern but in a sort of ritual invocation of 'the Holy Father and the Cardinals of Rome'(63), of 'St Joseph and St Patrick and St Brigid and St James'(65). In between is a group—one might call them the 'pseudo-Dionysians'—who waver between the two positions. Michael James, Philly and Jimmy rejoice in the Bacchantic excess of Kate Cassidy's wake, but when their security is threatened they opt for the domestic pieties. They salute the Dionysiac vigour and daring; in the person of Christy they try to accommodate it, even to use it. But their ambivalence is patent, and it provides a good deal of the play's comic incongruity, as with Jimmy's remark before leaving for the wake: 'Now, by the grace of God, herself will be safe this night, with a man killed his father holding danger from the door'(77).

Pegeen is torn between the two attitudes. Her intended marriage to Shawn clearly implies no acquiescence to his values. When he asserts that 'we're as good this place as another, maybe, and as good these times as we were for ever,' she replies with scorn:

As good, is it? Where now will you meet the like of Daneen Sullivan knocked the eye from a peeler, or Marcus Quin, God rest him, got six months for maiming ewes, and he a great warrant to tell stories of holy Ireland till he'd have the old women shedding down tears about their feet. Where will you find the like of them, I'm saying?(59)

The irony of her situation is, of course, that when she does encounter the likes of them in Christy she proves unequal to the challenge thus presented. She recognizes in Christy a kinsman of the poets—'fine fiery fellows with great rages when their temper's roused'(81)—and approves. But she tries to domesticate him, to tame his fire. When she is presented in the final scenes with the full reality of his fiery nature she fails. As Norman Podhoretz puts it, she 'can perceive greatness but cannot rise to it.'[19] She is the tragic figure of the play. But that is not to agree with T.R. Henn that the play is a tragedy, her tragedy.

The play is Christy's. It is about his escape to freedom between the Scylla and Charybdis of loneliness on the one hand and domination on the other. It is about his collision with settled society and his victorious rejection of it in favour of a new triumphalist attitude to the world. If the collision with society had resulted in his destruction the play would have been a tragedy. As it celebrates the victory of the aggressive individual will over the immoveable forces of society it must be deemed a Dionysiac comedy—the only great one of its kind that I know.

The core of this comedy is Christy's loneliness. Synge went to great pains to enunciate this theme, to build it up gradually till it achieves full expression half-way through the play. In the early drafts[20] Christy's loneliness is dwelt on at length in his conversation with Pegeen in the first act; but much of the material is later struck out with the marginal note—'Reserve this lonesome motif for II.'[21] Eventually it is towards the middle of Act II that the theme gets its full orchestration. There, when Pegeen threatens to send him away Christy replies with bleak realism, 'I was lonesome all times and born lonesome, I'm thinking, as the moon of dawn'(111). This is the crux of his condition. How is he to heal the wound of his lonesomeness? Can he do so without exchanging one kind of domination for another? Because it seems at this point that he can only have Pegeen on her own overbearing terms. At this point he is willing to accept those terms; as yet he knows no better, he has not fully discovered himself. When she relents ('Lay down that switch and throw some sods on the fire. You're pot-boy in this place, and I'll not have you mitch off from us now') his relief is painful:

CHRISTY   [*astonished, slowly*]. It's making game of me you were [*following her with fearful joy*], and I can stay so, working at your side, and I not lonesome from this mortal day.(113)

It will be helpful to trace Christy's development to this point of the drama.

## *III*

Christy comes in out of the darkness: he has been 'groaning wicked like a maddening dog' in the furzy ditch—'a dark lonesome place'(61). As he tells his story there is a touching contrast between the delight he is getting from such unexpected and appreciative company and the loneliness out of which he has emerged. He describes himself as 'a poor orphaned traveller, has a prison behind him, and hanging before, and hell's gap gaping below'(71). His home is 'a distant place . . . a windy corner of high, distant hills'(75). Since Tuesday was a week he has been 'walking forward facing hog, dog or divil on the highway of the road.' When Pegeen probes him about the girls he might have beguiled in his travels another, and important, aspect of his lonesomeness is revealed in his reply:

I've said it [his story] nowhere till this night, I'm telling you, for I've seen none the like of you the eleven days I am walking the world, looking over a low ditch or a high ditch on my north or south, into stony scattered fields, or scribes of bog, where you'd see young limber girls, and fine prancing women making laughter with the men.(81)

In the same sentence the deprivation of his past and his emerging sexual confidence are suggested.

The story of his domination by his father unfolds alongside the theme of his lonesomeness. In his description of Old Mahon in the horrors of drink the full Dionysiac chord is struck:

It's that you'd say surely if you seen him and he after drinking for weeks, rising up in the red dawn, or before it maybe, and going out into the yard as naked as an ash tree in the moon of May, and shying clods again the visage of the stars till he'd put the fear of death into the banbhs and the screeching sows.(83–5)

The presence of Old Mahon in Christy's life had in itself been ferocious and formidable. It became unbearable, we are told in the second act, when he tried to force Christy into marriage with the woman who had suckled him as a child. It is this that rouses his spirits to 'a deed of blood'(87). When Norman Podhoretz suggests that the play's underlying myth is 'rebellion against the father'[22] he gives us, I believe, precisely half the story. The other half is the recognition and acceptance of the father, and this is enacted in the reversal at the end, after the second and deliberate 'killing'. In the meantime Christy must discover and reject an alternative and different father in Michael James, a different form of female domination in Pegeen Mike. It is significant that Pegeen is the first person to offer him violence when he enters the Flaherty cabin, and that she behaves towards him with the most surly possessiveness *(seizing his arm* and *shaking him)* when the Widow Quin makes her play for him towards the end of Act I. Before she leaves, the Widow Quin warns him that 'there's right torment will await you here if you go romancing with her like'(91). Therefore, though Christy may be ingenuously happy with his 'great luck and company'(93), the audience watching the first curtain fall has its own well-founded reservations.

At the opening of Act II we find Christy transformed with the prospects of companionship which his new life seems to hold for him. He can henceforth spend his days 'talking out with swearing Christians in place of my old dogs and cat'(95). Immediately he has an audience of young girls to whom he retells the story which has now grown to heroic proportions.[23] He is praised for his eloquence as well as for his daring. The toast proposed to him and the Widow Quin by Sara Tansey compares them—both killers, and loners—to the 'outlandish lovers in the sailor's song'(105) and goes on to invoke the extravagant Dionysiac values to which Christy now aspires in his imagination, but which he has yet to embody and realize in life and action:

Drink a health to the wonders of the western world, the pirates, preachers, poteen-makers, with the jobbing jockies, parching peelers, and the juries fill their stomachs selling judgments of the English law.

It is at this moment that Pegeen returns, drives them from the house, and turns on Christy with quite gratuitous cruelty. Here we see some of the 'torment' that the Widow Quin had predicted for him. And it is here that the theme of loneliness is given its full expression. Christy is forced to choose between an obedient security with Pegeen on the one hand and the lonesome roads on the other. One could argue that this is Christy's first failure: he hasn't grown sufficiently into his new self to make the choice appropriate to his nature. As Synge seems to have worked harder on this than on almost any other scene in the play it is worth examining at length:

CHRISTY   [*loudly*]. What joy would they [the neighbour girls] have to bring hanging to the likes of me?

PEGEEN   It'd queer joys they have, and who knows the thing they'd do, if it'd make the green stones cry itself to think of you swaying and swiggling at the butt of a rope, and you with a fine, stout neck, God bless you! the way you'd be a half an hour, in great anguish, getting your death.

CHRISTY    [*getting his boots and putting them on*]. If there's that terror of them, it'd be best, maybe, I went on wandering like Esau or Cain and Abel on the sides of Neifin or the Erris Plain.

PEGEEN    [*beginning to play with him*]. It would, maybe, for I've heard the Circuit Judges this place is a heartless crew.

CHRISTY    [*bitterly*]. It's more than judges this place is a heartless crew. [*Looking up at her.*] And isn't it a poor thing to be starting again and I a lonesome fellow will be looking out on women and girls the way the needy fallen spirits do be looking on the Lord?

PEGEEN    What call have you to be lonesome when there's poor girls walking Mayo in their thousands now?

CHRISTY    [*grimly*]. It's well you know what call I have. It's well you know it's a lonesome thing to be passing small towns with the lights shining sideways when the night is down, or going in strange places with a dog nosing[24] before you and a dog nosing behind, or drawn to the cities where you'd hear a voice kissing and talking deep love in every shadow of the ditch, and you passing on with an empty hungry stomach failing from your heart.

PEGEEN    I'm thinking you're an odd man, Christy Mahon. The oddest walking fellow I ever set my eyes on to this hour to-day.

CHRISTY    What would any be but odd men and they living lonesome in the world?(109–11)

Two points are worth making here. Christy talks in the language and imagery of an outsider. It is the moving imagery of a traveller looking in at the settled world, wondering what it is like, certain that it alone holds the answer to his deprivation. Furthermore the warmth of this settled world is continuously seen in terms of sexual love. The one implies the other; his choice is between Pegeen Mike and exterior darkness. They slowly work towards a reconciliation, almost a declaration of love. But Pegeen's final remark before the entry of Shawn Keogh establishes her dominance in the relationship:

I'm thinking you'll be a loyal young lad to have working around, and if you vexed me a while since with your leaguing with the girls, I wouldn't give a thraneen for a lad hadn't a mighty spirit in him and a gamey heart.(113)

His 'wildness' is approved, so long as it dances to her tune.

Meanwhile the forces of society are working for his expulsion. Shawn Keogh, ambiguously abetted by the Widow Quin, tries to bribe him with a suit of clothes and a ticket for America. He fails, and the plot seems set fair for a romantic resolution, when Old Mahon appears. There is savage dramatic irony in the scene where Christy cowers behind the door and listens to his past being rehearsed for the Widow Quin in his father's contemptuous vision:

MAHON    [*with a shout of derision*]. Running wild, is it? If he seen a red petticoat coming swinging over the hill, he'd be off to hide in the sticks,

and you'd see him shooting out his sheep's eyes between the little
twigs and leaves, and his two ears rising like a hare looking out
through a gap. Girls indeed!

WIDOW QUIN    It was drink maybe?

MAHON    And he a poor fellow would get drunk on the smell of a
pint!(121–3)

It is now evident that Christy must defeat or outwit his father if he is to
realize his expectations. For the first time we find a genuine, if impotent,
anger rising in him; and this anger is embodied in rhetoric that becomes
more vivid and fearless as the play proceeds:

CHRISTY    [*breaking out*]. His one son, is it? May I meet him with one tooth
and it aching, and one eye to be seeing seven and seventy divils in
the twists of the road, and one old timber leg on him to limp into
the scalding grave. [*Looking out.*] There he is now crossing the
strands, and that the Lord God would send a high wave to wash
him from the world.(125)

The second act ends therefore with Christy poised between a past that
holds only humiliation, impotence and loneliness, and a future that seems
to offer him the vivid things—love, companionship, admiration and, more
problematically, freedom.

When Old Mahon reappears at the opening of Act III the resemblances
between him and Christy are deftly emphasized. He too has been walking
the roads and 'winning clean beds and the fill of my belly four times in
the day, and I doing nothing but telling stories of that naked truth'.(135)
He is as vainglorious about the resilience of his skull as Christy was about
his 'one single blow'. He has Christy's eloquence if not his lyricism. He
exults in the wildness of his excess: at one time he had seen 'ten scarlet
divils letting on they'd cork my spirit in a gallon can; and one time I seen
rats as big as badgers sucking the life blood from the butt of my lug . . .';
the authorities in the Union know him as a 'terrible and fearful case, the
way that there I was one time screeching in a straitened waistcoat with
seven doctors writing out my sayings in a printed book . . .'(143–5).

Furthermore, like his son, he is constantly described in the language
and imagery—whether his own or Christy's—as an outsider, a wanderer.
Though he owns a farm he never appears as a householder; he is consistently evoked in terms of the open air, the roads, the taverns, the prisons
and asylums. We recall how Christy had described him to Pegeen in Act I
as 'a man never gave peace to any saving when he'd get two months . . .
for battering peelers or assaulting men'(85), and we recall that Pegeen
had admired a certain Daneen Sullivan and another Marcus Quin who
not only boasted similar feats but who had the eloquence to make them
into a 'gallous' story. It is also notable that Old Mahon's descriptions of

Christy present him in terms of the hills, the fields and the road—never of the house. These clear indications of an elemental kinship between them tend subtly to offset their mutual antagonism throughout and help to prepare us not only for their reversal of roles, but also their reconciliation in the recognition scene at the end. This recognition is hinted at when Old Mahon, watching the races on the strand, sees his own son carrying all before him. But he is not ready yet for the real recognition—that Christy is truly his son, an even greater 'playboy' than himself. This insight can only be reached when Christy recognizes Mahon as his real father, thereby rejecting the men of Mayo and their law-fearing timidity, and by transcending his infatuation for Pegeen.

But first, in that remarkable love scene with Pegeen in Act III, we are permitted to see Christy in full possession of his powers of eloquence, passion and tenderness playing for 'the crowning prize'(147) and winning. Here Christy carries Pegeen triumphantly into his outdoor world: the language in which he woos her is redolent of movement, of the outdoors, of 'Neifin in the dews of night.' She baulks coyly for a moment at his 'poacher's love', but cannot help yielding to it: 'If I was your wife, I'd be along with you those nights, Christy Mahon, the way you'd see I was a great hand at coaxing bailiffs, or coining funny nicknames for the stars of night.'(149) Christy for the first time seems to be winning on his own terms. The play seems to be moving towards the resolution of traditional romantic comedy, with a wedding between Christy and Pegeen, and a possible second between Old Mahon and the Widow Quin—a victory for Apollo. But Pegeen is not Nora Burke; and the play turns swiftly towards a different and altogether more satisfactory conclusion.

Christy is now 'mounted on the spring-tide of the stars of luck'(157); Pegeen swears to wed him 'and not renege'; Michael James—not without fumbling reservations—gives them his drunken blessing. It seems the moment of extreme felicity: Christy has found status, love, a new father. But it is a false felicity, because his real father is still alive. The sudden appearance of Old Mahon changes everything. Immediately Pegeen reneges. Her reason is the social one: she thinks it bad 'the world should see me raging for a Munster liar and the fool of men'(161). Christy now goes through a series of traumatic insights. First he tries to deny Old Mahon. He then appeals vainly for help to the two women. Then a vision of his past loneliness drives him to desperation:

CHRISTY   And I must go back into my torment is it, or run off like a vaga-
          bond straying through the Unions with the dusts of August making
          mudstains in the gullet of my throat, or the winds of March blowing
          on me till I'd take an oath I felt them making whistles of my ribs
          within.(163)

The language and reference are strongly reminiscent of his father's. Now Old Mahon threatens him; the crowd jeers him; he begins to see the truth of his situation, the folly of his desire to be one of them:

CHRISTY    [*in low and intense voice*]. Shut your yelling, for if you're after making a mighty man of me this day by the power of a lie, you're setting me now to think if it's a poor thing to be lonesome, it's worse maybe go mixing with the fools of earth.(165)

His second insight comes after he has 'killed' Old Mahon the second time. He thinks that Pegeen will take him back now, will 'be giving me praises the same as in the hours gone by.' But he must transcend this vanity. She rejects him more emphatically: for her there is 'a great gap between a gallous story and a dirty deed'(169). Again invoking the social ethic she urges the Mayo men to take him to the peelers 'or the lot of us will be likely put on trial for his deed to-day.' As she prepares a lighted sod to 'scorch his leg', he realizes the foolishness of his love for her. Now he is utterly alone, and it is significant that now his terror disappears. His true nature emerges in all its fierceness. His language rises to a fine reckless crescendo:

CHRISTY    You're blowing for to torture me? [*His voice rising and growing stronger.*] That's your kind, is it? Then let the lot of you be wary, for if I've to face the gallows I'll have a gay march down, I tell you, and shed the blood of some of you before I die.

SHAWN    [*in terror*]. Keep a good hold, Philly. Be wary for the love of God, for I'm thinking he would liefest wreak his pains on me.

CHRISTY    [*almost gaily*]. If I do lay my hands on you, it's the way you'll be at the fall of night hanging as a scarecrow for the fowls of hell. Ah, you'll have a gallous jaunt I'm saying, coaching out through Limbo with my father's ghost.

SHAWN    [*to* PEGEEN]. Make haste, will you. Oh, isn't he a holy terror, and isn't it true for Father Reilly that all drink's a curse that has the lot of you so shaky and uncertain now.

CHRISTY    If I can wring a neck among you, I'll have a royal judgment looking on the trembling jury in the courts of law. And won't there be crying out in Mayo the day I'm stretched up on the rope with ladies in their silks and satins snivelling in their lacy kerchiefs, and they rhyming songs and ballads on the terror of my fate? [*He squirms round on the floor and bites* SHAWN's *leg.*]

SHAWN    [*shrieking*]. My leg's bit on me! He's the like of a mad dog, I'm thinking, the way that I will surely die.

CHRISTY    [*delighted with himself*]. You will then, the way you can shake out hell's flags of welcome for my coming in two weeks or three, for I'm thinking Satan hasn't many have killed their da in Kerry and in Mayo too.(169–71)

It is now that Old Mahon comes in again, 'to be killed a third time', and the two father figures, representing two different life-views, confront each other. Michael, sobered and diminished, pleads '*apologetically*'(173) for the safety of his little cabin and his daughter's security while Old Mahon rejoices in a future of bravado and adventure in which his son and he will 'have great times from this out telling stories of the villainy of Mayo and the fools is here.' It is here that Christy has his final insight and his ultimate victory. He now knows that he not only has mastered himself but subdued his father as well. He will go, but the roles will be reversed; he will be 'master of all fights from now'. He has at last discovered his true Dionysiac nature, and in discovering it he has shaken off all domination and transfigured his lonesomeness into a posture of gay, predatory adventure. In the parting speech the wildness of the father is elevated and transformed in the poetry and passion of the son:

CHRISTY   Ten thousand blessings upon all that's here, for you've turned me a likely gaffer in the end of all, the way I'll go romancing through a romping lifetime from this hour to the dawning of the judgment day . . .(173)

So the freebooters take to their proper element, the road, and the timid people of Mayo take to their drinks, their hopes, their lamentations. The astringent light of comedy has clarified each role, defined each relation.

# NOTES

First published in *A Centenary Tribute to John Millington Synge 1871–1909: Sunshine and the Moon's Delight*, edited by S.B. Bushrui (Gerrards Cross: Colin Smythe, 1972).

1   J.M. Synge, *Collected Works Volume IV: Plays Book II*, edited by Ann Saddlemyer (London: Oxford University Press, 1968; Gerrards Cross, Bucks: Colin Smythe, 1982; Washington, D.C.: The Catholic University of America Press, 1982), p. 153. All future references to Synge's *The Playboy of the Western World* are to this edition and will be incorporated in the text.

2   Quoted by David H. Greene and Edward M. Stephens, *J.M. Synge 1871–1909* (New York and London: New York University Press, rev. ed. 1989), pp. 258–9.

3   *Freeman's Journal* 31 January 1907, p. 8. The passage occurs in the prosecution of Patrick Columb [*sic*] for creating a disturbance at a performance of *The Playboy of the Western World*. Yeats is being cross-examined by Mr Lidwell, for the defendant, before Mr Mahony:

'Mr Lidwell: Did you read the play?
Yes, and passed it.
Mr Lidwell: Is it a caricature of the Irish people?
It is no more a caricature of Ireland than *Macbeth* is a caricature of the people of Scotland or Falstaff a caricature of the gentlemen of England. The play is an example of the exaggeration of art. I have not the slightest doubt but that we shall have more of these disturbances.

Mr Lidwell: Is the play typical of the Irish people?
No! It is an exaggeration.
Mr Lidwell: Then you admit it is a caricature?
An exaggeration.'

[Editor's note. For a comparable account of the exchange (from the *Dublin Evening Mail*), see Robert Hogan and James Kilroy, *The Abbey Theatre: The Years of Synge 1905–1909*; *The Modern Irish Drama: A Documentary History* 3 (Dublin: Dolmen Press; Atlantic Highlands, N.J.: Humanities Press, 1978), p. 133.]

4   Una Ellis-Fermor, *The Irish Dramatic Movement* (London: Methuen, 1954), p. 175.
5   Ann Saddlemyer, *J.M. Synge and Modern Comedy* (Dublin: Dolmen Press, 1967), p. 23.
6   *The Plays and Poems of J.M. Synge*, edited by T.R. Henn (London: Methuen, 1963), pp. 57–8.
7   Norman Podhoretz, 'Synge's Playboy: Morality and the Hero', *Essays in Criticism* 3 (July 1953), p. 337.
8    P.L. Henry, 'The Playboy of the Western World', *Philologica Pragensia*, Rocnik VIII, Cislo 2–3, 1965, pp. 189–204.
9   Stanley Sultan, 'A Joycean Look at *The Playboy of the Western World*', *The Celtic Master*, edited by Maurice Harmon (Dublin: Dolmen Press, 1969), p. 51.
10  Alan Price, *Synge and Anglo-Irish Drama* (London: Methuen, 1961), p. 162.
11  Saddlemyer, *J.M. Synge and Modern Comedy*, p. 21.
12  Greene and Stephens, *J.M. Synge 1871–1909*, p. 262.
13  Synge, *Collected Works Volume III: Plays Book I*, edited by Ann Saddlemyer (London: Oxford University Press, 1968; Gerrards Cross, Bucks: Colin Smythe, 1982; Washington, D.C.: The Catholic University of America Press, 1982), p. 59.
14  Synge, *Collected Works IV*, p. 49.
15  Daniel Corkery, *Synge and Anglo-Irish Literature* (Cork: Cork University Press, 1931), p. 185.
16  Northrop Frye, *Anatomy of Criticism* (Princeton, N.J.: Princeton University Press, 1957), p. 43.
17  *Ibid.*, p. 366. Low mimetic: a mode of literature in which the characters exhibit a power of action which is roughly on our own level, as in most comedy and realistic fiction.
18  Synge, *Collected Works IV*, p. 293 *et seq.*
19  Podhoretz, 'Synge's *Playboy*: Morality and the Hero', p. 337.
20  Synge, *Collected Works IV*, p. 82, notes 1–7.
21  *Ibid.*, p. 82, note 1.
22  Podhoretz, 'Synge's *Playboy*: Morality and the Hero', p. 337.
23  The heroic motif in this play is treated thoroughly and perceptively by P.L. Henry, 'The Playboy of the Western World'.
24  In the Methuen (edited by Henn, *op. cit.*) and in all other previous editions I have consulted the word is 'noising'. Ann Saddlemyer changes it to 'nosing' but provides no textual note on the emendation.

# – 5 –

## Priest and Artist in Joyce's Early Fiction

The first three stories of *Dubliners* were written concurrently with *Stephen Hero* in the years 1904–1905.[1] I will argue that these three stories and the rejected novel are concerned with an impasse which Joyce had reached in the development of his art, and which he did not fully resolve until he had written *A Portrait of the Artist as a Young Man*. The impasse concerned three main ideas: the Romantic idea of the artist as outcast, heretic and martyr; the notion of the artist as a priest of the occult; the concept of art as alchemy or transubstantiation. Most of these ideas are caught in a crucial passage of *Stephen Hero* towards the end of Chapter XXIII:

He repeated often the story of 'The Tables of the Law' and the story of 'The Adoration of the Magi'. The atmosphere of these stories was heavy with incense and omens and the figures of the monk-errants, Ahern [*sic*] and Michael Robartes strode through it with great strides. Their speeches were like the enigmas of a disdainful Jesus; their morality was infrahuman or superhuman: the ritual they laid such store by was so incoherent and heterogeneous, so strange a mixture of trivialities and sacred practices that it could be recognized as the ritual of men who had received from the hands of high priests, [who had been] anciently guilty of some arrogance of the spirit, a confused and dehumanised tradition, a mysterious ordination. Civilization may be said indeed to be the creation of its outlaws . . .[2]

Here, as it were in draft form, are the ideas and attitudes which Joyce was to expand and dramatize in the rhetorical pattern of *A Portrait*, especially in the final chapters. There, they are subsumed into an aesthetic theory which gives the fledgling artist mastery over the contending claims of his emotions, and victory—at least provisional—over his environment. Here, in *Stephen Hero*, he can do no more than ally himself with the Yeatsean rebels and heretics in a tentative baptism of desire:

These inhabit a church apart; they lift their thuribles wearily before their deserted altars; they live beyond the region of mortality, having chosen to fulfil the law of their being. A young man like Stephen in such a season of damp and unrest [had] has no pains to believe in the reality of their existence.[3]

What he achieves ultimately in *A Portrait is* to create for himself a personal version of this rebellious and occult priesthood. In doing so he invokes his own pantheon of heretical hero figures, Bruno of Nola, Joachim of Flora, Simon Magus, Gherardino da Borgo San Donnino. Whereas Aherne— in Yeats's 'The Tables of the Law'—had wavered between his esoteric priesthood and the biretta of the Dominicans, Stephen chooses between the priesthood of the Jesuits and that of the cabbalistic Simon Magus. Therefore, when the director of studies, in Chapter IV of *A Portrait*, is nudging Stephen towards the Catholic priesthood, the young man's thoughts are running at a subtle tangent to the discourse:

He listened in reverent silence now to the priest's appeal and through the words he heard even more distinctly a voice bidding him approach, offering him secret knowledge and secret power. He would know then what was the sin of Simon Magus and what the sin against the Holy Ghost for which there was no forgiveness. He would know obscure things, hidden from others. . . .[4]

The Jesuit expounds a priesthood that celebrates the sanctioned and orthodox mysteries, but Stephen's imagination is already pondering the mysteries of a darker hierarchy. When, in Chapter V, he tells E.C. that he was 'born to be a monk' she substitutes the word 'heretic'; immediately he sees himself as

. . . a profaner of the cloister, a heretic franciscan, willing and willing not to serve, spinning like Gherardino da Borgo San Donnino, a lithe web of sophistry . . . .[4]

Finally, he ordains himself 'a priest of eternal imagination, transmuting the daily bread of experience into the radiant body of everliving life'.[5] Thus, he transforms the negative rebellion, the longing, the unfocussed dissatisfaction and dampness of soul presented in *Stephen Hero* into a positive personal stance of aesthetic priesthood. It is significant, and proper, that by now all the Yeatsean allusions have been 'sublimed away'. He has replaced the alchemical metaphor with his own Catholic image of transubstantiation. He has earned his own triumphant posture in the face of society, orthodoxy, tradition and the world.

It is a hard victory for Joyce.[7] He began rewriting *Stephen Hero* as *A Portrait* in September of 1907 and by 1915 he had not completed it to his satisfaction.[8] This fact must be borne in mind when we turn to the first three stories in *Dubliners,* the work of a talent some ten years younger, a talent preoccupied with two related concerns: the need, carried through in the main body of *Dubliners*, to define and thereby subdue the environment of Dublin which threatened his independence as a person; the allied desire, expressed but not achieved in *Stephen Hero,* to find integrity and freedom in the role of rebellious artist. The two drives are implicit in a passage from the chapter already quoted from the discarded novel:

He was aware that though he was nominally in amity with the order of society into which he had been born, he would not be able to continue so. The life of an errant seemed to him far less ignoble than the life of one who had accepted the tyranny of the mediocre because the cost of being exceptional was too high.[9]

The bulk of *Dubliners* sets itself, with great success, to portray that mediocrity of the city's life-style, while the first three stories deal, in their central emphasis, with the struggle of the individual, the artist as a young boy, to recognize that mediocrity and to transcend it. In other words, these three stories look forward to *A Portrait*, while the body of the book looks forward to those central episodes in *Ulysses* which portray, through Bloom and his associates, the quotidian life of Dublin.

The first published version of 'The Sisters'[10] is a stark and disconcerting little sketch told in a style of 'scrupulous meanness'[11] rarely achieved—or attempted—elsewhere in the published form of the book. In this early version an observant child anticipates the death of an old priest with whom he had been friendly, but hears of it from his uncle and Mr Cotter. He recalls the old man taking snuff in his stuffy room, looked after by his spinster sisters, and the conversations which they had had together. The sketch ends with the boy listening at the wake while the old women sip sherry and recall, in fragmentary conversation, that the priest had broken a chalice once and that it had resulted in his mind being 'a bit affected'.

Joyce's re-working of the sketch has given rise to a remarkable body of ingenious, elaborate and contradictory exegesis and criticism.[12] It is certainly a problematical story, and its difficulty arises, I would argue, from its divided emphasis: its role as key-note to the collection and its pretensions as a story in its own right.

When Joyce re-wrote the story he added a number of new ideas and motifs—the word 'paralysis' with all its symbolic overtones, the oriental imagery, the intensified boy-priest relationship, the eucharistic symbolism—if we admit it to be operative—of the wine and wafer, the words 'simony', 'gnomon' and 'Rosicrucian'.

There are two clear trends in these revisions. The priest is now to act as a symbol for the 'paralysis'[13] of Dublin and the Catholic Church in Ireland, his down-at-heel and docile sisters to represent the ignorance and subservience of the Irish laity towards their clergy. On this level the story succeeds. The grey, inert body of Father Flynn is powerfully rendered; his presence, at once repulsive and mysterious, throws its shadow over the stories that follow. The second trend concerns the boy—who is also the hero of the two stories that follow—and his curious relationship with the priest and with the elderly lay adults, male and female, in the story itself.

The boy in the first version of the story is not especially remarkable. He is observant, but is also obedient and respectful. His role is largely that of uninvolved observer and recorder of the events. He is mildly irritated that old Cotter has been before him in the discovery of the priest's death, but his hostility to his elders goes no further than that. The boy narrator of the revised version is remarkable in several ways. He regards Cotter with angry contempt—'Tiresome old fool. . . . Tiresome old red-nosed imbecile'(10–11). His hatred has an added motivation: Cotter is suggesting that there is something unwholesome in the relationship between him and the priest. The boy is angry because Cotter is so close to the mark while at the same time missing the subtlety of the boy's fascination with the old priest and the mystery he represents.

The young hero is first of all obsessed by words. As the story opens he is standing beneath the priest's window, repeating, almost as a magical incantation, the word 'paralysis':

It had always sounded strangely in my ears, like the word *gnomon* in the Euclid and the word *simony* in the Catechism. But now it sounded to me like the name of some maleficent and sinful being. It filled me with fear, and yet I longed to be nearer to it and to look upon its deadly work.(9)

The fascination with words, their texture and symbolism, is that of the artist. In *Portrait,* the young Stephen Dedalus pondered words like belt, heartburn, cancer, canker, tundish and enchantment of the heart. The desire to penetrate beyond the word to the mystery of the paralysis, the priesthood, and the sin, is the impulse of the artist as a young boy. Already he is a boy apart, offending against Cotter's hearty ideal of childhood—'"let a young lad run about and play with young lads of his own age"'(10). Already he is acquainted with the 'pleasant and vicious'(11) areas of the psyche. When the uncle calls him a 'Rosicrucian' he has a richer intuition than he imagines. The child's secret imaginative life, his withdrawal from the extrovert virtues and the orthodox pieties, foreshadow the more formal rejections of Stephen Dedalus and his hunt after secret and forbidden knowledge.

The theme of artist is complicated by that of priesthood. The child is aware that the priesthood has failed for Father Flynn. Yet the old priest had 'a great wish for him'(10). Before the stroke that had paralysed him he had tried to initiate the boy into the ministry in which he himself had faltered and atrophied:

. . . he had explained to me the meaning of the different ceremonies of the Mass and of the different vestments worn by the priest. Sometimes he had amused himself by putting difficult questions to me . . . whether such and such sins were mortal or venial or only imperfections. His questions showed me how complex and mysterious were certain institutions of the Church which I had always regarded as the simplest acts. The duties of the priest towards the Eucharist and towards the secrecy of the confessional seemed so grave to me that I wondered how anybody had ever found in himself the courage to undertake them. . . .' (13)

The priest's approach, as the movement of the clauses so skilfully enforces, has been insistent and insidious, its emphasis on mystery, sin and secrecy. It has got inside the child's psychic defences, partly with his assent. In his sleep the boy is pursued by 'the heavy grey face of the paralytic', and he finds his mind receding 'into some pleasant and vicious region', in which he tries feebly to 'absolve the simoniac of his sin'. The sin, I would argue, is not simony in the literal sense—any more than the priest is a 'gnomon' or the boy a 'Rosicrucian'[14]—but that of enticing the boy towards a priesthood in which he himself had failed. In doing so he barters the sacred mysteries and the secrets of his office to secure the boy's fascinated, and eventually morbid, interest. This is why, in the dream, their roles become reversed; the boy's unconscious reveals to him what the waking mind could not rationalize. But in escaping from the Catholic priesthood—as represented by Father Flynn—the young hero swerves towards another, and Yeatsean, form of priesthood, as suggested in that otherwise inexplicable oriental image:

I remembered that I had noticed long velvet curtains and a swinging lamp of antique fashion. I felt that I had been very far away, in some land where the customs were strange—in Persia, I thought. . .(13–14)

It is an echo from the Yeatsean reveries of *Stephen Hero*, transposed and largely unabsorbed into the structure. So, as the old priest lies dead, 'solemn and copious, vested as for the altar' the young Rosicrucian approaches the table and, on his own terms, sips the sacramental sherry, while the elderly ladies discuss in terms of very prosaic mystery what had 'gone wrong'. The broken sentences with which the story ends are one kind of Joycean epiphany—'a sudden spiritual manifestation . . . in the vulgarity of speech. . .'.[15] Like the enigmas and evasions of old Cotter at the beginning they go well beyond their immediate meaning and suggest the stunted values, moral and cultural, by which these adults live. It is from this set of values that the boy has begun to disengage himself. By the end of the story he has encountered paralysis, looked upon 'its deadly work', and, in so far as he can with his fledgling resources of insight and imagination, rejected it.

It is in the limitation of the hero's imaginative resources that the weakness of the story lies. The boy cannot be shown to have the intellectual command necessary to judge his environment adequately and escape from it. In *A Portrait* the conscious and adequate process of judgement, rejection and flight is achieved only in the final chapter when the hero has created his aesthetic theory and transcending myth. Here, Joyce is forced to present the flight in terms of dream and reverie. To do this he invokes the vague symbolism of the orient, the hints of Rosicrucianism and of an occult priesthood, a tissue of images which the child could hardly have had access to. In the two following stories such images as these are handled with greater clarity and assurance. Here, because the story is called upon to serve purposes outside itself—in striking the key-note to the volume—and because of Joyce's current difficulty with the self and the city, the story falters in its emphasis. The framework of the original sketch is hung with a weight of symbolic suggestion that it cannot evenly support. This, I suggest, is why so many critics disagree about both its meaning and merit, why such an experienced reader as Frank O'Connor can remark that 'the point of it still eludes me'.[16]

While the youngster who listens to his aunts' conversation at the end of 'The Sisters' has not gained imaginative control over his world, and while his rebellion against that world is wholly secret and interior— 'hermetically sealed' in every sense—he has clearly begun to detach himself from it, a necessary step in the growth of an artist's sensibility. His priesthood will not be according to the order of James Flynn, but of the dissenting and creative imagination. The first three stories have in common this theme of the imagination, the vivid but treacherous force which can be to its possessor a means to insight or delusion. The child in 'The Sisters' differs sharply from his elders in having imaginative energy. There is a sustained counterpoint between what the young hero imagines and what he sees: at the outset he imagines that he will see the candles behind the blind, but finds that they have not yet been lit; as he walks the streets he wonders that neither he nor the weather is in mourning for the dead priest; when he goes to the wake he expects to find the corpse smiling in the coffin, but is mistaken. But most importantly it is through his imagination that he penetrates to the priest's paralysis and its cause. His conscious brooding on the matter brings him revelation in a dream. There he sees the old man's state as repulsive and pitiable—the 'grey face . . . moist with spittle'(11) begging to be absolved from sin. The child alone has dared to confront the reality of the priest's spiritual malaise, to feel the full charge of its 'deadly work'. The adults lack either the courage or the imaginative sympathy. They are typical Joycean Dubliners: in their different ways they too are paralysed. The boy is exceptional. He is a

Joycean artist figure—detached, observant, silent and cunning behind his mask of conformity, compassionate in his sympathy yet cold and implacable in his moral judgement, darkly inquisitive, a heretic in the making. If we omit the two stories that follow, we find no-one like him in the rest of *Dubliners*.

A similar counterpoint between imagination and reality creates the pattern in both 'An Encounter' and 'Araby'. In each the young hero is at once betrayed and illumined by the importunity of his imagination. Each story dramatizes an attempt on the part of the hero to make real a vision formed in the imagination, the first in terms of reverie, the second in terms of Romantic self-dramatization. The action of the imagination becomes consecutively more deliberate in each of these three stories. If Joyce had continued in the first person he could hardly have avoided a pattern similar to that of *A Portrait*, in which the artist-hero uses the developed imagination to subdue and transform the work-a-day world. What happens in *Dubliners* is that, from this point on, we see a world where the creative imagination has failed; where it has taken refuge in futile dreams of escape, sentimental songs of love or patriotism, drunken fantasies of erotic conquest, weak visions of literary success, feeble dreams of domestic comfort, shoddy versions of the kingdom of heaven.

The similarities between 'The Sisters' and 'An Encounter', where the young hero feels threatened by the old pervert, are so striking that one is surprised they have not received more attention: the hero-narrator, the dream of escape, the role of the imagination, the emphasis on ritual, sin, mystery, the similarity of the demands made by the two old men on the boy, the lonely plea to be understood, the manner in which the boy, alone among his associates, has the empathy to understand and perhaps even to pity while taking the full charge of fear and revulsion.

Here Joyce has, from the outset, a more satisfactory image for the vivid life than the oriental fantasies of 'The Sisters'. The boys find life flat and dull, but they can escape into the world of the Wild West. They can enact its adventures in their playtime. The young hero is rather more precocious than his companions in preferring American detective stories because they were 'traversed from time to time by unkempt fierce and beautiful girls'(20)—which hints at his nascent sexuality and later makes poignant the version of sexual reality which finally he confronts.[17] The makebelieve grows wearisome and he longs for 'wild sensations' and 'real adventures' which 'do not happen to people who remain at home: they must be sought abroad'(21). It is the hero who plans the expedition. He stands apart from the extrovert fierceness of Joe Dillon, who is older, but who remains in the Wild West fantasy when the hero has abandoned it; and who significantly opts later for the priesthood. He differs also from Leo Dillon in that the latter backs out at the last minute, and from Mahony who brings his catapult along, thereby making the quest an extension of their childhood play rather than a break with it. In other words, while the 'spirit of unruliness' permitted them to waive their 'differences of culture and constitution'(20), the waiving is temporary and superficial.

The climax of the quest for 'real adventures' is sharply ironical. The young quester finds himself enmeshed in the dreams and fantasies of the old pervert. Mahony, the extrovert, evades and deflects the experience with a deftness which would have won the approval of old Cotter. But the young hero, despite his fear and distaste, sees it through, hears the old man out. Like Father Flynn the old man is physically repellent, with 'great gaps in his mouth between his yellow teeth'(25). What the old man says about girls seems 'reasonable' and liberal, but as he proceeds the boy 'disliked the words in his mouth'. When he talks about the beauty of a girl 'her nice white hands and her beautiful soft hair'(26), his voice like that of Father Flynn becomes insistent and incantatory:

At times he spoke as if he were simply alluding to some fact that everybody knew, and at times he lowered his voice and spoke mysteriously as if he were telling us something secret . . .

Then he goes and performs his squalid ritual and returns, soured but no less vehement, with another mystery to unfold:

He said that if ever he found a boy talking to girls or having a girl for a sweetheart he would whip him and whip him. . . . He said that there was nothing in this world he would like so well as that. He described to me how he would whip such a boy as if he were unfolding some elaborate mystery. He would love that, he said, better than anything in this world; and his voice, as he led me monotonously through the mystery, grew almost affectionate and seemed to plead with me that I should understand him.(27)

I would suggest that the story's rhetorical emphasis is this. The young artist begins by compensating for the flatness of life through fictional fantasy, first in his reading, then in an attempt to make these fantasies come alive through play. He tires of this. He determines to seek for an equivalent to his imaginations in the unknown world beyond the daily round of home and school and playground. Instead of finding a vivid adventure in the real world he discovers a reality beyond the expectations of the most squalid realist. In confronting the reality of the old pervert he finds the embodiment of a morbid fantasy, a diseased imagination. He recognizes a possible and sinister outcome to imaginative excess. As with Father Flynn he sees a frightening version of himself. Having seen he recoils. As he goes he is afraid that the old man may 'seize me by the ankles', a foreshadowing of Icarus.[18] As the story ends the extrovert, Mahony, comes running across the field 'as if to bring me aid'(27). The hero feels penitent as 'in my heart I had always despised him a little'. It is not the last time in Joyce's fiction that the artist is to be comforted by earthbound normality.

'Araby' shares with 'The Sisters' the family pattern of an imaginative boy living with kindly but unintelligent adults. In both stories the boy is silent, lonely and secretive, sustaining his own private perceptions and their attendant fantasies. In both stories the memory of a dead priest infects the atmosphere with dampness and decay. The boy in each case has an artist's obsession with words, their sound and symbolism, their power of invocation: in the latter story the infatuated boy repeats to himself '*O love, O love*'(31); and 'the syllables of the word *Araby* were called to me through the silence in which my soul luxuriated and cast an Eastern enchantment over me'(32). A sense of the occult and the exotic which it shares with the first story is casually reinforced by the aunt's inquiry as to whether the bazaar is 'some Freemason affair', which works roughly on the same level as the uncle's use of 'Rosicrucian' in 'The Sisters'.

'Araby' shares with 'An Encounter' the Romantic theme of quest and vision; and again the quest is undertaken in partial response to the conjurations of literature—the knight-errantry of Scott's *The Abbot,* the erotic adventures of the sinister Vidocq. The third book which the child finds in the old priest's room, *The Devout Communicant,* is obviously related to the imagery of priesthood which operates in all three stories, especially that of the chalice which here symbolizes the boy's devotion to his beloved:

I imagined that I bore my chalice safely through a throng of foes. Her name sprang to my lips at moments in strange prayers and praises which I myself did not understand.(31)

The religious imagery is used to celebrate a secular mystery of romantic love wherein the young hero holds firmly the chalice which the old priest had dropped. As in 'An Encounter' the quest is the attempted realization of a vision first conceived in the imagination. But now the quest is clearly defined: the boy has now found a real focus in the actual world of Dublin for his fantasies, a goal which is definitely located yet magically named. The possibility of fusing dream and reality at last seems possible.

But when he arrives the enchantment has gone from the word and the occasion. In a series of subtle and cumulative religious images the boy senses the disenchantment—the silence is 'like that which pervades a church after a service'(34); the 'stalls' are mostly closed; in the temple of romance 'two men were counting money on a salver'(35). The epiphany of the banal is in the broken, trite exchanges of the bored attendants. The young knight-errant departs in the darkness with a sense of self-knowledge more formal and articulate than anything we have seen previously— 'a creature driven and derided by vanity' whose 'eyes burned with anguish and anger'(35).

All three stories are what Mordecai Marcus defines as 'stories of initiation'.[19] The initiation in each case seems at first to reveal some exotic mystery conceived in the creative imagination then offered by the quotidian world. But as the child reaches towards the preferred vision he finds instead the bleak reality behind the mystery. In other words they are initiations into life, in this case Dublin life. The final story, in which the child is old enough to perceive and articulate his disillusion, brings the hero and Joyce his creator to an impasse. If he continues with a sequence of first person narratives the hero must either succumb to the material world or begin formally to rebel against it. That process of formal rebellion is already being dramatized, as yet unsuccessfully, in *Stephen Hero*, particularly in that passage already quoted in part:

A certain extravagance began to tinge his life. He was aware that though he was nominally in amity with the order of society into which he had been born, he would not be able to continue so. The life of the errant seemed to him far less ignoble than the life of one who had accepted the tyranny of the mediocre because the cost of being exceptional was too high.[20]

Stephen has already chosen the priesthood of the artist. His rebellion, or flight, must be through the creative, transmuting imagination, through the exercise of his role as artist. There are two subjects for his creative imagination—the self and the city. The first three stories in *Dubliners* are, as I have shown, about the self. The city is there in a secondary capacity, to show the growth of the rebellious self in its early phases. But to go on with the process would have been to relegate the city continuously to a secondary role in the fiction. After 'Araby', therefore, the self withdraws to reshape itself in *A Portrait* while the artist turns his attention to those who have remained earthbound in Dublin, who have accepted the tyranny of the mediocre because the cost of being exceptional was too high. With few exceptions these portraits are harsh and unaffectionate. In view of their place in Joyce's artistic development they have to be. They are the embodiment of the paralysis from which he must escape. By the time he comes to write 'The Dead', Joyce, having expelled the charge of his contempt into the body of the collection, begins to repent of his harshness: 'I have reproduced (in *Dubliners* at least) none of the attraction of the city . . . its ingenuous insularity and hospitality'.[21] These absent qualities are in some measure supplied in the final story, though they had begun to appear in such a late story as 'Grace'. And, of course, in *Ulysses* he finds the means of dramatizing in a genial and elaborate relationship, through the affinity of Bloom with Stephen, the bond between the aesthete and the common man, the self and the city, the artist and his material.

# NOTES

First published in *Anglo-Irish Studies*, Volume II, edited by P.J. Drudy (Chalfont St. Giles, Bucks: Alpha Academic, 1976).

1   See Theodore Spencer's Introduction to his edition of *Stephen Hero* (New York: New Directions, 1963), pp. 8–10. See also the Viking Critical Edition of *Dubliners*, edited by Robert Scholes and A. Walton Litz (New York: The Viking Press, 1969), pp. 463–9. All future references to *Dubliners* will be to this edition and will be incorporated in the text.

2   Joyce, *Stephen Hero*, p. 178.

3   *Ibid.*, p. 178.

4   James Joyce, *A Portrait of the Artist as a Young Man*, edited by Chester G. Anderson (New York: The Viking Press, 1968), p. 159.

5   *Ibid.*, pp. 219–20.

6   *Ibid.*, p. 221.

7   The 'victory' is of course the writing of the book which the metaphors of transubstantiation and flight made possible. The night itself, if we are to credit *Ulysses*, Episode 9, was a failure.

8   There were two lacunae in the serial version published in *The Egoist* (London, February–September 1915).

9   Joyce, *Stephen Hero*, p. 179.

10  Published in *The Irish Homestead*, 13 August, 1904.

11  Letter from Joyce to Grant Richards of 5 May 1906 'I have written it [*Dubliners*] for the most part in a style of scrupulous meanness. . .'. *Letters of James Joyce*, Volume II, edited by Richard Ellmann (New York: The Viking Press, 1966), p. 134.

12  For a summary of this criticism see 'The Opening of *Dubliners*, a Reconsideration' by Donald T. Torchiana in the *Irish University Review*, Vol. 1, No. 2, Spring 1971, where he advances an interpretation of striking eccentricity.

13  Letter from Joyce to Grant Richards of 5 May 1906: 'I chose Dublin for the scene because that city seemed to me the centre of paralysis.' *Letters of James Joyce*, Volume II, ed. Ellmann, p. 134.

14  The priest is a gnomon in the Euclidean sense: a part of him is missing. As used by the uncle 'Rosicrucian' simply means 'dreamer'. Of course the primary cause of the boy's fascination with the three words is the one given, they 'sound strangely' (9). None of them is pronounced as it is written. This would make them initially interesting to the kind of boy described. Critics in pursuit of more exotic explanations have overlooked this basic and characteristic example of Joyce's psychological insight.

15  The relevant sentence from *Stephen Hero*, Chapter XXV, p. 211, is: 'By an epiphany he meant a sudden spiritual manifestation, whether in the vulgarity of speech or of gesture or in a memorable phase of the mind itself'.

16  Frank O'Connor, *The Lonely Voice: A Study of the Short Story* (London: Macmillan, 1963), p. 114.

17  Critics have argued about what the old man does when he withdraws; it is impossible
    to be certain. My view is that he does something furtive and indecent. His change of
    mood and attitude on the subject of courting suggests, but does not prove,
    masturbation. In a story where mystery plays such a large role Joyce was wise to keep
    the matter vague.
18  One recalls, for instance, how Stephen in *A Portrait*, poised for flight, fears
    Mulrennan's old peasant with his 'redrimmed horny eyes' and feels that he must
    struggle with him all through the night. See Joyce, *A Portrait of the Artist as a Young
    Man*, ed. Anderson, p. 252.
19  Mordecai Marcus, 'What is an Initiation Story?', *Critical Approaches to Fiction*, edited
    by Shiv K. Kumar and Keith McKean (New York, 1968), p. 201.
20  Joyce, *Stephen Hero*, p. 179.
21  Letter from Joyce to Stanislaus of 25 September 1906. *Letters of James Joyce*, Volume
    II, ed. Ellmann, p. 166.

# Sin and Secrecy in
# Joyce's Fiction

When invited to reflect on my reactions as an Irish Catholic to the fiction of James Joyce I found my mind swooping back to a number of dramatic moments in my reading experience, moments when a shock or shudder of recognition registered a strange accord between personal experience and artistic revelation. These moments cannot be unique to me, or even to those who share my upbringing, but I suspect that those brought up in another tradition may not feel them with such force. Further, I feel reasonably certain that the power of Joyce's writing derives in part from the urgency and pain with which these moments are suffused. They involve religious taboo, the Catholic sense of purity, defilement and repentance, a dramatic distinction between the inner and the outer self, the confessional impulse and the concept of secrecy. I was brought up in a world similar in its theology and religious practice to that of Joyce. It is a world that was virtually overthrown by the Second Vatican Council in the mid-1960s, so that I think it unlikely that more recent generations of Irish readers or Catholic readers anywhere will have read Joyce quite as I did. But as my reaction to the books on first reading is somehow bound up with their narrative strategy, the response may be worth recording, insofar as it can be honestly and accurately recalled.

The issue was vividly recalled for me when I was asked to review Richard Ellmann's edition of the *Selected Letters*[1] some years ago, with their notorious Fontenoy Street letters to Nora in the year 1909. These letters brought back the passages that had shocked me in *A Portrait of the Artist as a Young Man* when I read it as a first year undergraduate. These passages were not the hell fire sermon—which I took in my stride, nothing new there, Thomas Merton notwithstanding—but those passages where Stephen reviews his sins of the flesh and braces himself for Confession:

Could it be that he, Stephen Dedalus, had done those things? His conscience sighed in answer. Yes, he had done them, secretly, filthily, time after time, and, hardened in sinful impenitence, he had dared to wear the mask of holiness before the tabernacle itself while his soul within was a living mass of corruption.[2]

Confess! He had to confess every sin. How could he utter in words to the priest what he had done? Must, must. Or how could he explain without dying of shame? . . . Confess! O he would indeed be free and sinless again!(140)

The antiphon between secrecy and confession, the sense of an occluded and furtive inner life and a composed and fraudulent exterior dominates the three central chapters of *Portrait* from that mysterious, jolting epiphany the hero undergoes in the Cork anatomy theatre where he confronts the word *Foetus* carved on the desk while his father's extrovert chatter continues in the background. He is forced to hide his flushed face:

But the word and the vision capered before his eyes as he walked back across the quadrangle and towards the college gate. It shocked him to find in the outer world a trace of what he had deemed till then a brutish and individual malady of his own mind. His recent monstrous reveries came thronging into his memory. . . .
—Ay, bedad! And there's the Groceries sure enough! cried Mr Dedalus.(90)

The recurrent imagery of filth, slime and bestiality—the goat connotations of 'capered' may be intended—within, and the mask of urbanity, even of sanctity, without, unfolds itself as a powerful resource of rhetoric as the novel develops. The narrative structure of *Stephen Hero* employs no such sophisticated antinomy. Between writing the two books Joyce seems to have felt the weight of this confessional desire in his personal life before, perhaps, he determined upon it as a device of narrative. Indeed the publication of the Fontenoy Street letters makes it clear that his marriage to Nora Barnacle had provided the confessional which allowed him to release the pressure of this inner guilt, to heal the wound of his shame and loneliness, and clear the way for the remarkable experiments of his prose in delivering to fiction those secret processes of the unconscious that had never previously been dramatized in respectable fiction.

The letters in question were written from 44 Fontenoy Street, Dublin, in 1909, and were occasioned by the false assertion of Cosgrave—Lynch in *A Portrait*—that Nora had been unfaithful to Joyce in those crucial days in summer 1904 when they had fallen in love. The sense of betrayal released in Joyce an outpouring of erotic longing, tender, obscene and poetic at turns, which he embodied in a series of the most remarkable love letters ever published, to Nora in Trieste. It is probable that this uncensored display of hitherto occulted desire in prose, however private, may have awoken him to the possibility of similar revelations in fiction. For the present purpose it is sufficient to note the different registers of eros canvassed in the letters and its consistency with the theme and tone of Stephen's inner reveries and outer gestures.

The letters range passionately from masochism and self abasement through fetishism, coprophilia, auto-eroticism, bestiality and joyful carnality to raptures of exquisite spiritual tenderness. In short, the one thing that can be absolutely predicated of these letters is that they are emphatically love letters, that they seem to have been received and answered with a commensurate frankness, and that the relationship between the Joyces was one of exceptional sexual spontaneity and candour. Thus within their discourse James could conclude a letter in terms like these:

Nora, my faithful darling, my sweet-eyed blackguard schoolgirl, be my whore, my mistress, as much as you like (my little frigging mistress! my little fucking whore!) you are always my beautiful wild flower of the hedges, my dark-blue rain-drenched flower.[3]

But more frequently the imagery of bestiality and ordure is deliberately and zealously indulged: 'the act itself, brief, brutal, irresistible and devilish'. 'My love for you allows me to pray to the spirit of eternal beauty and tenderness mirrored in your eyes or to fling you down . . . like a hog riding a sow, glorying in the very stink and sweat.' There is nothing of Lawrence's 'sense of health' in Joyce's sexual reveries. On the contrary it exults in the drama of its privacy: 'O, I wish that you kept all those things *secret, secret, secret*. . . . As you know, dearest, I never use obscene phrases in speaking. . . . When men tell in my presence here filthy or lecherous stories I hardly smile. Yet you seem to turn me into a beast.'[4] In confirmation of this last point, Italo Svevo wittily recalls that 'Joyce one day called me to task because I allowed myself to make a rather free joke. "I never say that kind of thing," said he, "though I write it." So it seems that his own books cannot be read in his presence.'[5]

When I read these letters for the first time, though I was mildly shocked, I was not surprised. I was meeting face to face what I had already perceived through the prism of the fiction, through the refractions of Stephen, Leopold, Molly. There the sudden and the more gradual shifts between public and private, conscious and unconscious, the willed and the involuntary act of the imagination, had engendered a large measure of the narrative excitement. These tensions and transitions had in fact supplied the traditional resources of suspense and reversal, replacing them with a new sense of drama as vivid, to adopt Henry James's phrase, 'as the surprise of a caravan or the identification of a pirate'.

As he crossed the square, walking homeward, the light laughter of a girl reached his burning ear. The frail gay sound smote his heart more strongly than a trumpetblast, and, not daring to lift his eyes, he turned aside and gazed, as he walked, into the shadow of the tangled shrubs. Shame rose from his smitten heart and flooded his whole being. The image of Emma appeared before him and, under her eyes, the flood of shame rushed forth anew from his heart. If she knew to what his mind had subjected her or how his brutelike lust had torn and trampled upon her innocence! Was that boyish love? Was that chivalry? Was that poetry? The sordid details of his orgies stank under his very nostrils: the sootcoated packet of pictures which he had hidden in the flue of the fireplace and in the presence of whose shameless or bashful wantonness he lay for hours sinning in thought or deed; his monstrous dreams, peopled by apelike creatures and by harlots with gleaming jewel eyes; the foul long letters he had written in the joy of guilty confession and carried secretly for days and days only to throw them under cover of night among the grass in the corner of a field or beneath some hingeless door or in some niche in the hedges where a girl might come upon them as she walked by and read them secretly. Mad! Mad! Was it possible he had done these things?(115–16)

The counterpoint of images is now familiar: light laughter, frail gay sound, smitten heart, boyish love, innocence, chivalry, poetry, all the sanctioned values and aspirations; then the familiar bestiary—brutelike lust, monstrous dreams, apelike creatures, the furtiveness of sootcovered packets and hingeless doors. But more significant, perhaps, for our understanding of Joyce's art is 'the joy of guilty confession' in which the young hero wallows. The secrecy in which he clutches his moral enormity must find vent in this sort of perverse revelation, and in the hope that a kindred spirit, 'a girl', might be ambushed by and share in that defilement. It is hardly fanciful to suggest that Stephen's surreptitious confessions in A Portrait have an affinity with their author's epistolary confessions in the Fontenoy Street letters. Or that the release afforded by the latter may well have shown their author the way in dramatizing the crisis of conscience in his teenage hero.

What is certain is that the crisis of conscience is Irish and Catholic in its terror, its ardour and its intensity. It is closely related to the extravagant reverence for the Blessed Virgin which has characterized Irish Catholic education for at least a century. Her cult is surrounded with liturgy and theology of very great beauty, and there is every evidence that Joyce responded with remarkable fervour and veneration to that devotion in his early years. It was inevitable that it coloured his earliest apprehensions of women, the beloved mother figure in the early pages of A Portrait and his friend Eileen Vance, whom he consciously identifies with the imagery of the Litany of Our Lady: 'Eileen had long thin cool white hands too because she was a girl. They were like ivory; only soft. That was the meaning of Tower of Ivory. . . . Her fair hair had streamed out behind her like gold in the sun. Tower of Ivory. House of Gold. By thinking of things you could understand them'(42–3). The association persists with the years. As he wrestles with his conscience during the Retreat and tries to raise his soul from its 'abject powerlessness' he reflects:

God and the Blessed Virgin were too far from him: God was too great and stern and the Blessed Virgin too pure and holy. But he imagined that he stood near Emma in a wide land and, humbly and in tears, bent and kissed the elbow of her sleeve.(116)

Then, in a plangent phrase from Newman, Joyce enacts the Virgin's forgiveness: 'it had not offended her whose beauty *is not like earthly beauty, dangerous to look upon, but like the morning star which is its emblem, bright and musical.'* Victorian schoolboys everywhere had, I'm sure, to deal with agonies of sexual suppression and guilt, but only Irish Catholics had to cope with such piercing symbols of purity and virtue. The very poet in Joyce made his case the more traumatic. Consequently the transgressions of coarser natures, like those of Lynch and Temple, are mere routine by comparison with those of the young Stephen Dedalus. Therefore, when Stephen makes the final break, dramatized in the fourth chapter of *A Portrait*, there is nothing temperate or gradual about it. It is a radical rejection of the world of grace, a deliberate fall into 'the swoon of sin'(101) which he had welcomed at the close of Chapter Two on his return from Cork.

There are three critical phases in Chapter Four. Dorothy Van Ghent has argued convincingly that Stephen's consciousness is always circling outwards in time and space: her model is the inscription on his textbook which begins with 'Stephen Dedalus/Class of Elements' and spirals outwards to end with 'The World/The Universe'.[6] But there is also a circling inwards, towards secrecy, silence and cunning. The third chapter had opened with Stephen circling furtively inwards on the brothel area of Dublin and proceeded to reveal the manner of his hypocrisy at the college Sodality. Chapter Four begins with an account of his amended life with its secret and elaborate mortifications of the flesh:

To mortify his smell was more difficult as he found in himself no instinctive repugnance to bad odours, whether they were the odours of the outdoor world such as those of dung and tar or the odours of his own person among which he had made many curious comparisons and experiments.(151)

Then abruptly he is talking to the director of vocations in the parlour at Belvedere. Here Stephen's carefully cultivated mask of propriety manages the conversation with the Jesuit, while his secret self acts as an occult chorus to the dialogue. When the director tries to draw him into a manly Jesuit conspiracy at the expense of the Capuchins with his reference to their cassocks as '*les jupes*' Stephen smiles assent, but his thoughts are at a tangent to the suggestion: 'The names of articles of dress worn by women or of certain soft and delicate stuffs used in their making brought always to his mind a delicate and sinful perfume.'(155)

The counterpoint between his words and thoughts continues through the interview. The director dwells on Stephen's exemplary conduct as prefect of the Sodality of Our Lady and asks him to consider the priestly vocation:

He listened in reverent silence now to the priest's appeal and through the words he heard even more distinctly a voice bidding him approach, offering him secret knowledge and secret power. He would know then what was the sin of Simon Magus and what the sin against the Holy Ghost for which there was no forgiveness. . . . He would know the sins, the sinful longings and sinful thoughts and sinful acts, of others, hearing them murmured into his ears in the confessional under the shame of a darkened chapel by the lips of women and of girls.(159)

The obsession with 'soft stuffs', 'sinful perfume', 'secret knowledge', a subverted priesthood—Simon Magus is a cult figure in Hermeticism and Rosicrucianism—remind us that the novel is set in the Nineties, the shag-end of the Decadence. The pathos of Stephen's fantasies derives in part from the fact that he is a sort of Herod without a Salome, Des Esseintes without the enabling income. More significantly, however, he has determined upon his own strategy of man and mask, silence and cunning—exile is yet to come.

As he leaves Belvedere he has decided against the priesthood. He now resolves that he will wander in the 'ways of sin'(162), that he will fall because 'Not to fall was too hard'. As he crosses the Tolka a disenchanted image of the Blessed Virgin standing 'fowlwise' in a 'faded blue shrine' marks the end of his affair with grace. The secular beauty of the girl on the beach and the 'outburst of profane joy'(171) with which he greets it set him on his way to becoming what he terms in the final chapter 'a priest of eternal imagination, transmuting the daily bread of experience into the radiant body of everliving life'(221). It must be noted, however, that this proud formulation does not wholly compensate him for the fact that Emma will not resort to his priesthood but to that of the 'priested peasant', Father Moran, when she comes to 'unveil her soul's shy nakedness' in confession. The husband of Nora Barnacle does much better.

There used to be an old preacher's trick of rhetoric in which a churchful of youngsters on 'retreat' would be assured on a rising note of menace: 'And when you commit that sin, my dear boys, I may not see you, your parents may not see you, but God sees you!' It is not often remarked that more of the action in *Ulysses* is solitary, the thoughts and deeds of private individuals, than of any major novel before or since, with the exception, perhaps, of *Robinson Crusoe*. And often when the action is not entirely solitary—as in 'Nausicaa'—it is frequently surreptitious or furtive. Joyce, in the role of an unaccusing and unretributive god, sees it all. The reader becomes a sort of artful voyeur, spying benignly on the sins and secrecies of other voyeurs:

Mr Bloom, alone, looked at the titles. *Fair Tyrants* by James Lovebirch. Know the kind that is. Had it? Yes. . . .

He read the other title: *Sweets of Sin*. More in her line. Let us see.

He read where his finger opened.

—*All the dollarbills her husband gave her were spent in the stores on wondrous gowns and costliest frillies. For him! For Raoul*! . . .

Warmth showered gently over him, cowing his flesh. Flesh yielded amid rumpled clothes. Whites of eyes swooning up. His nostrils arched themselves for prey. Melting breast ointments (*for him! For Raoul!*). Armpits' oniony sweat. Fishgluey slime (*her heaving embonpoint!*). Feel! Press! Crushed! Sulphur dung of lions![7]

The transition from titillation to disgust, from erotic romance to physiological realism, is typical of Bloom's sensibility. Yet he carries his novelette, his dark secret, through all the vicissitudes of his day: 'by Moulang's pipes, bearing in his breast the sweets of sin, by Wine's antiques in memory bearing sweet sinful words, by Carroll's dusky battered plate, for Raoul'(331).

Stephen, artist, whose role it is to 'wrest old images from the burial earth'(330), indulges his typically more strenuous and structured reverie outside the window of Russell's jewelry:

dull coils of bronze and silver, lozenges of cinnabar, on rubies, leprous and winedark stones.

Born all in the dark wormy earth, cold specks of fire, evil lights shining in the darkness. Where fallen archangels flung the stars of their brows. Muddy swinesnouts, hands, root and root, gripe and wrest them.

She dances in a foul gloom where gum burns with garlic. A sailorman, rustbearded, sips from a beaker rum and eyes her. A long and seafed silent rut. She dances, capers, wagging her sowish haunches and her hips, on her gross belly flapping a ruby egg.(310)

No other fictional form or method could accommodate a reverie so private, so thorough—in which the implications of precious stones as wealth, idolatry, slavery, beauty, evil, sexual adornment, are tracked back to their aboriginal essence—so seemingly gratuitous. That thrust of secret exploration, that challenge of the forbidden regions of the psyche, which were begun in the first stories of *Dubliners* and pursued in the apostasies of Stephen in *A Portrait*, have here developed into the radical fictional adventure of which this passage is one of the supreme achievements. They are, of course, to develop in turn to the phantasmagory of Bella Cohen's den and the nightmares of Earwicker in *Finnegans Wake*.

It is a commonplace that before Joyce—if we except the limited experiments of Dujardin which Joyce generously acknowledged—novelists confined themselves largely to narrative, paraphrase, action, dialogue, and in certain rare cases such as *Moby Dick,* interior monologue; and that their plots, comic, tragic, satiric or romantic, were mostly taken over from the drama. Characters revealed themselves to each other, or less frequently to the reader, through the mediation of the authorial voice—as in *Portrait of a Lady,* Chapter XLII. Like theatre, fiction was a public art where the inner workings of the mind found resolution and expression through social forms—conversations, letters, confessions, actions, hints, explanations. Joyce frequently remarked to Bugden and others that literature had still left too much unsaid, that even Shakespeare had been forced, by the formal restraints, to leave unsaid so much that matters deeply to mankind.[8] Joyce's 'stream of consciousness'— we cannot avoid the term—was his means of getting to that unexpressed world, of catching movements of mind, fancy and reverie, often before these movements had achieved the finality of thought. It was a colossal undertaking, like trying to turn up the light fast enough to see the darkness. The uniqueness of *Ulysses* resides in the marvellous variety of tone, mood and rhythm achieved within its pages. Therefore the term should at least be changed to 'streams of consciousness'. Because while the method may have been primarily useful in exploring the murkier regions of the private conscience which I've been discussing—and for which its inventor paid the bitterest price—it afforded him opportunities in comic freedom and intellectual elaboration unknown to the novel as he had found it.

Bloom is in Westland Row watching for a flash of ankle as a lady prepares to ascend a carriage across the street. M'Coy stands insensitively before him with the tedious story of how he had come to learn of Paddy Dignam's death from Hoppy Holohan:

> —*Why?* I said. *What's wrong with him?* I said.
> Proud: rich: silk stockings.
> —Yes, Mr Bloom said.
> He moved a little to the side of M'Coy's talking head. Getting up in a minute.
> —*What's wrong with him?* he said. *He's dead*, he said. And, faith, he filled up. *Is it Paddy Dignam?* I said. I couldn't believe it when I heard it. I was with him no later than Friday last or Thursday was it in the Arch. *Yes*, he said. *He's gone. He died on Monday, poor fellow.*
> Watch! Watch! Silk flash rich stockings white. Watch!
> A heavy tramcar honking its gong slewed between.
> Lost it. Curse your noisy pugnose. Feels locked out of it. Paradise and the peri. Always happening like that. The very moment. Girl in Eustace street hallway. Monday was it settling her garter. Her friend covering the display of. *Esprit de corps.* Well, what are you gaping at?
> —Yes, yes, Mr Bloom said after a dull sigh. Another gone.
> —One of the best, M'Coy said.(90–1)

It is hard to decide which of our heroes may feel his sense of loss the keener as life and death, paradise and Hades, are caught on the same hook of dialogue. The drama is hardly less lively when Bloom is alone with his curious visions of bliss:

Do ptake some ptarmigan. Wouldn't mind being a waiter in a swell hotel. Tips, evening dress, halfnaked ladies. May I tempt you to a little more filleted lemon sole, miss Dubedat? Yes, do bedad. And she did bedad.(223)

This sprightly prelude leads into the charged erotic passage in which he recalls his lovemaking with Molly on Howth Head, which leads in turn to his cool curiosities about goddesses, their diet, the perforations of statuary in the National Museum.

The 'Nausicaa' scene where Bloom and Gerty MacDowell hold their wordless, distant intercourse—'A long seafed silent rut'?—on Sandymount Strand takes the language of secrecy to a new pitch of elaboration, a more nuanced sense of the human comedy. One side of Gerty's mind knows exactly what is going on, the other side screens this knowledge, insists on translating it into the gush and rapture of the novelette:

O! then the Roman candle burst and it was like a sigh of O! and everyone cried O! O! in raptures and it gushed out of it a stream of rain gold hair threads and they shed and ah! they were all greeny dewy stars falling with golden, O so lovely! O so soft, sweet, soft!
. . . She glanced at him as she bent forward quickly, a pathetic little glance of piteous protest, of shy reproach under which he coloured like a girl. He was leaning back against the rock behind. Leopold Bloom (for it is he) stands silent, with bowed head before those young guileless eyes. What a brute he had been! At it again? A fair unsullied soul had called to him and, wretch that he was, how had he answered? An utter cad he had been.(477–8)

As Bloom moves on from his telepathetic conquest his mood brightens to a sort of jaunty self-gratulation: 'Anyhow I got the best of that . . . *Lingerie* does it.'(479–80) The guilt is transitory, if not actually enjoyable. We have travelled a long way from the trapped mortification of the sixteen year old Stephen. In the case of the wily Ulyssean Dublin Jew the outer and the inner man have a more genial working relation, at least during the hours of daylight. With the fall of night the moods and techniques change so often and so radically as to put these later episodes beyond the general scope of the present inquiry.

Similarly the Stephen we meet in 'Proteus' is a livelier, wiser man than the hero of *A Portrait*. Walking along Sandymount Strand he can mock the solemnity of his secret lusts: 'Cousin Stephen, you will never be a saint. . . . You prayed to the devil in Serpentine avenue that the fubsy widow in front might lift her clothes still more from the wet street. *O si, certo!* Sell your soul for that, do, dyed rags pinned round a squaw.'(49–50) But his jauntiness cannot slide round his guilt with the ease of a Leopold Bloom. Steeled in the school of old Aquinas and drilled in the moral disciplines of Loyola, he can never escape the need for analysis and self-accusation, however jocular the tone. He is seldom more engaging than in this episode where he discloses his artistic vanities, assuring us in passing that he did not have to travel far for the comic fantasies of that potential poet, Little Chandler:

Reading two pages apiece of seven books every night, eh? I was young. You bowed to yourself in the mirror, stepping forward to applause earnestly, striking face. Hurray for the Goddamned idiot! Hray! No-one saw: tell no-one. Books you were going to write with letters for titles. Have you read his F? O yes, but I prefer Q. Yes, but W is wonderful. O yes. W. Remember your epiphanies on green oval leaves, deeply deep, copies to be sent if you died to all the great libraries of the world, including Alexandria? Someone was to read them there after a few thousand years, a mahamanvantara. Pico della Mirandola like.(50)

It is clear that Joyce is enjoying the double-take: no-one saw; no-one need ever know. But he insists on telling. He is the great betrayer of secrets. His art is a monstrous and sustained breach of confidence. He gives us all away. That is why he has been treated for so long with such distrust. Our rage has been that of Caliban on seeing his reflection in a two-way mirror, Joyce's 'nicely polished looking-glass'.[9] He may even feel a little guilty himself at what he has been doing, and this may account for the strangled solemnity of parts of *Portrait*. But in the passage just quoted that mood has been replaced by a sort of erudite glee, epitomized in that last sentence.

The green oval leaves echo the 'Emerald Tablet' of Hermes, god of writers, whose cult was from Alexandria, and who gave the Egyptians laws and letters. He has been invoked as Thoth in the last chapter of *A Portrait* where he is imaged as 'writing with a reed upon a tablet'(225). Pico had been a devotee of Hermes's secret cult. So much for learned allusion. On the demotic level Italians still regard Pico as the epitome of learned omniscience. If asked a difficult question an average Roman or Triestine might well reply: 'Chi son' io? Pico della Mirandola?' (Who do you think I am? Pico della Mirandola?) Dubliners, on the other hand, have a trick of language by which they append 'like' as a detached suffix to nouns, adjectives and adverbs to achieve a sort of conspiratorial intimacy: 'He came up to me sort of quiet like, you know?' It was kinda Sunday like, you know what I mean?' Stephen is walking; the whole passage is pedestrian in the rhythm of its phrasing: ambulatory, self-mocking, idiomatic, secret, erudite like—in short Pico della Mirandola like.

All fiction involves a conspiracy of understanding between writer and reader, a tonal accord by means of which the fictive message can pass reliably back and forth between the reader and the text. In one sense or another there is always a shared secret. The first sentence of *Pride and*

*Prejudice* draws one immediately into such a conspiracy, and to the end of the story that pact never falters. But the arcana of Jane Austen's Meryton or Netherfield could be spoken of without blushes, certainly without that 'flame' that so often burns on Stephen Dedalus's cheek. James Joyce's milieu and upbringing presented him with a vivid and dangerous challenge to which his artistic nature responded with extraordinary subtlety and courage. To meet that challenge, to explore those regions of the psyche that beckoned to him, he was forced to invent a range of technical and linguistic resources unequalled in power and range through the length and breadth of modern literature. The sound barrier of his enterprise was that of social reticence, the wall—at least the façade—between the public and private self that Victoria's reign had so consolidated and which the Catholic Church in Ireland had so reinforced. Breaking through to those secret chambers was a heroic undertaking. Bringing generations of readers into sympathy and accord with that occluded world inside, getting the fictive current running both ways, was the supreme achievement of his literary genius. At least so it seems to one Irish reader.

## NOTES

First published in *James Joyce: An International Perspective*, edited by Suheil Badi Bushrui and Bernard Benstock (Gerrards Cross, Bucks: Colin Smythe, 1982; Totowa, New Jersey: Barnes and Noble Books, 1982).

1   *Selected Letters of James Joyce*, edited by Richard Ellmann (London: Faber, 1975).
2   James Joyce, *A Portrait of the Artist as a Young Man*, edited by Chester G. Anderson (New York: The Viking Press, 1968), p. 137. All future references to *A Portrait* are to this edition and will be incorporated in the text.
3   *Selected Letters of James Joyce*, ed. Ellmann, p. 181.
4   *Ibid.*, pp. 180, 181, 182.
5   Italo Svevo, *James Joyce*, translated by Stanislaus Joyce (New York: City Lights Books, 1950), unpaginated.
6   Dorothy Van Ghent, *The English Novel: Form and Function* (New York: Holt, Rinehart and Winston, 1953), pp. 275–6.
7   James Joyce, *Ulysses* (London: The Bodley Head, 1960), pp. 302–3. All future references to *Ulysses* are to this edition and will be incorporated in the text.
8   See Frank Budgen, *James Joyce and the Making of 'Ulysses' and Other Writings* (Oxford and New York: Oxford University Press, 1972), pp. 15–16.
9   The phrase is in a letter from Joyce to Grant Richards of 23 June 1906 regarding the troubled publication of *Dubliners* and Richards's fear of prosecution: 'I seriously believe that you will retard the course of civilization in Ireland by preventing the Irish people from having one good look at themselves in my nicely polished looking-glass.' *Letters of James Joyce*, Volume I, edited by Stuart Gilbert (London: Faber, 1957), p. 64.

# – 7 –

# Novelist and City: The Technical Challenge

Perhaps the most radical feature of Joyce's *Ulysses* is the relaxed neutrality of its tone in conveying a day in Dublin's life. For once, a major novel presents a capital city without investing it with social or moral significance. After a century which included Balzac, Dickens, Dostoevsky, Zola and Conrad this was a remarkable achievement. It is arguable that the chief strategy in that achievement was Joyce's elimination of conventional 'plot' from the novel's action and the consequent sense of a city's life suspended in the present, its multifarious activity presented without the stimulus of narrative suspense. A happy reading of *Ulysses* does not concern itself with what is going to happen next, but with what is happening now, on the page before us. This is not because—as so many critics tend modishly to say—the 'real hero of *Ulysses* is its language', but because Joyce's technique, of which language is a major part, manages to convey, minute by minute, the feeling of a city in which many things are happening at the same time.

The mini-plot of Throwaway's victory in the Gold Cup shows that Joyce, like Damon Runyon, could write a story of suspense and ironic reversal if he chose to. But its greater function is to frame the time between 10.15 a.m. and 5.15 p.m., when its consequences descend on Bloom in Barney Kiernan's, and to animate a complex moment for the hero in Westland Row where he is trying at once to feign interest at news of a death, get rid of a bore and catch a flash of female ankle in the same civil manoeuvre.

The radical nature of the *Ulysses* narrative technique, whereby the sense of a suspended present survives all the changes in *style*, is the more sharply appreciated when one ponders the implication of the remark that Joyce did for Dublin what Dickens did for London, what Balzac and Zola did for Paris. Joyce's methodology is so radically different, especially in the point of 'plot', that no symposium on the city in Irish fiction[1] can safely ignore the technical struggle that distinguishes *Ulysses* from previous novels of the city.

Taking a hint from Vladimir Propp in his *Morphology of the Folktale* one can generalize that the most persistent narrative pattern in novels of the city before Joyce is the Dick Whittington fable.[2] This naive plot in which the provincial innocent sets out for the distant city, enters and engages with it, and finally masters it, underlies novels as disparate in other respects as *Tom Jones*, *Vanity Fair*, *Père Goriot* and Dickens's three great novels of the 'self', *Oliver Twist*, *David Copperfield* and *Great Expectations*. The uncontrolled rush to the cities resulting from the Industrial Revolution tarnished the optimism of the Dick Whittington story as the quest for fortune carried with it an increasing threat of defeat and corruption.

Proleptic images of the doomed modern city were quickly identified in the Bible and widely deployed in moral rhetoric of the Victorian novel: Sodom, Gomorrah, Babylon. In one of his morning reveries Bloom mistakenly adds Edom to the list; and Henry James in *The Tragic Muse* styles London 'that great grey Babylon'. Hardy's innocent hero, Jude, discovers that his radiant vision of Christminster had been a cultural mirage; and Thackeray's intrepid worldling, Becky Sharp, proves barely equal to the pitfalls of 'Vanity Fair'—a phrase culled from Bunyan and bristling with moral implication. Mrs Barton and her daughters are forced to retreat 'bootless home and weather-beaten back' to the Galway countryside after their hopeful pilgrimage to George Moore's Dublin Season in *A Drama in Muslin*. Pip's departure from the village as he pursues his 'great expectations' is deliberately suggestive of Adam's loss of Eden. As the chapter ends 'the world lay spread before me' and as the next begins we find him 'scared by the immensity of London . . . ugly, crooked, narrow, and dirty.'[3]

Two points can be made about these great novels of the city: they employ the same plot, tell the same basic story; and in terms of that story the city is never neutral, it is always charged with moral significance. The plot employed is one of the most primitive of narrative forms, the journey or quest romance which developed into the picaresque and found in the modern city its ambiguous goal and grail. Very often the prime object of the writer may have been to delineate the city, but he found this impossible without the scaffolding of a plot, what E.M. Forster called 'this low atavistic form' which 'runs like a backbone—or may I say a tape-worm'— through the most sophisticated fictions.[4] The trouble for the writer, to stay with Forster's terms, is that his reader's attention is now held by the primitive pleasure of suspense: 'What would happen next?' Whereas he might be interested in conveying the life and texture of a city, the reader is on tenterhooks to know what is going to befall David, Pip or Alice Barton.

To sense the vitality and persistence of this atavistic narrative form one has only to compare the story of Oliver Twist with that of Spenser's *Faerie Queene*, Book 1. The only morphological difference is that Dickens projects his hero into a city and Spenser his into a forest. Oliver enters the labyrinth of London and is taken to Fagin's den; the Knight enters the forest and is taken to Archimago's cell. Archimago brings the guiles of Duessa to bear on the Knight, Fagin sets Nancy to gain Oliver's confidence. Each undergoes corrupt indoctrination. The Knight is saved by the virtuous ministrations of Una, Oliver by the kindness of Rose Maylie. Oliver is captured by Sykes, the Knight by Orgoglio. The Knight is finally rescued by supervenient grace in the person of Arthur, while Oliver finds a secular but no less miraculous deliverer in the benign and powerful Mr Brownlow. Similar correspondences could be found easily in the stories of Pip and David—one thinks of Uriah Heep, Creakle, Dora, Agnes and the avenging Micawber; or of Magwitch, Estella, Biddy, Bentley Drummle, Orlick, Jaggers. As the question of influence can hardly arise between Spenser and Dickens we can only conclude that there is a deep-seated need in the human psyche for this form of narrative, and that it migrates effortlessly from age to age, from forest to city, using whatever set, props and locations are to hand to rehearse its essential gestures. At the same time a sharp distinction must be made between Spenser's story and Dickens's: the former has no interest in the forest as such, using it merely as a background for the Knight's ordeal; but the depiction of London was a major part of Dickens's purpose, so that he constantly holds up the story of Pip's adventures to dilate upon its streets, buildings, shops, courtrooms and tenements.

Balzac was equally fascinated with Paris and his depiction of the city in all its moods and manifestations is arguably his prime achievement as a novelist. But his entire world is sustained by this primitive organ of suspense narrative, especially the quest romance. When the young provincial, Rastignac, has buried the old man at the end of *Père Goriot* he has learned by ordeal that the city has yet to be conquered:

Lights were beginning to twinkle here and there. His gaze fix almost avidly upon the space that lay between the column of the Palace Vendome and the dome of the Invalides; there lay the splendid world that he had wished to gain. He eyed that humming hive with a look that foretold its despoliation, as if he already felt on his lips the sweetness of its honey, and said with superb defiance,
'It's war between us now!'[5]

The city is still a version of the forest and 'enchantments drear' of medieval romance, and the events of *Père Goriot* that lead to Rastignac's gesture of defiance present a cast of characters and a web of motive remarkably close to the Dickensian pattern. While the city does not necessarily take second place in Balzac, it is either embodied in the hero's progress or accommodated in intervals of the plot where the author pauses to describe, reflect or ruminate on its glamour and danger. Zola in his Paris novels expanded upon this latter device by the use of what Angus Wilson called his 'interspersed lyrical passages' during pauses in the narrative.[6] Sometimes Zola could brilliantly *embody* the Parisian panorama in the action, as in the visit to the Louvre of the wedding-guests in *L'Assommoir*, yet his narrative mainstay remained the story of social adventure. At the end of *L'Assommoir* we see the child, Nana, wandering down the slum alley-way with a flower towards her fate at the pinnacle of the *demi-monde* in a novel that is to bear her name. Even the father of Naturalism, the fictional form most calculated to render life as it is lived, did not succeed in devising a technique which would embody the drama of a city's life without the support and the distraction of a traditional success story.

It may well have been this unfilled need that sent other novelists of the city to turn from the social climber to the detective as an agent of exploration in the urban jungle. The social climber could negotiate the societal tiers that led from the cheap boarding house to the gorgeous salon, but the sleuths of Wilkie Collins, Conan Doyle—even Dickens himself—could, by virtue of their licence, probe, interrogate, eavesdrop, penetrate the City's labyrinth and pick out the guilty and the innocent from its huge anonymity. This *genre* became Conrad's enabling instrument in his dark anatomy of London, *The Secret Agent*. The progress of detectives 'down these mean streets' has become one of the potent myths of our time.

But other fictional devices were being tried, and Dickens, being the most obsessed with his city, proved the most inventive in finding ways of conveying its reality through the novel. Raymond Williams, in *The English Novel from Dickens to Lawrence*, daringly and justly stood traditional criticism on its head when he outlined Dickens's faults as a novelist and then claimed them as virtues:

His characters are not 'rounded' and developing but 'flat' and emphatic. They are not slowly revealed but directly presented. Significance is not enacted in mainly tacit and intricate ways but is often directly presented in moral address and indeed exhortation. Instead of the controlled language of analysis and comprehension he uses, directly, the language of persuasion and display. His plots depend often on arbitrary coincidences, on sudden revelations and changes of heart. He offers not the details of psychological process but the finished articles: the social and psychological products.[7]

These techniques of narrative, Williams argues, are Dickens's means of responding to a challenge which he was the first to take up—that of expressing the new 'popular culture' of great cities where human relations are 'obscured, complicated, mystified, by the sheer rush and noise and miscellaneity of this new and complex social order'.[8]

Though Dickens revelled in the headlong momentum of narrative, and though he had a natural zest for aboriginal fable—note the ease with which he filled his tales with witches, dwarves, ogres, fairy god-fathers and heroic innocents—the artist in him struggled hard to break the tyranny of suspense narrative in his fiction One thinks of the thematic assault and battery in the symbolism at the opening of *Bleak House* or *Hard Times*. In each of these the human story—of Esther and Louisa—is firmly subordinated to the satiric and social purpose of the author. Though the plotting of *Our Mutual Friend* is absurdly ingenious, it is neither the human stories nor the individual characters that dominate our memory of the book but the massive symbolism of the river and the dust-heaps. This is a triumph of technique for an artist who had confided in his memorandum book his hopes of

representing London—or Paris, or any great place—in the light of being unknown to all the people in the story, and only taking the colour of their fears, their fancies and opinions. So getting a new aspect and being unlike itself. An odd unlikeness of itself.

The two love stories that are woven through the city's life—that of Bella Wilfer and John Rokesmith and that of Lizzie Hexam and Eugene Rayburn—are dwarfed by the vision of London itself, vast, anonymous, multicellular, at times like and unlike the London of *Great Expectations* where Pip's search for identity—and for Estella—had taken precedence over the city, at times reducing it almost to the status of background.

Dickens provides both comparison and contrast to Joyce's handling of his two obsessive themes, the artist and the city: what was going on in the mind of his artist-figure, Stephen Dedalus, and what was going on around the city of Dublin. After a number of confused beginnings—most notably in *Stephen Hero* where the two emphases trip each other up—he expressed the artist's inner life in his *Bildungsroman, A Portrait of the Artist as a Young Man*, and concentrated the city's life in *Dubliners*. Later, in *Ulysses*, he found the means of bringing both concerts to fictional life in the large contrapuntal unity of a single work. *A Portrait* corresponds roughly to *Great Expectations* in so far as it traces the growth of a sensitive adolescent in the context of a city's mazes. While the city is often vividly evoked in its pages, the main interest is on the protagonist. Dublin, like Clongowes and Cork, acts as a background and sounding-board for the hero's developing consciousness.

*Dubliners* and, more emphatically, *Ulysses* correspond to *Our Mutual Friend* in that they formally set about the delineation of a city's life as a literary objective. The city is no longer merely to be glimpsed, sketched or even elaborately contemplated in the intervals of a story but presented as foreground, theme and *heroine* of the fictional enterprise. Joyce came slowly to the realization that he was entering upon what Milton termed 'Things unattempted yet in prose or rhyme' and much of his middle years was devoted to finding appropriate forms and answerable style. But the main objective, from the earliest sketches, was seldom in doubt. In a letter to C.P. Curran in 1904 he determines to 'betray the soul of that hemiplegia or paralysis which many consider a city.'[9] To Stanislaus in 1905 he reflects that no writer 'has given it [Dublin] to the world . . . though it has been a capital of Europe for thousands of years'.[10] His attitude to his material is still moral and denunciatory: 'I think people might be willing to pay for the special odour of corruption which, I hope, floats over my stories.'[11] He is still a long way from the relaxed neutrality of tone which is to characterize *Ulysses*, but the larger perspectives of that novel are foreshadowed in the progress of *Dubliners*: sketch gives way to story, the canvas widens and the technique expands to give the sense of a city in perpetual—albeit aimless—motion. As 'Two Gallants' opens, the city, which in 'After the Race' had worn 'the mask of a capital',[12] exhibits a more alluring character and perspective:

The grey warm evening of August had descended upon the city and a mild warm air, a memory of summer, circulated in the streets. The streets, shuttered for the repose of Sunday, swarmed with a gaily coloured crowd. Like illumined pearls the lamps shone from the summit of their tall poles upon the living texture below which, changing shape and hue unceasingly, sent up into the warm grey evening air an unchanging, unceasing murmur.[13]

The caress of these rhythms is meant to display the city as an entity, if not indeed a personality. When the camera moves in to pick up Corley and Lenehan it has the air of seeking random samples of the town's humanity. Writing to his brother Joyce insisted that 'after all "Two Gallants"—with the Sunday crowds and the harp in Kildare street and Lenehan—is an Irish landscape.'[14] While Corley goes about his greedy business in the long grass of Donnybrook the murmur of Dublin goes on: Lenehan strums the harper's melody on the railings of the Duke's Lawn and describes a futile circle of the inner streets as he waits for his friend to return. His encounters are haphazard and pointless:

Lenehan said that he had been with Mac the night before in Egan's. The young man who had seen Mac in Westmoreland Street asked was it true that Mac had won a bit over a billiard match. Lenehan did not know: he said that Holohan had stood them drinks in Egan's.[15]

These banal details are a deliberate offence to the economy of 'plot', but they are vivid samples of a city's atmosphere. And they establish one emphasis that distinguishes Joyce's Dublin from the London of *Our Mutual Friend*: in the latter Dickens strives to make the metropolis alien and unknowable to the individual characters, whereas in *Dubliners*—and more emphatically in *Ulysses*—everyone in the fictional *milieu* tends to know everything about the others by dint of guess, gossip, observation, innuendo and slander. It is clear how Joyce is testing his techniques for the larger perspectives of *Ulysses*. Holohan will reappear in 'A Mother', Lenehan and Corley will figure in *Ulysses*, and in the motions of Chandler, Farrington, Duffy, Maria, Henchy, Hynes and Jimmy Doyle through the city's streets the vast pedestrian comedy of *Ulysses* is rehearsed and pre-figured.

In a celebrated passage in *Dombey and Son* Dickens wishes that some good angel would for a moment take the roofs off the houses of London to reveal the private lives of its citizens. His interest is humanitarian as well as artistic. Without any philanthropic distraction Joyce in his stories exposes a whole range of Dublin interiors: a wake, a schoolroom, a bazaar, a law office, a church, a sick-room, two house parties, two kitchens, a committee room, several pubs and restaurants, a boarding-house. The technical challenge of bringing these separate cells into one fictional organism has yet to be met. The solution is found partly in 'Grace' where the lavatory into which Kernan falls stands for Dante's hell, the sick-room for purgatory and the retreat at Gardiner Street for paradise. He has discovered what Eliot was to christen the 'mythical method',[16] the invisible 'plot' beneath the surface, a recipe to purge the 'tape-worm' of conventional narrative. Meanwhile the impulse to portray the city, *qua* city, was growing in the consciousness of the exiled writer. In September 1906, writing to Stanislaus, he repents of having been 'unnecessarily harsh' in his depiction of Dublin, and having reproduced 'none of the attraction of the city . . . its ingenuous insularity and its hospitality.'[17] In 'The Dead' which he was soon to write he redresses the balance on both these counts. Meanwhile, in 1906 he requests 'a Xmas present made up of tram-tickets, advts, handbills, posters, papers, programmes', and wishes for a 'a map of Dublin on my wall'.[18]

At home in the centre of the 'Hibernian Capital' James Stephens is working on the urban lyrics that go into his *Insurrections*, the city sketches that make up *Here Are Ladies*, and what must be the first thorough-going novel of the Dublin slums, *The Charwoman's Daughter* which was serialized as *Mary: a Story* in the Irish Review of 1912. It is not surprising that Stephens, incorrigibly a fabulist, should employ one of the oldest folk patterns, the Cinderella story, for his plot. His ingenuity reveals itself by the manner in which the traditional tale is adapted to dramatize the growth of the heroine to sexual awareness and discrimination, the class structure which makes a domestic servant the natural prey to a policeman—is it significant that the predatory Corley is a policeman's son?—the grinding squalor of the tenements, redeemed, as in O'Casey, by the humour and solidarity of their inhabitants.

A more vivid contrast could not be found as that between the city of *Dubliners* and that of *The Charwoman's Daughter*. The key word in Stephens is sunshine, in the early Joyce 'dampness' of soul and body. For Mary the city is an adventure playground, for Joyce's Eveline it is a constriction and a tyranny. Each writer had a precise eye for detail, and both describe the same thoroughfares, bridges, parks and rivers; yet the difference in atmosphere is so great that one could not envisage such passages as these inserted into a single story of *Dubliners*:

The sun was shining gloriously, and the streets seemed wonderfully clean in the sunlight. The horses under the heavy drays pulled their loads as if they were not heavy. The big, red-faced drivers leaned back at ease, with their hard hats pushed hack from their foreheads and their eyes puckered at the sunshine. The tram-cars whizzed by like great jewels. The outside cars went spanking down the broad road, and every jolly-faced jarvey winked at her as he jolted by.[19]

But its atmosphere, as distinct from its style, is not incompatible with the general ambience of *Ulysses* wherein the fictional weather has so improved since the depression of *Dubliners*. It may not be irrelevant that Mary Makebelieve, heroine of Stephens's novel, is based upon 'Cynthia' Kavanagh whom the writer had recently taken from her husband, and that the June day in which *Ulysses* is set was the first time Joyce went for a walk with Nora Barnacle. But though Stephens's Dublin is presented in the spirit of romance and optimism it has its moral configurations. Mary's daily journey through its streets implies a sense of peril—as in its folk archetypes—and this peril takes actual form in the sinister transformation of her first suitor. Equally there is a shrewd symbolism in the two parks she frequents: in Stephen's Green we find her indulging child-like fantasies of parenthood as she observes the ducks and fish with their 'children'; in the Phoenix Park she first meets the policeman, and thereafter it stands for adult experience, sexual love and duplicity. A crucial moment in Mary's—and the novel's—development is when, having set out for the Green to 'look at the ducks and the flower-beds and the eels', she reaches O'Connell Bridge where 'she blushed deeply, and turning towards the right, went rapidly in the direction of the Phoenix Park'.[20]

When Stephens had brought his young heroine through the pitfalls of experience to happiness with the right partner, and wealth with the supervention of Uncle Patrick's American legacy he hesitated before closing the book on her: 'Thus far the story of Mary Makebelieve'[21] is how the volume ends. In fact he proposed in a letter to Alice Stopford

Green in December 1914 to write 'La Comedie Humaine of Ireland'.[22] Nothing came of the ambition. But though radical prose fantasy occupied most of his creative activity thereafter, his sporadic raids on city experience yielded at least three dark masterpieces in the short story form: 'Desire', which is based on a folk motif that might be enacted in any city; 'Hunger', which is probably the most powerful short fiction to arise out of the Dublin Lock-out of 1913; and 'A Glass of Beer', a memorable study in alienation and misogyny centred on a side-walk cafe in Paris.

Meanwhile Joyce was refining those techniques and strategies which were to make *Ulysses* the one indisputable watershed in the course of the modern novel, and Dublin the most famous city in literary history, with the possible exception of Troy. These devices are so well known that they need only be listed here. The first, from which all the others stem, is that grid substitute for traditional plot, the 'mythical method' which received Eliot's *imprimatur* in a famous *Dial* review of November 1923:

In using the myth, in manipulating a continuous parallel between contemporaneity and antiquity, Mr Joyce is pursuing a method which others must pursue after him. They will not be imitators, any more than the scientist who uses the discoveries of an Einstein in pursuing his own, independent further investigations. It is simply a way of controlling, of ordering, of giving a shape and a significance to the immense panorama of futility and anarchy which is contemporary history . . . Instead of narrative method, we may now use the mythical method.[23]

Eliot had already picked up the idea from following the serial progress of *Ulysses* in *The Little Review* and deployed it to express his own 'Unreal City' in *The Waste Land*. (I take it that the carbuncular clerk who seduces the typist and leaves 'Finding the stars unlit' is a latterday, comic Oedipus.) Thus Joyce, by a fine irony, stole the plot of the first picaresque novel to underpin the action of the first modern novel to survive without a plot.

Feeding into this mythical grid was the 'stream of consciousness' borrowed, Joyce claimed, from Dujardin, which made it possible to show at once the outer man and the secretive private man, whether alone or deviously confronting the world of his friends and enemies. A new fictive idiom, fluid and allusive, emerged to carry the flotsam and jetsam of the passing moment together with fragments and particles of philosophy, myth and history, presented with apparent randomness yet organized with elaborate art. Bloom's mind is richly but casually allusive; Stephen's is erudite and formally allusive, constantly turning the matter of life into the language of literature. Thus while Stephen broods on his begetting by 'the man with my voice and my eyes and a ghostwoman with ashes on her breath', Bloom is musing on the probable moment of his son's conception: 'Give us a touch, Poldy. God, I'm dying for it. How life begins.'[24] When these correspondences take on mythic or symbolic overtones their resonance doubles. Stephen's contemplation of the milk woman in the first episode calls up a world of ancestral memory:

They lowed about her whom they knew, dewsilky cattle. Silk of the kine and poor old woman, names given her in old times.

Meanwhile Bloom's racial memory is given flesh in Eccles Street:

A dead sea in a dead land, grey and old. Old now. It bore the oldest, the first race. A bent hag crossed from Cassidy's clutching a naggin bottle by the neck.[25]

Stephen ruminates upon the milkwoman's 'unclean loins, of man's flesh made not in God's likeness'. Bloom in a mood of uncharacteristic desolation thinks of his scattered people 'multiplying, dying, being born everywhere. It lay there now. Now it could bear no more Dead: an old woman's: grey sunken cunt of the world.'[26]

There are the intertwining melodies and lyrics of songs by which the reader's ear is at turns teased and caressed, helping to shape a movement of prose that is itself symphonic, until music reaches its own prose apotheosis in the Ormond Bar in the late reaches of the afternoon. There is the peristalsis of Bloom's progress through the city's digestive tract at lunchtime, and the parallax of his movement relative to that of Boylan and Stephen. There are the recurrent motifs, the proliferating theories of life and afterlife,—*amor matris* and *lex aeterna*—the wide variety of styles, all contributing to the vast verbal energy that keeps the imaginary city ticking over from sentence to sentence. If I single out one device in particular it is because it is at once so obvious and unobtrusive that critics have tended to ignore it. Yet it is of central importance to the sense of the city's ordinary life. This is the continuous movement of bodies—human, embryonic, marine, celestial, inanimate, mineral, organic, animal—across our vision.

One of the first is the ship, *Rosevean*, which Stephen sees from Sandymount Strand, which moves in to meet the crumpled handbill thrown over O'Connell Bridge by Bloom at lunchtime, and from which able seaman Murphy disembarks in time to exchange words with Bloom and Stephen at the cabman's-shelter in the small hours of the following morning. Then come Wisdom Hely's sandwich men, mad Mr Breen with his law-books and his distraught wife in pursuit, Cashel Boyle O'Connor Fitzmaurice Tisdall Farrell—a one-man procession of names—the blind piano-tuner, the one-legged sailor whose song is casually echoed in Murphy's dialogue—Dilly Dedalus and Patrick Dignam, Father Conmee going north, Sir William Humble going south, the two midwives wending from Sandymount back to the Liberties. The examples could be multiplied.

Their unobtrusive motion registers mostly on the corner of the eye and provides the human flux, the elaborate 'strandentwining' patterns of continuity which create the pulsation of a living city.

## NOTES

First published in *The Irish Writer and the City*, edited by Maurice Harmon (Gerrards Cross, Bucks: Colin Smythe, 1984; Totowa, New Jersey: Barnes and Noble Books, 1984).

1  This was originally delivered as a plenary lecture at the fifth triennial conference of the International Association for the Study of Anglo-Irish Literature held at University College Dublin in July 1982, where the theme was the Irish writer and the city.
2  Vladimir Propp, *Morphology of the Folktale* (Austin and London: University of Texas Press, 1968), pp. 50–1.
3  Charles Dickens, *Great Expectations* (London: Penguin, 1965), p. 186, p. 187.
4  E.M. Forster, *Aspects of the Novel* (London: Hodder and Stoughton, 1974), pp. 17–18.
5  Honoré de Balzac, *Old Goriot*, translated by Marion Ayton Crawford (London: Penguin, 1951), p. 304.
6  Angus Wilson, *Emile Zola: An Introductory Study of his Novels* (London: Secker and Warburg, rev. ed. 1964), p. 67.
7  Raymond Williams, *The English Novel from Dickens to Lawrence* (London: Chatto and Windus, 1970), p. 31.
8  *Ibid.*, p. 33.
9  *Letters of James Joyce*, Volume I, edited by Stuart Gilbert (London: Faber, 1957), p. 55.
10  *Letters of James Joyce*, Volume II, edited by Richard Ellmann (New York: The Viking Press, 1966), p. 111.
11  Letter to Grant Richards on 15 October 1905. *Ibid.*, p. 123.
12  James Joyce, *Dubliners*, edited by Robert Scholes and A. Walton Litz (New York: The Viking Press, 1969), p. 46.
13  *Ibid.*, p, 49.
14  *Letters of James Joyce*, Volume II, ed. Ellmann, p. 166.
15  Joyce, *Dubliners*, ed. Scholes and Litz, p. 58.
16  T.S. Eliot, '*Ulysses*, Order and Myth', *James Joyce: The Critical Heritage*, Volume One 1902-1927, edited by Robert H. Deming (London: Routledge and Kegan Paul, 1970), p. 271.
17  *Letters of James Joyce*, Volume II, ed. Ellmann, p. 166.
18  *Ibid.*, p. 186.
19  James Stephens, *The Charwoman's Daughter* (London: Macmillan, 1912), p. 48.
20  *Ibid.*, p. 74.
21  *Ibid.*, p. 228.
22  *Letters of James Stephens*, edited by Richard J. Finneran (London: Macmillan, 1974), p. 150.
23  T.S. Eliot, '*Ulysses*, Order and Myth', *James Joyce: The Critical Heritage*, Volume One 1902-1927, ed. Deming, pp. 270-1.
24  James Joyce, *Ulysses* (London: The Bodley Head, 1960), p. 46, p. 110.
25  *Ibid.*, p. 15, p. 73.
26  *Ibid.*, p. 16, p. 73.

# Section Two

## *Inherited Dissent*

# 8

# Inherited Dissent: The Dilemma of the Irish Writer

The relations between the Irish artist and his society have been strained and uneasy since our literature emerged from the nineteenth century. One could make a nasty collection of comments from the writings of Irishmen, since, say, the publication of George Moore's *The Untilled Field* in 1903, down to Austin Clarke's *Flight to Africa*, sixty years later. These comments would refer to the apparent difficulty which the literary artist finds in living among and writing about his countrymen. For Joyce Ireland was among other things the old sow that ate her farrow; a country dedicated to the banishment of her artists.

This situation is sometimes puzzling to innocent students who can find no case of an artist who was actually banished, and who are puzzled to find that some of our most trenchant satirists occupy positions of public trust in Irish society. Another collection might also be made, a great deal more massive and amorphous than the first, illustrating the image of Ireland which such writers have projected down through the decades. This image of Irish society, promoted in fiction, drama and poetry, would be found to be consistently unflattering; it would also be found that it had undergone very little essential change since the turn of the century. Raymond Mortimer, surely an alert observer, in reviewing the late Michael Farrell's *Thy Tears Might Cease*, stated it thus:

The best Irish writers of Farrell's generation (unless they were Protestants) believed that independence would remould their country nearer to their hearts' desire. Now they complain that it has become provincial, complacent and philistine—a waterlogged boat slowly sinking, in which the priest and the publican grow sleek, while the dwindling population seek to escape. Presumably they exaggerate, but what room is there for intellectuals in a society that bans their books?

This passage puts one side of the picture very neatly: the artist as a pariah, at odds with his smug, philistine society. In essentials it hardly differs from the image of Ireland put out by Joyce and Moore in the early years of the century. It is the picture of Ireland that continues to dominate our literature; unquestionably this is the sort of situation which the majority of literary foreigners expect to find in Ireland. As an image it is certainly as well established as the nineteenth-century image of the imbecilic peasant and hard-riding gentry which Croker, Lover and Lever had impressed on an overseas reading public, and which George Moore was so rightly anxious to discredit.

Now the universality, stamina and persistence of this twentieth-century 'waterlogged boat' image poses two allied questions. Firstly, is it a true image? Has the spirit of the nation stood still in a state of complacent and sluggish decay for all this time? Or alternatively, has the image itself become moribund? The writer has consistently chastised his society for being lifeless, inert and complacent. Is it possible that the writer may have himself fallen victim to these very vices in being satisfied with outmoded stereotypes of a society which has, in the meantime, shaken off its lethargy and moved forward unnoticed by its literary chroniclers? To pursue this second alternative a little further: there have been considerable and noticeable changes in both the temper and the pattern of Irish life particularly since the war. In such areas as industry, housing, agriculture and education these changes have rapidly accelerated over the past ten years. Have any, or all, of these social changes been reflected in contemporary Irish writing? And if they have not—as I believe they have not—why?

This essay is an attempt to answer these questions, to examine the relationship that exists and has existed between the Irish writer and his society, to glance at some of the more urgent problems and difficulties that confront the young creative writer in Ireland to-day. And lest my position may be misunderstood in this land where secret novelists and poets are said to abound, I write not as a practitioner but as an onlooker, a reader, and a critic in a small way. From this point of vantage it appears to me that Irish writing has reached some sort of cross-roads, a time demanding re-appraisal and renewal and perhaps a greater degree of intellectual awareness than has been necessary for some years past. It is being said, for instance, by responsible commentators—e.g. Robin Skelton in *The Critical Quarterly*—that there is a revival of literature going on in Ireland to-day. If this is so, then the need for the sort of definition mentioned above is all the more urgent.

## Tradition and Environment

The creative consciousness of a writer is normally under pressure from two forces: on the one hand there is the literary tradition which he has received

from the past, remote or proximate; and on the other there is his environment, the society in which he lives and which must inevitably become his
subject matter. Ideally both forces should cooperate: under the control of
his own inspiration the tradition ought to furnish him with models,
suggest technical possibilities, indicate areas of life and experience which
he might explore; at the same time it ought not to come between him
and the living scene which is in one way or another to be his material.
This is ideally the case, but in practice the two forces do not always fuse
profitably. Literary history is strewn with the corpses of talented writers
who allowed an inherited mode or sensibility to blind them to the
realities of their own age and place. At the end of great literary movements
there is always this period of decline, when otherwise competent writers
continue to work through a derived rather than an experienced sensibility.

It is easy to see the progressive decay in romantic sensibility from
Tennyson through the pre-Raphaelites and the Decadents down to the
Georgian lyricists. It is not merely a matter of semantic decadence,
though it is in the gradual dislocation of word and meaning that it is
most clearly manifest. It is a general process which involves the uncritical
acceptance of second-hand imagery, symbols, postures, thought patterns,
ideas, even opinions. When this condition sets in, the time has come to
renew the creative apparatus, break with the immediate past or at least
take a more ruthlessly selective attitude towards it, seek more remote,
less dominating models, and open up new areas of the mind and the
landscape for exploration. Eliot did this for English poetry in the teens of
the century and now he, in turn, has become part of the tradition. Young
English poets are, at the moment, struggling to get free from his very
powerful influence. We, in Ireland, could perhaps afford to watch the
process with amused detachment were it not for our own parallel and
even more urgent predicament. In fact our own modest tradition has
fallen under the immense and crippling shadows of Joyce and Yeats; and
when two such giants throw their shade over a social landscape as small
as Ireland's, things are likely to get very difficult for the fledgling writer
who is trying to bring that raw material into artistic focus.

## The Influence of Joyce and Yeats

It would be difficult to exaggerate the influence of Joyce and Yeats on
the young Irish aesthete of to-day. Having travelled the world their
reputations have come back to Ireland to receive, in full, belated
homage. Great effort has been put forth by the younger generations to
see that justice be done to their vast achievements. The activities which
now surround the Martello Tower and the Sligo Summer School, while

admirable in terms of piety, have served to intensify the influence exerted by both writers on the creative consciousness of an emerging generation. This influence manifests itself in various, subtle ways. In the works of younger writers their names keep recurring like pious invocations; in the latest publications of Ewart Milne, Richard Weber, Basil Payne, James Liddy, Desmond O'Grady and Roy McFadden there are formal allusions to the works of Yeats and Joyce. One could also instance the proliferation of their more celebrated phrases, both on the literary pages and in the literary pubs: Joyce's 'silence, exile and cunning', 'signatures of all things', 'the old sow that ate her farrow', 'forge in the smithy of my soul' and then Yeats's 'dog that praised its fleas', 'rocking the cradle of genius', 'words alone are certain good', 'the foul rag-and-bone-shop of the heart', 'call the muses home', 'a terrible beauty', 'no petty people'. When Brendan Behan died Roy McFadden, as if in an attempt to clinch my conviction in the matter, commemorated him with such lines as:

> The  broth of an Irish boy no doubt;
> But, Joyce be with us, don't neglect
> The learning and the intellect . . .  ('Brendan Behan')

Joyce, in fact, is now become a god. Surely Eliot has not got such a cultish grip on the younger English writers. A great deal of water has flowed under London Bridge since Evelyn Waugh's Anthony Blanche recited 'The Waste Land' from Sebastian's balcony! But we are a small country, rather given to extremes of rejection or adulation, and we have received a good deal of flattery from abroad of late. The result is that these two great writers have become a pair of benevolent incubi for the young writer who is trying to find his feet.

If Joyce and Yeats were orthodox, typical writers, their influence might be a great deal more salutary; if like Wordsworth, Shakespeare or Thomas Mann they had absorbed and transfigured the pieties of their country's ethos into art, then their successors might have selected with greater ease from the many lessons bodied forth in their work. But, in different ways, both writers repudiated the social and religious pieties of Ireland; both were philosophical eccentrics; Joyce in particular, seeing Dublin as a 'centre of paralysis', deals destructively with his material and the vision of Ireland which he embodies is so grievously compelling that one is inclined to forget that it is so intensely personal and subjective. Two generations later this fierce personal vision is capable of coming between our eyes and the Irish scene—which has changed out of recognition since then—and even colouring our view of it. This is an example of a literary tradition becoming so strong as to impair the second factor: the dialogue between author and environment. The resulting tension in the mind of the Irish writer has been stressed by Benedict Kiely in his admirable survey, *Modern Irish Fiction*, where he writes:

Irish literature and particularly the modern Irish novel is tugged this way and that, now by the rejection that meant so much to Joyce, now by the acceptance that contains as a skin contains an apple the stories of Daniel Corkery.

Here tradition and environment come together in one ineluctable, complex pressure on the novelist. Kiely, no doubt, has not only seen the tension at work in the writings of others, but perhaps has had to control it within the rigorous equilibrium of his own excellent novels. It would be false and overdramatic to say that the Irish artist had to choose between two sharply divided, ready-made attitudes to his society, between rejection and acceptance; but the 'tug', however subconsciously, is still there. In his struggle for expression he must cope with this ante-cedent tension, and this tension will be one of the factors in determining his final attitude towards his material. Consequently the question is not whether he will be sympathetic or hostile to his society. The real question is whether his hostility or acceptance will be derived or experienced. Will it be the result of a highly fashionable traditional bias, or will it be the result of a hard personal confrontation with the realities of that society? Will it be literature nourishing itself on its own entrails, or literature drawing its sustenance from the springs of life?

It is only natural that a tug between Corkery and Joyce should result in a clear victory for Joyce. When Ernest Boyd set out to compare *A Portrait of the Artist as a Young Man* with Daniel Corkery's *The Threshold of Quiet* he was really laying aside his critical judgment temporarily. It is not just that rejection is more attractive and dramatic than acceptance; it is simply that Irish fiction has had its James Joyce and still awaits its Thomas Mann. It is human to look around for someone to fill the role, and in 1922 it was natural to elect Corkery for the honour. Early last year (1964) a critic in *The Irish Times* cast Joseph Brady, author of *In Monavalla*, for the part. But the plain fact is that he does not measure up; and so far the forces of rejection are winning hands down—on sheer merit at that! They have been at work much longer than many of us care to admit, and the movement cannot be laid solely at the door of Joyce.

Thirteen years before Stephen Dedalus pronounced his *non serviam* George Moore's alter ego, John Rodney in *The Untilled Field*, had made his choice:

He was leaving Ireland. On this point his mind was made up, . . . He had enough of a country where there had never been any sculpture nor any painting, nor any architecture to signify. They were talking about reviving the Gothic, but Rodney did not believe in their resurrection or in their renaissance, or in their anything . . . he was going . . . to where there was the joy of life, out of the damp, religious atmosphere in which nothing flourished but the religious vocation.

This stance of national and religious apostasy on the part of the Irish artist in the person of Moore/Rodney was rapidly reinforced by Moore's immediate successors. Yeats, Stephens, A.E. and, of course, Joyce expressed in different ways their distrust of Catholic Ireland as a centre of artistic energy. Yeats, Stephens and A.E. abandoned different forms of Protestantism for a more mystical religious concept, while Moore and Joyce left Catholicism for a religion of art. It would be impossible, and presumptuous, to try to unravel or pronounce upon the individual subtleties of faith and dialectic which dictated these several defections. One point, however, might be noted—that each of them replaced his original faith with blends of the mystical and aesthetic. They seem to have been needled into apostasy by a Christianity which at that time, in both systems, appeared to be extremely philistine, anti-intellectual, disciplinarian and above all anti-mystical. It was Christianity smug in the dry complacency of nineteenth century apologetics, suspicious of everything outside devotionalism and observance. It would take too long to establish the point by argument, but a quotation from Father Martin D'Arcy, S.J. (in his preface to the poems of St John of The Cross, translated by Roy Campbell) provides independent witness to the official frame of mind:

As is well known, many leading Protestant divines refused to give mysticism a place within the Christian faith, and for a period Catholic spiritual writers advocated a vigorous practice of the virtues in preference to what savoured of illuminism and quietism. In the last fifty years [he writes in 1951] this open or veiled hostility has changed into a marked degree of appreciation.

This 'veiled hostility', prevalent in the Christian world at large, was if anything more intense in Ireland. And as the artistic impulse is essentially mystical it might explain the recoil of so many Irish artists. To some extent it might explain why so many obviously intelligent men turned enthusiastically to Madame Blavatsky's incredible cult of theosophy; it helps to explain the movement of Stephens, Yeats, Russell and others towards Celtic paganism. As Austin Clarke points out, three orthodox Christian authors of 'acceptance', Pearse, MacDonagh and Plunkett attempted to set up a counter-trend of Christian mysticism. But the minor nature of their talents and the finality of a British firing squad severely limited their influence. Younger writers were affected by a spirit which seems to have been almost inherent in the age: in his *Drums Under the Window* we find the young O'Casey reading Fraser and Darwin as if they were sacred books; later it was Marx—always it was the doctrinal catalyst of an antecedent dissent.

By now nearly all the greater builders of our tradition have been mentioned, and the balance has been heavily weighted in the direction of revolt and rejection. The image has been that of the artist as maverick, if not exactly pariah. It might fairly be said too that the cleavage between artist and average society has been a genuine, a spontaneous thing, rather than a perverse cult of withdrawal. The standard of literature produced is guarantee enough that a solid impact between artist and material had been consistently made. Further evidence of this spontaneity is shown in the reaction of artistic Ireland to the Insurrection in 1916. Yeats, with that honesty which characterized his social attitudes, made a public confession of his previous blindness in a poem which became the finest existing tribute to his country's dead; Russell concurred; Stephens celebrated it in two passionate books; O'Casey saluted it in one splendid play—the rest were excused by death or exile.

In fact the teens of the century promised greatly, producing a steady upsurge of positive writing. Daniel Corkery, Padraic Colum and that now neglected fiction writer Seamus O'Kelly were taking up the torch from a tradition which had been predominantly Anglo-Irish and Protestant, and the dialogue between sow and farrow began to lose much of its acrimony. But abruptly the kissing had again to stop. The ugly horror of the Civil War broke in and the quarrel was renewed. When the smoke settled the air was heavy with disillusion. The dominating figures of O'Flaherty, O'Connor, O'Faolain who had shared the dream of a free and beautiful Ireland made no secret of their disappointment that—in Benedict Kiely's phrase—'the birth of a terrible beauty in 1916 ended only in the establishment of a grocer's republic.' Ironically O'Connor and O'Faolain began as pupils of Corkery; but being sincere and original writers they absorbed from him all that was consistent with their own visions and then went their own ways. Austin Clarke, once a dutiful son of the same cultural matrix, returned from England in the thirties and lamented over a land

> . . . . . where every woman's son
> Must carry his own coffin and believe,
> In dread, all that the clergy teach the young.
> ('The Straying Student', 1937)

It may be significant also that while his two brilliant pupils dominated the thirties with fiction and controversy, the old master, Corkery, lapsed into silence—his only contribution to the decade being in 1939, *Earth out of Earth*, his final book.

This 'echo of learned controversy' obscured somewhat the merits of two considerable novelists who emerged in the early years of the decade,

Kate O'Brien and Francis MacManus. It was a pity, because both of them reflected a calm contemplative relationship with their material. If we except Kate O'Brien's one impatient swipe at the newly formed censorship board, we can see them both as novelists of 'acceptance' in the healthiest possible sense. Both showed a deep, penetrating understanding of the society they depicted, its social standards, its religious leaven, and both succeeded in exposing it to the roots with a relentless, yet placid, objectivity. In most other respects they were and are utterly different writers, though they share the unjust neglect of their countrymen. Yet the attitude of disinterested contemplation, free from either enthusiasm or bitterness—surely the ideal state for the realistic artist—bore fruit in the forties when a post-revolutionary, post-civil-war generation had come of age. They were joined by Mary Lavin—for whose pen a 'grocer's republic' might have been specifically invented—Michael MacLaverty and later Benedict Kiely, all of whom found a calm exploratory attitude to Ireland quite natural. In their work there was no dramatic hostility, no sharp sense of disillusion nor, on the other hand, no wild doctrinaire enthusiasm. Bryan McMahon's celebration emerges organically from a folk tradition in which he had steeped himself, and on the other side of the coin Patrick Kavanagh's harsh, affectionate, implacable investigations in *Tarry Flynn* and *The Great Hunger* came direct from life as it was lived, owed nothing to bookish presuppositions. Even the satirists, Mervyn Wall and Flann O'Brien, exhibited a spirit of delightful liberty. Wall's brilliant and self-mocking anticlericalism had nothing of Joyce's or Clarke's fierce, bitter involvement; O'Brien made it a point to mock at Joyce, and at all that was pompous and pretentious in his cult.

The only two considerable figures of the fifties, James Plunkett and Thomas Kinsella, spoke with clear individual voices; and they might be seen as fore-runners of the present 'movement' which we alluded to at the outset. But it is only fair to stipulate that while the movement may break down, or be found not to exist, both these writers have staked indisputable claims to distinction, and that much of our hope for the future of Irish writing is centred on them both.

This has been a rapid and rather crude survey of the modern Irish tradition, carried out as a search for a single theme—the writer's relationship to his country, and implicitly his attitude towards his tradition. It has roughly demonstrated that *in fact* there is no question of a consistent, monolithic attitude; that different writers and different generations have reacted individually, differently; that the movement has been broadly from rejection to enthusiastic acceptance, back to disillusioned rejection, back to calm detached acceptance down to the present time.

*The Hardening 'Cliché'*

But while the scene has varied in detail, the more spectacular figures form a near-continuous line of dissent down through the half-century: Moore, Joyce, O'Connor, O'Casey and, most significantly, Austin Clarke whose influence on the present is incalculably powerful. Furthermore, these dissenting writers have been so influential that they have conveyed the *impression* of a monolithic attitude. Because the most vocal of our writers have been distrustful of Irish values it has been assumed, both at home and abroad, that all sensitive Irish artists feel the same. The image of which we have spoken has formed and the tendency has been to read Irish literature in the light of the image, often importing ideas and ascribing prejudices where they have no relevance or meaning.

A recent example will serve to show how intelligent readers can fall victim to this error. When John McGahern's brilliant first novel *The Barracks* was reviewed in an English Sunday paper, the critic immediately assumed that the author implied a hostile comment on rural Irish life. It is an erroneous assumption, for there is no writer—with the possible exception of Francis MacManus—more free from didacticism than John McGahern. This would be insignificant, however, if it were not for the manner in which the reviewer seized on one detail in the book to clinch his point. In describing the scene around the village church the author mentions an authentic detail—rosary beads twined round the church railings. As every Irishman can tell the beads are lost property which have been picked up off the ground and displayed where their owners may find them. But the reviewer, apparently mistaking the custom for a superstitious rite, wonders sadly what one can do for people who piously twine rosaries round railings. The reader in this case has fallen victim to a *cliché*, because the vision of Ireland which the misreading implies is the result of a powerful and relentless *cliché*. He has seen something in an Irish novel which was not there; he has mistaken John McGahern who was born in 1934 for Frank O'Connor who was born in 1903.

It has become firmly established in the majority of literate minds that Ireland is a backward, insanitary, inert, despairing country; a people priest-ridden and superstitious, which despises its artists and intellectuals, treats its autocratic, avaricious and crafty clergy with a sanctimonious servility; a people soaked in dreams and booze, fixated backwards on the events of Easter Week, 1916, blind to the meaning of the present and the future, without economic hope, helpless in the face of emigration, ignorant of the facts of life, overcome with a Jansenistic fear of sex and the body, bemused with the opium of past splendours—yet in spite of it all, a people friendly, poetic, with a certain gentle unreliable charm. This set of traits cannot be ascribed to the pages of any one writer: they are the cumulative end-product of half a century of writing which was by turns hostile, embittered and penetrating. Whatever the contemporary social veracity of these portrayals, I do not think that any observer of provincial Ireland over the past ten years would claim that the picture holds good for to-day.

## The New Ireland

Except for rare exceptional cases, eccentricities and survivals, that picture of Irish life has changed in every single aspect mentioned, changed radically, and in most cases changed for the better. This change has been noted in such an unexpected quarter as *Time* magazine, and symbolized by a leprechaun pulling back a shamrocky curtain to reveal a power station. But, sad to say, no such sign of recognition has appeared in the pages of Ireland's younger writers. I must make one exception in the case of that perceptive expatriate writer John Montague who returned to Ireland last year and attended a Fleadh Ceoil. The experience gave birth to a witty little poem with the refrain:

> Puritan Ireland's dead and gone,
> A myth of O'Connor and O'Faolain.
>     ('At the Fleadh Cheoil in Mullingar')

But the mass of the younger writers—where their work impinges on the topic—John Broderick, Brendan Kennelly, James Liddy, Desmond O'Grady, Aidan Higgins, Edna O'Brien, Ewart Milne and of course the elder dominating figure of Austin Clarke, show few signs of recognizing the fact.

Even apart from the Jansenistic charge—which can be readily refuted by taking the writer in question to any of the great ugly dance halls which dominate the provinces—the provincial life of Ireland is at the moment in a ferment of change and development. Here is something that outstrips completely in dramatic potential anything that the emergence of the co-operative movement delivered over to the imaginations of George Moore or Peadar O'Donnell. The traditional water-logged insularity has been rapidly disturbed by the influx of foreigners—continental business men, executives, representatives, technicians. The social patterns are going through an exciting and salutary change; soon the problems attendant on inter-marriage with Irish Catholics will begin to emerge. The relationship between lay-man and priest has moved on to a completely new platform where they co-operate or disagree on equal terms in every area of rural and provincial activity from community development to amateur dramatics. There is probably a greater degree of sophistication, and of materialism; there is a parallel upsurge of idealism among lay-organizations which has brought energy and hope to previously stagnant communities. There is a new feeling in the air, a stimulation and excitement in rural life that I find is totally unknown to Dubliners and, in particular, to literary Dubliners.

There is, too, a new openness to artistic matters. Narrow-mindedness and philistinism and autocracy still survive (they always will in a free society), but they no longer have the force or the influence to hinder the cultural and sociological advances which have got firmly under way.

Another change in Irish life which has been overlooked is the huge advance in education since the Second World War. The proportion of Irishmen to receive secondary education has rocketed. There is therefore a higher degree of literacy, a wider accessibility to new ideas, a greater intellectual independence than ever before. Yet, as has been mentioned, none of these changes has been significantly reflected in Irish fiction. Part of the reason is, I believe, the factor mentioned at the outset—the powerful influence of the literary tradition which the younger writers have received: the spectacular return of Joyce and Yeats; the just celebration of their long-neglected greatness; and the rather irrelevant insistence on the bitter struggle which they both had waged with their philistine society. The attitude of the Irish artist to his people, in other words, had been defined: his was the high disdain of Yeats and the 'silence exile and cunning' of Joyce. Society was not worthy; consequently the artist must despise and repudiate it. The stance was historically valid for Joyce and Yeats but it is not *necessarily* valid for the young writer who, more than a generation later, has to wrest a totally different literature from a radically changed society. Yet one gets the impression that this attitude of withdrawal and hostility has been adopted, uncritically, almost as a sacred duty by many of the present day heirs to the Irish tradition.

Another factor has been the dramatic rise of Austin Clarke's reputation, his well-deserved recognition after a lifetime of arduous, neglected and brilliant writing. Clarke, too, chose the path of withdrawal. His latest work exhibits a fierce articulate antagonism to almost every aspect of Irish life, lay and clerical. There is no doubt as to his integrity, his intense scorching sincerity. There is also no doubt that he has more to teach young poets in terms of technique and language than any living poet anywhere. But it would be carrying adulation too far to imagine that it is necessary to share his vision of Irish society. His vision is his own; it has been formed and conditioned by factors, historical and personal, which have no genuine relevance to the younger generation. It would be as ludicrous for our generation to try to see Ireland through Austin Clarke's eyes as it would be impossible for him to see it through ours.

## The Artist as Freak

Sean O'Faolain, who could never manage to conceal his deep love and concern for the country and its people, has written as devastatingly as any artist of his generation about the position of the artist here. The writer, to him, is unavoidably a man apart, 'an outcast', a mistrusted interloper trying to extort significance from a society where 'sin is furtive, convention rigid, courage slight and honesty scant', where 'the policeman and the priest are in a perpetual glow of satisfaction'. The passionate reasonableness of this author's controversy down through the years has struck home where disdain or bitterness might not have penetrated. But, as we shall see presently, O'Faolain would not suggest for a moment that his attitude was valid for anyone but himself.

Finally, take Frank O'Connor's definition of the Irish artist's position *vis-à-vis* Irish society. Perhaps the most satisfactory statement of his views comes in his chapter on the stories of Mary Lavin in his study of the short story, *The Lonely Voice,* where he digresses to comment on the novels of C.P. Snow. He wonders whether a series of novels such as *Strangers and Brothers* could be written on Irish society by an Irish author. He believes that it could not be done, and his chief reason for the opinion is quite startling. It could not be done, he holds, because a narrator like Snow's Lewis Elliot would not be viable for an Irish novelist. Lewis Elliot represents the normal view in Snow's novels, but he could have no counterpart in the Irish novel because, as O'Connor asserts,

. . . the narrator could never have regarded himself as representing normality. On the contrary, he would have realized as Yeats realized that he owed his position to having always been a bit of a freak. . . .

So there it is. The young Irish writer has had his position in society defined, stated, ramified and laid down for him. He is above it, beyond it, persecuted by it, outcast from it. He is so much an outsider that he cannot create and sustain a character/narrator who represents that society's concept of normality! He is a freak!

## Breaking the Mould

Now, as I have been stressing to the point of boredom, it would be egregiously foolish for the younger writer to step into the position which his elders have so minutely defined for him. I cannot say whether Frank O'Connor's remarks were true of his period, but I gravely doubt their validity for to-day. (In fact the evidence of his own stories would seem to suggest an extraordinary *rapport* between the author and the plain people of Ireland.) To accept his pronouncement, and those others quoted above, would be to limit the range of the writer's sympathies disastrously. It would be to throw up a barrier of extraneous prejudice between him and his fellow countrymen. Its final effect would be to drive the artist into an ivory tower or a literary pub; the result is the same in both cases—literature drawing its strength from literature; literature losing its vital contact with life.

The present vogue of literary palesmanship is one symptom of this withdrawal. Most of our writers are inevitably Dublin-based. Most modern writing, consequently, treats of either an urban milieu or else a rural background recollected in suburbia. Both modes have of course produced distinguished work. But neglect has been the lot of the real modern challenge. There is neglect of that great provincial hinterland represented by Mullingar, Roscrea, Kilkenny and Athlone where the real dynamism of change and development is centred. When our city writers go down the country they invariably head for exotic and exceptional places like Ballyferriter and Achill, passing by a whole provincial ethos in a blur of alternating grey and green. Now it is not suggested that the writer should be asked to gird himself and go forth from the literary village of Grafton Street as a mere pop sociologist. It is not too much, however, to ask him to open his mind and his consciousness to the spirit of his time and place. There is hardly an example in literature of a great writer who was not first a man of his own era. If it is not an essential it is certainly a distinct advantage for a writer to be, in F.R. Leavis's phrase, 'alive to his times'.

I am not suggesting for a moment that the resultant literature ought to be uncritical celebration of the Irish pieties. It might indeed turn out to be an even more deadly indictment of Irish values than ever went before. It would be, however, alive and authentic; and, whatever the result, it would be ultimately not only for the good of literature but for the good of society. It would compel the writer to know his people directly, minutely, omnivorously; to know them in the flesh rather than by the literary images of their fathers. It is only when this effort has been made that the act of acceptance or rejection is either possible or meaningful. Joyce earned the right of artistic rejection, just as Corkery earned the right of acceptance; in neither case was it a facile choice. But it would be intolerably facile for a young Irish writer to take his stand on either side without having won through to that conviction *via* life. It has been truly said that the artist's first duty is disloyalty. But the principle cuts both ways: if the writer is to clear his mind of pious prejudice towards faith and fatherland, he must be equally ruthless with the influences and prejudices of his literary tradition.

Sean O'Faolain, when he turns to the positive side of the Irish literary question (in *Studies:* Spring 1962), foresees this very problem, when he writes of the dangers which beset a 'writer's battle for honesty':

The danger of becoming embittered, or twisted, threatens creativity itself, and here we come to the real battleground of contemporary Irish writing. For the first time Irish writers have to *think* themselves into personal release. . . . We need to explore Irish life with an objectivity never hitherto applied to it. . . . But to see clearly is not to write passionately. An artist must, in some fashion, love his material, and his material must, in some fashion, co-operate with him. It is not enough for an artist to be clinically interested in life: he must take fire from it. This has been the great rub in Ireland for some thirty years.

I wonder did O'Faolain mention thirty years with direct realization that it covered precisely the period of his own productive career at the time of writing; his first book, *Midsummer Night's Madness,* had come out in 1932, exactly thirty years previously. But it is significant that his latest book, *I Remember, I Remember,* has the mellow warmth of a writer who had made the effort of sympathy, who had literally *'thought* himself into personal relief'. The effort is surely less exacting for the young writer who comes freshly upon the scene—provided he does not come loaded with presuppositions.

## The Anti-Clerical Stereotype

How might this process of fruitful objectivity, this new literary frontier, be facilitated? The answer lies, of course, both with society and the author. Firstly the author, in his attempts to establish salutary contact with his community, must learn to curb and control the influence of tradition. The artistic consciousness that accepts the formal and technical lessons of Joyce must be careful not to take over uncritically Joyce's fierce, irrational anti-clericalism. His attitude towards the Irish clergy must be his own. This is only one example, but it is a significant one, because the clerical *cliché is* perhaps the most threadbare in our tradition. The facile, doctrinaire anti-clericalism which has dominated Irish fiction since George Moore's time still stands as a mark of our failure.

One is not concerned with the search for an Irish Mauriac. But it is surely something in the nature of a national disgrace that we have not produced one really powerful portrayal of priesthood; a portrayal like that of Bernanos, which might convey the complexity of the priest's spiritual ministry against the background of his humanity. Our disgrace would be complete, were it not for the distinguished work of Francis MacManus who has grappled successfully with aspects of the problem. But compare our record in this century with France's, with Mauriac,

Bernanos, Bloy, Claudel as it comes down to the present generation in the persons of Beatrix Beck, Anne Huré and Jean Montaurier. Against a line-up like that one becomes a little self-conscious about a Catholic tradition and its clerical offspring in the persons of Fathers Ring, Conmee, Maguire, Milvey, Gogarty, and Dowling. It is quite evident to everyone that a fresh approach will have to be made to the priest in Irish fiction, or else he had better be left alone. Anti-clericalism is clearly flogged to death. It has had a substantial innings; for more than sixty years the Irish priest has been lambasted from every conceivable angle. It is most unlikely that anything new can be added to the catalogue of reproach, and we can rely on Honor Tracy to keep up a steady supply of the old. But supposing a serious attempt were made to explore the priestly personality afresh, how many of our writers appear to be equipped intellectually or theologically to do it? And it is here that some of the blame must be laid at the door of the clergy themselves who have been in control of Irish education long enough to have produced a more informed and spiritually alive laity. But the challenge still stands; and will stand till some Irish writer has equipped himself sufficiently with knowledge and sympathy to meet it.

## The Tyranny of the Past

A similar, though less obvious, obstacle to the writer's task is the Irish literary attitude to the past. It has not been sufficiently noted that Irish writing, since Standish James O'Grady, has been almost morbidly fixated with the past. First there was the absorption with legends and their resuscitation which sapped the vitality of James Stephens—when he should have been exploring the Dublin slums—Lady Gregory, Yeats, Russell, Douglas Hyde, Austin Clarke, Padraic Colum and which is at the moment weaving spells on Frank O'Connor. Then there was the folklore rage, involving many of the same writers. Synge immersed himself in the life of western islands knowing that a medieval world would have to be rendered before it died. Even at the moment Thomas Kinsella is calmly engaged in yet another prose telling of the *Táin*. Is our past so unique that we must always be gazing backwards lovingly at it? Of course every country has its historical novelists—a small proportion! But in general they leave the past to the historians and the archaeologists. But we look over the heads of the present, wade through the welter of life to revive the ghosts of the past.

Again this attitude infects our view of the present. It is easier to write of a past that is petrified and will stand still, rather than to try to fix and render a present that is in flux, that changes before our eyes. Similarly it is easier to write in terms of last year's image than in terms of this year's reality. I wonder has this anything to do with the elegiac mood of some recent Irish writing. John Broderick—one of the few of our writers who both lives in the provinces and writes about them—addressed himself to the life in a provincial town in his second novel, *The Fugitives*. But he dealt specifically with the decayed side of the town, the disintegrating 'old-town' on the wrong side of the river, not the thriving, advancing community on the other side which had left it behind. Similarly Brendan Kennelly in his sour little fable *The Crooked Cross* deals in allegorical form with a village in Ireland altogether untypical of to-day—and predictably a society utterly devoid of hope or energy. I wonder if it is this preoccupation with the past that gives most of modern Irish writing its elegiac mood. James Plunkett and Benedict Kiely have written with great verisimilitude on the modern Irish scene; but strangely their characters seem to be without a future, as if trapped in an immobile present. The majority of Mary Lavin's and Kate O'Brien's characters and situations go back twenty years or more. Though Sean O'Faolain strives strenuously with the present, his dominating theme is reminiscence. Compare this situation with that in England, with the rigorously contemporary quality of Angus Wilson, Graham Greene, C.P. Snow, John Wain, Kingsley Amis, Muriel Spark, and poets like Thom Gunn, Philip Larkin and Ted Hughes. Could this be another sympton of withdrawal, another barrier between the artist and his society, his material? (Perhaps one might risk the statement that the only writers who strike us as really involved in society are Jack White and Terence de Vere White, each of whom inherits an aspect of the Anglo-Irish tradition.) The young Irish writer is the inheritor of an elegiac convention and he must be careful that it does not overwhelm him completely.

## Publisher and Critic

All the prerequisites for a new literary renaissance are present to-day. Irish publishing, spear-headed by Liam Miller's Dolmen Press, has undergone a powerful revolution. If the talent is to be found the future seems very promising in this regard. Furthermore there are five literary magazines flourishing at the moment; about ten years ago, unless I am mistaken, there was no more than one. There is also an impressive body of young writers coming on the scene. In this latter connection the new energy and criticism coming from under-graduate organs and platforms promises solidly for the future. In order to give all this endeavour proper direction and shape, one thing more is lacking: an intelligent and dedicated criticism. Our efforts in this direction have been too sporadic; a more continuous and cumulative tradition is necessary if they are not to be undone by irregular bursts of spleen and self-gratulation. It is fashionable nowadays to decry the school of criticism based on the concept of an 'Irish mode', pioneered by Thomas MacDonagh and perpetuated by Daniel Corkery and Robert Farren. But is it not time that some consistent and useful alternative has been developed and expressed? The other trend, the penetrating, uncommitted survey work done by Ernest Boyd and Benedict Kiely, has similarly been left in isolation. Perhaps the time has come to bring these two trends into healthy synthesis. The 'Irish mode' was, in fact, valuable for its time; it is up to us to find an equally useful stance for our own. In the absence of a broad synthesizing mind, however, there is an important obligation on our reviewers, critics and editors to exercise a rigorous and impartial discrimination with regard to current Irish writing. We are a small country and the bulk of our literary life is centred in a small area of one city; it is natural that criticism should be threatened with all kinds of personal alliances, that the tendency towards what John Jordan called 'protection societies' should be hard to control. But, in the end, all that is required is a little courage and integrity, and the writer who fails to exercise them should really yield what limited critical platforms there are to those who will.

## Challenge to Society

The final obstacle to the young writer—this creature of mine is beginning to take on the stature and mystery of a literary myth—in seeking a new frontier is perhaps the greatest of all, because it is the one over which he has least control. This is Ireland, its people, his environment, his raw material. If the cleavage between writer and society is not to go on widening, then society will have to re-appraise its attitudes towards the whole position of the artist and his problems. Something has been seriously wrong with Irish aesthetic attitudes over the past few generations. More than in any modern society, I would say, the writer in Ireland is suspect. Seldom while alive is he accorded the respect which is his due. And part of his hostility, his policy of withdrawal is due to this state of social tension and insecurity. Irishmen overlook the fact that the writer is an unusually sensitive person; that this sensitivity is, in fact, part of his equipment as an artist. It is not going to help him in forming an objective picture of his countrymen if they automatically treat him as an outcast.

Not only do Irishmen distrust writers, they distrust literature. Basically it is our educational approach to reading that has been at fault. The Irish educator is naturally and commendably concerned about the moral development of the children under his care. Especially in the case of boarding schools, he is anxious that improper literature should not circulate among them. Automatically the educator takes on the role of censor. Students are constantly having their reading examined for its moral propriety. Inevitably the notion that reading is a dangerous business, a moral hazard permitted reluctantly, builds up in the student's mind. For him the phrase 'bad book' means evil book; the 'goodness' of a book similarly has nothing to do with its literary merit but with its mere, negative harmlessness. Hence Baroness Orczy is elected a 'good writer' while Evelyn Waugh is conceivably declared a 'bad writer'. This whole attitude may seem harmless, but its cumulative effect is damnable. Every teacher knows that out of every good English class there will be one or two pupils who love literature: pupils for whom reading is something very precious, something which occupies a prominent and permanent place in their consciousness. These are the people who are later to be cultural leaders and leaveners in society; they will be the informers of public taste; they may, in certain cases, turn out to be writers. The damage done to this type of personality is immense if this cautionary and negative attitude is carried out too strenuously. In the first place a young person will get the idea that there is something guilty and evil in his passion for reading; slowly there is built up in his mind the false notion that religion and art are opposed; he will feel alienated, disapproved of, a little suspect. In time he will come to associate the Church—in the majority of cases his educators will be clergy—with philistinism. If he becomes a writer in time he may easily sublimate his unconscious resentment into anti-clericalism—even apostasy. The *non serviam* of Irish writers does not necessarily come out of thin air; the society itself is often partially responsible for, and utterly oblivious of, what really has happened.

So much for the exceptional sensitive pupil in the class. But the unliterary majority can do equal harm. In time they will become teachers, priests, parents; they will carry their prejudices with them. They will sit on library committees and on censorship boards and pass narrow judgments. And all the time the gap between the artist and his countrymen will be widening, and the bitterness will increase. But all this difficulty can be eliminated at the root if the educator—priest, teacher and parent—will make a slight basic adjustment of emphasis: provide suitable books from the available masses of excellent paperbacks, and *encourage* the pupil in the habit of reading. This, happily, is being done in most schools to-day and the results are already becoming apparent. Irish television is also making an invaluable contribution by means of its discussion programmes and self-portraits. The difficulty, the complexity, the essential dignity of the writer's task is beginning to be better appreciated. The time for an artistic *aggiornamento* may have arrived.

Before finishing, it might be well to anticipate two possible objections to the thesis advanced in this essay. Firstly it may be claimed that I am laying down the law for writers, drawing up blueprints for artists, walking roughshod over the concept of the writer's autonomy. The other objection may be that I am ascribing a social function to the writer, making him into a propagandist of his country's image. If at times I seem to have been advancing either of these views it is because I have chosen to oversimplify rather than overload my thesis with excessive qualification. What, in fact, I am suggesting is that there must be a living bond between the artist and his society. Unless this bond is constantly renewed there is a real danger of art separating from life, leading to a barren aestheticism, a doctrine of *l'art pour l'art*. Such a movement is unhealthy in any situation, but the mere idea of it at this stage in our young tradition borders on the ludicrous. But the danger is there; so also is the antidote. Donald Davie remarked some years ago that in Ireland 'the ties between poetry and society had not yet snapped as they have in England and America', but that they were still 'very near breaking point'. My own view would be that we compare unfavourably with both England and America in this regard. In either case it is the peculiar duty of this generation to renew these ties and as far as possible to strengthen them. Genuine literature, whatever the *genre,* must, in the last analysis, be 'the book of the people', the product of a 'lover's quarrel' between the writer and his world. One gets the feeling that Irish writing has come to one of those cross-roads where new bearings must be taken, old obstacles removed, new problems solved. The present essay has been an attempt to define some of these problems, and very diffidently to suggest possible solutions. I would be most interested to hear of other and perhaps better questions, or other and better answers; indeed I should be glad to be assured that there is no problem at all, and that all is as it should be between sow and farrow.

First published in *Studies*, Volume LIV, Spring 1965.

# 9

# Anglo-Irish Literature: The Protestant Legacy

'No rootless colonist of an alien earth . . .'
Samuel Ferguson, 'Mesgedra'[1]

If an Irish Anglican were asked to write on the role of Roman Catholicism in Anglo-Irish literature he would have no hesitation, I imagine, in choosing his line of emphasis. He would notice that writing by Irish Roman Catholics from William Carleton at the beginning of our period down to Edna O'Brien at the end of it is penetrated with religious faith and doubt. He would see a spiritual vista at once fearsome and inspiring; he would be aware of the same religious light— at once a glare and a radiance—being reflected and refracted through a wide variety of human sensibilities: Canon Sheehan's erudite piety, Joyce's elaborate dissent, Austin Clarke's drama of conscience, Daniel Corkery's passionate acceptance, Mervyn Wall's satire, Patrick Kavanagh's celebration and thanksgiving. The governing emphasis would be spiritual or theological; it would have to do with sin, grace, guilt, obedience, forgiveness, repentance, apostasy; it would have its social dimension, but that dimension would be secondary. It would be a promising area of investigation.

The Church of Ireland scene yields no such emphasis. Though—in his essay on Shaw—Ernest Boyd could boast truly of the number of 'distinguished heretics, in literature, politics and religion, who have been born into Irish Protestantism',[2] he could hardly point to a work of literature in which the Anglican *non serviam* achieves any sort of memorable resonance. There is a paragraph in Forrest Reid's *Apostate* where he formally renounced his religion '. . . its doctrines, its theory of life, the shadow it cast across the earth';[3] Synge takes two paragraphs in his fragmentary *Autobiography* to record the 'terrible experience' of his apostasy;[4] Yeats describes his break with 'the simple-minded religion of my childhood' in a sentence of *Autobiographies*;[5] the work of Shaw shows little evidence of anguish or remorse at the loss of his Anglicanism; and with A.E. (George Russell) the withdrawal from Christianity seems to have been no more than a graceful prologue to the endless adventure of his mystical speculation. James Stephens is, perhaps, an exception among the 'distinguished heretics'. Such early poems as 'What the Devil Said' and 'The Lonely God' may certainly be taken as an attempt to dislodge the icons of a dead belief from their dominance in his imagination. But then Stephens was reared in a Protestant orphanage where Jehovah tended to merge with the headmaster and with those policemen who loom so large and menacingly in the fiction of his maturity.

Similarly with the belief of those who did not dissent. Lady Gregory was a devout member of the Church of Ireland all her life, but the religion that appeared in her plays—as, for instance, in *The Story Brought by Brigit* and *Dave*—was as close to the mystery and wonder of peasant Catholicism as to the benign reasonableness of Anglican theology. Standish O'Grady reserved his religion for his private life, and no one would suspect from her fiction that Edith Somerville played the organ at the parish church at Castle Townsend. His Protestantism seems to have been the one subject on which Douglas Hyde was not voluble. In his case and that of Lady Gregory there were sound practical reasons for such reticence. Both were devoted to cultural aims in which they hoped increasingly to involve the mass of their Roman Catholic countrymen; it was natural that they did not brandish the symbols of their separateness. It was also true—as it is today—that the Irish Anglican did not wear his religion on his sleeve. Yet the contrast with Irish Roman Catholicism is dramatic, and might be rendered in a comparison between the experiences of two seven-year-olds of the two different Communions, Elizabeth Bowen and Austin Clarke. In *Seven Winters* Bowen recounts how, on Sundays, she went to St Stephen's Church, Upper Mount Street, Dublin:

The round-topped windows let in on us wintry, varying but always unmistakably Sunday light, and gas burned where day did not penetrate far enough. The interior, with its clear sombreness, sane proportions, polished woodwork and brasswork and aisles upon which confident feet rang, had authority—here one could feel a Presence, were it only the presence of an idea. It emphasized what was at once august and rational in man's relations with God. Nowhere was there any intensity of darkness, nowhere the point of a small flame. There was an honourable frankness in the tone in which we rolled out the General Confession—indeed, sin was most felt by me, in St Stephen's, as any divagation from the social idea. There was an ample confidence in the singing, borne up by the organ's controlled swell.[6]

Though the light of irony is not wholly absent from this portrait of her congregation, it is obvious that no young artistic rebel would need the wings of Daedalus to escape from its demands, its ambience. The religious is embedded in the social, and in studying the literary work of the Church of Ireland writer one must bear this constantly in mind. How different, for instance, was the case of the young Austin Clarke, making his private and specific confession on the other side of Dublin:

> Closeted in the confessional,
> I put on flesh, so many years
> Were added to my own, attempted
> In vain to keep Dominican
> As much i' the dark as I was, mixing
> Whispered replies with his low words;
> Then shuddered past the crucifix,
> The feet so hammered, daubed-on blood-drip,
> Black with lip-scrimmage of the damned.[7]

To complete the parallel, the contrast, one might read Austin Clarke's account of his attendance at a service in the Protestant Black Church as a child where he noticed—after the stained-glass mystery of his own church—'a plain and temperate daylight' that came through the lancets.[8]

Elsewhere in her book Elizabeth Bowen recalls that while the bells of her churches had the good taste to ring only on Sundays, the 'other' bells kept calling their faithful to devotion all through the week. 'This pre-disposition to frequent prayer,' she remarks, 'bespoke, to me, some incontinence of the soul.'[9] One could almost prophesy that the fiction of the mature Anglican would hardly obsess itself with the agonies or the triumphs of the 'Anglican conscience' in action. And in as far as the Anglican conscience does operate as a force in Elizabeth Bowen's fiction, it does so implicitly, with tact and continence. One could equally predict that the Roman Catholic conscience would play a vivid part in any body of genuine creative literature which the mature Austin Clarke might produce. Indeed he himself chose to characterize that work as enacting 'the drama of racial conscience'.[10] One might generalize and say that with the majority of good Irish Roman Catholic writers the religious concern forms much of their working material, while with the majority of Irish Anglicans the religious is either assumed or ignored—the creative adventure begins after the question of orthodoxy has been settled, one way or the other.

The distinction is well exemplified in the work of our two greatest modern writers. The motive power of Yeats's poetry comes from his positive effort to fabricate a new religion to replace the Protestantism which he had found inadequate to the needs of his nature. With Joyce much of the motive power comes from a life-long effort to dislodge and exorcise from his consciousness a religion which he found himself unable and unwilling to sustain, its terror and its ardour. The bias evident in

Yeats manifests itself in all the Irish Protestant writers, almost without exception. After that brief struggle in his teens when Synge opted for 'nature' rather than religion,[11] he went on to explore the natural, the pre-Christian in the consciousness of peasant Ireland. The drama that had taken place off-stage achieved its subliminal—if significant—articulation in a dramatic vision that was at once passionate and simple and profoundly ironic. James Stephens arrived at his finest effects not through his struggle with Christianity—which was, after all, sharp and perfunctory—but in the discovery of a new, ecstatic paganism which finds early and eloquent expression in *The Crock of Gold*. With A.E. formal Christianity is simply forgotten in the endless fervour and excitement of his mysticism. With Sean O'Casey the rejection of Protestantism is quickly overshadowed by the discovery of Fraser, Shaw and Marx, while his later satire is not directed against the Anglicanism which he had personally rejected but against the Roman Catholicism which he felt was choking the springs of Irish life. Denis Johnston could hardly be classed as a Protestant dramatist. Samuel Beckett had clearly settled the question of his Anglicanism long before he embarked on his powerful formulation of modern despair. Lady Longford, when she raises the question of Anglicanism formally, as for instance in her hilarious novel, *Mr Jiggins of Jigginstown*, does so with a profound detachment and a wicked irony, as when Mr Jiggins reassures his worried Rector that he is not 'going over to Rome':

'I'm not sir. You should be proud of Irish Protestantism' (The Rector bowed his head). 'The religion of Swift and Molyneux and the great Bishop Berkeley! Of Wolfe Tone and Emmet, Mitchel and Parnell! What a training in critical thought!'

The Rector is not reassured; he is 'not too sure about some of those'. But these names, Swift, Molyneux, Berkeley, Tone, Emmet, Mitchel and Parnell, are to arise with increasing frequency in discussions of the 'Protestant Nation' and its place in Irish political and literary tradition. And it is names such as these that lead us to a just appreciation of what the Church of Ireland has done not only for Anglo-Irish literature, but for the political and cultural well-being of our country as a whole.

The line from Ferguson quoted in the subtitle now becomes especially relevant. It comes from his poem on the death of Mesgedra, King of Leinster, who was killed by the Ulster warrior, Conall Carnach, at the 'Hurdle-ford' where Dublin now stands. In a sudden swerve from heroic redaction, towards the end of the poem, Ferguson apostrophizes the Dublin of the future, granting her all virtues and charms 'to please the manly mind, but one', and goes on to formulate what seems to me the most significant aspiration and achievement of the 'Protestant Nation' through the decades that followed:

> For, thou, for them, alas! nor History hast
> Nor even Tradition; and the Man aspires
> To link his present with his Country's past,
> And live anew in knowledge of his sires;
>
> No rootless colonist of an alien earth,
> Proud but of patient lungs and pliant limb,
> A stranger in the land that gave him birth,
> The land a stranger to itself and him.[12]

The problem of identity which is reaching its crisis with Ferguson had troubled the Anglo-Irish conscience for two centuries or more. As Thomas Flanagan has pointed out[13] it was first voiced by Shakespeare's Captain Macmorris: 'What ish my nation? Ish a villain, and bastard, and a knave, and a rascal. What ish my nation? Who talks of my nation?' It was a disturbing question for William Molyneux and for the later Swift. It had been obliquely posed by that great Irish woman, Maria Edgeworth, in *Castle Rackrent* and positively if partially answered by her Lord Colambre, hero of *The Absentee*. What Maria Edgeworth had seen as a social problem—the failure of landlords in their stewardship—Davis, Gavan Duffy and the *Nation* journalists saw as a political challenge. It was Ferguson who saw first, and most clearly, the importance of a common Gaelic culture, based on an enlightened and disinterested exploration of the past, as a means of forging a unity between all Irishmen—a common sense of cultural nationality which might transcend mere Nationalism. Yeats saw the many-sided significance of Ferguson's achievement. In an article published in *The Dublin University Review* in 1886 he declared Ferguson 'the greatest poet Ireland has produced, because the most central and most Celtic' and saw his poems as possible precursors of 'a truly great and national literature'.[14] Ten years later he underlined the social significance of Ferguson's choice: 'He lived in a class which, through a misunderstanding of the necessities of Irish Unionism, hated all Irish things, or felt for them at best a contemptuous and patronizing affection. . .'.[15]

It would be hard to overrate the importance of Ferguson for the literary generation that followed his and for a movement which was to find its leaders among those of his religion and class—Standish O'Grady, W.B. Yeats, Lady Gregory, J.M. Synge. He had the humility and insight to see the cultural hinterland that lay beyond the blasted horizon of Gaelic, Catholic Ireland, and he had the courage to cross the barriers of his class to explore it. He now had a simple, authentic answer to Captain Macmorris's question. His nation was not the 'Protestant nation' but the Irish nation. He was an Irish writer writing on Irish subjects for Irish readers. More than any other writer of his time, therefore, he deflected the Irish creative impulse from the shallow regionalism of Lever and Lover and made possible a metropolitan consciousness among Irish writers. As Ernest Boyd has written:

He was able to see the past with the eyes of a scholar and to interpret it with the mind of a poet. It was thus his privilege to possess the key that unlocked the gates through which the stream of modern Irish literature was to pass. He set free the Celtic spirit, imprisoned in the shell of an almost extinct language, and obscured by the dust of political turmoil.[16]

Standish James O'Grady who is universally acknowledged as 'the father of Ireland's Literary Renaissance' was also a scholar, but like Ferguson a scholar with a larger vision. He might be viewed under three heads: a literary historian might consider him as the founder of the literary revival, a social historian might choose to view him as the Cassandra of the Anglo-Irish landlords, a political historian as that *rara avis*, a Fenian Unionist. What seems certain is that he possessed a profound unity of vision that encompassed all three roles, and that this inner certitude came from his religious upbringing. During his childhood the Evangelical movement was at its zenith and his father, Church of Ireland rector at Castletownbere, was one of its most ardent adherents. In a tribute to him his son, Hugh Art, has recorded that O'Grady 'grew to manhood with two possessions, a deep religious feeling, and a minute knowledge of the Bible. The religious feeling, which he never expressed in conversation, came out in his writings on social questions'.[17] His upbringing was in several respects exceptional. He seems, for instance, to have learned Irish from the Roman Catholic children of his locality and it is a matter of record that he was an expert hurler. He was uniquely equipped to step across the barriers that so intimidated his contemporaries. His exhortation to the landlords in his pamphlet, *Crisis in Ireland*, recalls the Bible both in its apocalyptic ardour and the roll of its periods:

To the mass of the people the Irish Aristocracy appear as the deadly foe of the Irish nation—a foe which eighty-one years since sold to England the independence of their country and their own great future as leaders of a nation, for a paltry sum of money, or for still paltrier baubles and trappings, and exchanged, for ignoble sloth and abject, uneventful lives, a career of high effort, beneficent activity, and glorious responsibility. To them our class has ever since presented itself as the chief and most potent engine by which England has enslaved and fettered her sister, free-born as she. They hate us because anti-national, and despise us because anti-national for such mean rewards. The day of absolute democratic power in Ireland draws nigh—the day of reckoning and vengeance; while through half-shut eyes we look out and murmur, 'It is all well; England is bound to protect us'.

O'Grady felt passionately that the landlords should abandon their position of privilege, sell their estates at a just price and invest their money in

Irish industry. In this way they would earn the right to lead the Irish people, a role for which so many of them were fitted by education and tradition. This was O'Grady's solution to a problem that was to exercise both Shaw and Yeats: the role of an aristocracy in a modern egalitarian society. O'Grady's appeal to both factions reads ironically in the present perspective of history:

In the interest of democratic republican Ireland, if for no other reason, I call upon the people's leaders to beware how they press beyond recall a class, the costly product of centuries, containing elements of moral, personal, intellectual wealth, which this nation will yet sorely need, and which, with all its gifts, and with all circumstances consenting and conspiring, it cannot again of that kind produce.

But few listened to O'Grady as few had listened to Maria Edgeworth two generations before, and those who did listen were not the young politicians but the young writers and, through them, the young patriots who were to go to the barricades in 1916. The matter can be put very simply: O'Grady gave Cuchulain to the young Irish imagination; he gave him to Yeats and he gave him to Pearse.

O'Grady had remarked that his parents saw the world as being full of good and bad spirits, ministers of God and of his enemy: 'Neither of them would have been greatly surprised had they seen angels, or if the arch-enemy himself had taken shape before them'. It is a similar spirit that permeates his heroic romances; a naïve but powerful enthusiasm that can call up the war-demons, 'the Bocanahs and Bananahs', the 'estrays out of the fold of hell' who give such barbaric dimension to his epic redactions. In everything he wrote we feel an extraordinary gusto, a combination of enthusiasm and vision that springs ultimately from a profoundly religious attitude to the world. The effect of his books on the Irish psyche is quite incalculable. A sentence from A.E. gives some idea of its force:

I owe so much to Standish O'Grady that I would like to leave it on record that it was he who made me conscious and proud of my country, and recalled my mind, that might have wandered otherwise over too wide and vague a field of thought, to think of the earth under my feet and the children of our common mother.[18]

Similarly Yeats in one of his several tributes to O'Grady described him as 'a man whose rage was a swan-song over all that he had held most dear, and to whom for that very reason every Irish imaginative writer owed a portion of his soul'.[19]

I have stressed the role of Ferguson and of O'Grady because each of them tried hard to bridge the divisions, to heal the wounds in the Irish psyche for which their own people, the Anglo-Irish Ascendancy, had been responsible. Their choice was deliberate and it involved a turning against the majority opinion of their own class. The choice may indeed have been religiously motivated—it is in line with their Church's claim to continuity with the past, to be 'the Ancient Catholick and Apostolick Church of Ireland'—but it is in social terms that it is expressed. To use Elizabeth Bowen's phrase again, one could say that their lives were in a sense devoted to a heroic 'divagation from the social norm'. This element of deliberate choice is found in most of their literary descendants, and gets its most explicit and interesting formulation in a remark of Yeats in the *Freeman's Journal* in January of 1924:

There are two kinds of Patriotism in Ireland . . . the patriotism of Catholic Ireland, which is inherited, and to which a man holds because he will not change. Then there is the patriotism of those who are brought up in the Church of Ireland, and that has its own special meaning—but in it there is always a choice.

Yeats himself makes such a choice when in 'To Ireland in the Coming Times' he wrote:

> Know, that I would accounted be
> True brother of a company
> That sang, to sweeten Ireland's wrong,
> Ballad and story, rann and song
> . . .
> Nor may I less be counted one
> With Davis, Mangan, Ferguson . . . [20]

So does Synge, as he records in that tantalizing fragment of his *Autobiography* which has survived. Having wrenched himself free from the fierce and bigoted Evangelicalism of his mother—who was a daughter of the vehement Dr Traill—Synge backed into the arms of Irish nationalism:

Soon after I had relinquished the Kingdom of God I began to take a real interest in the kingdom of Ireland. My politics went round from a vigorous and unreasoning loyalty to a temperate Nationalism. Everything Irish became sacred . . . [21]

His mother viewed his activities among the rebels and peasants of the Abbey Theatre with profound disapproval, and no member of his family was ever to see a play of his performed in his lifetime.

The death of Synge in 1909 was a grievous loss to the theatre and to the literary movement as a whole. Yet Yeats and Lady Gregory persevered. With Lady Gregory it was a patient and unrelenting labour of love; with Yeats it was often an angry lover's quarrel with the people whose culture he and his colleagues had set out to rebuild. His mystique of aristocracy was beginning to emerge and from this stance the money-grubbing Paudeens who would not contribute to a gallery to house the Lane Pictures seemed increasingly unworthy. More and more he harked back to the great patriots of his Protestant ancestry:

> Was it for this the wild geese spread
> The grey wing upon every tide;
> For this that all that blood was shed,
> For this Edward Fitzgerald died,
> And Robert Emmet and Wolfe Tone . . . [22]

He was also to turn more and more to Georgian Ireland—to Burke, Goldsmith and 'God-appointed Berkeley'[23]—for their aristocracy of intellect. Yet his faith in the new Ireland was restored with the chivalry and heroism of the Easter Rising and he recognized the birth of a new and equally potent mythology:

> I write it out in a verse—
> MacDonagh and MacBride
> And Connolly and Pearse
> Now and in time to be,
> Wherever green is worn,
> Are changed, changed utterly:
> A terrible beauty is born.[24]

He found a new playwright for the Abbey, Sean O'Casey, an Anglican too, who made the choice, the commitment to resurgent Ireland. In *Drums under the Window* one finds O'Casey's vivid account of how he wore an Irish kilt and campaigned for Father O'Hickey and the cause of Irish in the National University, how he worked under Connolly and Larkin in the Citizen Army, how he garnered the experience and the insight to become the dramatist of the Rising, the War of Independence and of the Civil War. We find too, in that volume, his withdrawal from the Protestantism of his childhood:

Under the darkened sky, in the midst of a flash of lightning, Sean saw the low brow, the timid eye, the shivering step of Adam had changed to the alert walk, the gleaming eye, the lofty brow, and the reddish thrust-out beard of Bernard Shaw. And Sean, bending low under the Golden Bough, followed close behind him.[25]

The story of the 'Troubles' and their implications for the landed Protestant gentry does not fall within the scope of this essay. But it is clear that by the end of the Civil War the first great thrust towards an Irish national literature is coming to an end. A symptom of the change is the number of writers, Catholic and Protestant, who went into permanent or temporary exile in the years that followed. For our purpose we may mention James Stephens, A.E., Sean O'Casey, Elizabeth Bowen, Louis MacNeice, Samuel Beckett, W.R. Rodgers. One notices also a change of tone in the fiction and poetry of the younger writers, a change from romanticism to irony, from enthusiasm to detachment, from celebration to satire. Yeats might go on extolling the past of his people, lamenting the passing of the great houses. But his vision was not shared by such a brilliant young ironist of the new generation as Louis MacNeice who noted that 'in most cases these houses maintained no culture worth speaking of—nothing but an obsolete bravado, an insidious bonhomie and a way with horses.'[26]

In their practical and patient way Yeats and Lady Gregory continued to nurse the Abbey Theatre which, with the appointment to the Board of the Anglican playwright, Lennox Robinson, and the Anglican poet, F.R. Higgins, continued to be a centre for artistic collaboration between the two cultures. There remained a conscious will to achieve a unified Irish sensibility. Yeats, F.R. Higgins and Lady Gregory would have agreed with Lennox Robinson when, in his introduction to an edition of Thomas Parnell's poems, he saw it as the tragedy of eighteenth-century Ireland 'that these two cultures, the Gaelic and the Anglo-Irish, never met, never seem to have been aware of each other's existence'. He goes on:

We think we understand the value of both cultures a little better now. We strain back to them, we fumble in old manuscripts and put fragments of Gaelic verse together, we read again Berkeley, we read Swift, read Burke, and as a small part of our great Irish heritage, reprint now a few poems of Thomas Parnell.[27]

But the creative side of his mind was composing an elegy for his people in his play *The Big House,* which stands roughly in the tradition of Maria Edgeworth's *Castle Rackrent, The Big House at Inver* by Somerville and Ross, Elizabeth Bowen's *Bowen's Court.*

In his great Senate speech on divorce, Yeats wondered whether the Anglo-Irish—the people of Burke, Grattan, Swift, Emmet and Parnell— might have lost their stamina. I suspect it was a serious, even an agonizing, speculation for him. He had always shared O'Grady's vision of the Anglo-Irish playing a large part in the leadership of the new Ireland. In 1925 that vision was by no means unrealistic, even on the political level, while on the cultural level he and his colleagues at the Abbey had made it a reality. The subsequent years must have been for him a disappointing pageant. The sense of a common quest that had characterized the great days of the literary revival became dissipated, and his attempt to recreate it with an Irish Academy of Letters was no more than a modest success. Lady Gregory and A.E. died. The intellectual leadership was now passing into the hands of Sean O'Faolain and his collaborators on *The Bell,* Roman Catholics who could fight the Paudeens of the new state at ground level. That there was no loss of stamina in the Anglo-Irish strain is attested by a remarkable body of good writers for such a minority of the population, writers like Beckett, Joyce Cary, Cecil Day Lewis, William Trevor,

Elizabeth Bowen, Monk Gibbon, Jack White, Iris Murdoch, Louis MacNeice, W.R. Rodgers, Stephen Gwynn and others. But with few exceptions these writers went their own ways, ways which frequently not only led them well beyond the tradition that Yeats had laboured to create, but beyond the shores of their country as well.

There is no space, nor real need, to analyse why this was so. It may have been due to a loss of faith in the new nation, a traditional tendency towards cosmopolitanism or the contemporary tendency of the writer to be a private and often a lonely man. But looking back to the time of disestablishment, and beyond it to the greatness of the eighteenth century, one has no difficulty in assenting to the proposition that, in literary terms, these were 'no petty people'.[28]

# NOTES

First published in *Irish Anglicanism 1869–1969: Essays on the role of Anglicanism in Irish life presented to the Church of Ireland on the occasion of the centenary of its Disestablishment by a group of Methodist, Presbyterian, Quaker and Roman Catholic scholars*, edited by Michael Hurley S.J. (Dublin: Allen Figgis, 1970).

1  *Poems of Sir Samuel Ferguson* (Dublin: The Talbot Press, 1917; London: T. Fisher Unwin, 1918), p. 132.

2  'An Irish Protestant: Bernard Shaw', Ernest A. Boyd, *Appreciations and Depreciations* (Dublin: The Talbot Press, 1917; London: T. Fisher Unwin, 1917), p. 115.

3  Forrest Reid, *Apostate* (London: Constable, 1926), p. 204.

4  'Autobiography', J.M. Synge, *Collected Works Volume II: Prose*, edited by Alan Price (London: Oxford University Press, 1966; Gerrards Cross, Bucks: Colin Smythe, 1982; Washington, D.C.: The Catholic University of America Press, 1982), p. 11.

5  W.B. Yeats, *Autobiographies* (London: Macmillan, 1955), p. 115.

6  Elizabeth Bowen, *Seven Winters: Memories of a Dublin Childhood* (London: Longmans, Green and Co., 1943), p. 43.

7  'Ancient Lights', Austin Clarke, *Later Poems* (Dublin: Dolmen Press, 1961), p. 47.

8  Austin Clarke, *Twice Round the Black Church* (London: Routledge and Kegan Paul, 1962; Dublin: Moytura Press, 1990), p. 24.

9  Elizabeth Bowen, *Seven Winters*, pp. 44–5.

10  Austin Clarke, *Later Poems*, p. 90.

11  'Autobiography', J.M. Synge, *Collected Works Volume II:Prose*, ed. Price, p. 7.

12  *Poems of Sir Samuel Ferguson*, p. 132.

13  Thomas Flanagan, *The Irish Novelists* (New York: Columbia University Press, 1959), p. 1.

14  'The Poetry of Sir Samuel Ferguson—II', W.B. Yeats, *Uncollected Prose 1886–1896*, Volume One, edited by John P. Frayne (London: Macmillan, 1970), p. 103.

15  'An Irish Patriot', *Ibid.*, p. 405.

16  Ernest Boyd, *Ireland's Literary Renaissance* (Dublin: Maunsel, 1916; New York: Alfred A. Knopf, 1916; Dublin: Allen Figgis, 1968), p. 25.

17  *Standish James O'Grady: Man and Writer*, edited by Alfred P. Graves (Dublin: The Talbot Press, 1929), p. 29.

18   *Ibid.*, p. 74.

19   W.B. Yeats, *Autobiographies,* p. 220.

20   'To Ireland in the Coming Times', *The Variorum Edition of the Poems of W.B. Yeats,* edited by Peter Allt and Russell K. Alspach (New York: Macmillan, 1957), pp. 137–8.

21   'Autobiography', Synge, *Collected Works Volume II: Prose*, ed. Price, p. 13.

22   September 1913', *The Variorum Edition of the Poems of W.B. Yeats,* ed. Allt and Alspach, p. 290.

23   'Blood and the Moon', *Ibid.*, p. 481.

24   'Easter 1916', *Ibid.*, p. 394.

25   Sean O'Casey, *Drums under the Window* (London: Macmillan, 1945), p. 218.

26   Louis MacNeice, *The Poetry of W.B. Yeats* (London: Faber, 1967), Chapter V.

27   *Poems by Thomas Parnell*, selected by Lennox Robinson (Shannon: Irish University Press, 1971; facsimile reprint of 1st ed., Dublin: Cuala Press, 1937), no pagination.

28   *The Senate Speeches of W.B. Yeats*, edited by Donald R. Pearce (London: Faber, 1960), p. 99.

# Section Three

## The Irish Prose Tradition

# 10

# James Stephens's
# The Crock of Gold

## The Apocalyptic Form

Critics of James Stephens have been content to classify *The Crock of Gold* as 'prose fantasy' on the perfectly valid grounds that it is not realistic fiction, that it creates for its purposes a fantasy world with its own laws or its own indigenous anarchies. It is a convenient label but it has two disabilities. It tends to associate *The Crock of Gold* with the children's fantasies of English writers such as Kenneth Grahame and Walter de la Mare whose methods and intentions were sharply different from those of Stephens. It distracts, in a limiting way, from the serious dimensions of satire, allegory and prophecy which give the book its richness of intellectual content and artistic wholeness. It is therefore more fruitful to approach the book in terms of its natural antecedents, the prophetic poems of Blake and, more immediately, the apocalyptic stories of Yeats.

Blake's prophetic poems, notably 'The Four Zoas', dramatize the dissolution of the human personality in his peculiar version of the Fall, and forecast the ultimate reunion of its faculties and members in a final apocalyptic vision. We have Stephens's word for it that he conceived of *The Crock of Gold* in similar terms:

In this book there is only one character—Man—Pan is his sensual nature, Caitilin, his emotional nature, the Philosopher his intellect at play, Angus Og his intellect spiritualized, the policemen his conventions and logics, the leprecauns his elemental side, the children his innocence, and the idea is not too rigidly carried out, but that is how I conceived the story.[1]

The rhetorical structure of the fable can be seen as a sort of allegory in which the human faculties are, at the outset of the story, dislocated, and are finally reunited in the apocalyptic flourish with which the book ends.

This pattern in which the ancient pagan gods, classical and Celtic, are represented as awakening and returning to Ireland to be the catalysts of a new dispensation, had already found expression in the occasional writings of A.E. and in the *Secret Rose* stories of Yeats. A passage from A.E., with which Stephens would have been familiar, appears in *The Irish Theosophist*, March–April, 1895 under the title of 'The Ancient Legends of Ireland':

The Golden Age is all about us, and heroic forms and imperishable love. In that mystic light rolled round our hills and valleys hang deeds and memories which yet live and inspire. The Gods have not deserted us. Hearing our call they will return. A new cycle is dawning and the sweetness of the morning twilight is in the air. We can breathe it if we can but awaken from our slumber.

Yeats, in 'Rosa Alchemica', the culminating story of his volume, *The Secret Rose*, as it first appeared in 1897, gives the following lines to his Rosicrucian, Michael Robartes:

A time will come for these people also, and they will sacrifice a mullet to Artemis, or some other fish to some new divinity, unless indeed their own divinities, the Dagda, with his overflowing cauldron, Lu, with his spear dipped in poppy-juice, . . . Angus, with the three birds on his shoulder, Bove Derg and his red swine-herd, and all the heroic children of Dana set up once more their temples of grey stone.[2]

I have argued at more length elsewhere[3] that *The Secret Rose* is organized in its entirety around a concept of apocalyptic structure, that each of the stories ends in a 'thrust into the numinous' and that the book as a whole moves through 'twenty centuries of stony sleep' towards the birth of a new Dionysiac dispensation involving the return of the old gods. Stephens's version of apocalypse differs in many respects from those of Russell and Yeats. It is presented in the idiom of comedy, and sometimes of conscious parody. Yeats's prophecy is solemn and terrible, where Stephens's is exultant, humorous and optimistic. But it shares with both Yeats and Russell a vision of a world transformed by the return of ancient, magical and elemental forces represented by the pagan gods.

## Parody and Satire

To write of satire and parody in *The Crock of Gold* is to risk giving them excessive prominence within its organization. The purpose in raising them at this early stage of the discussion is at once to get them out of the way, and to create an awareness of their presence in the unfolding of the book's overall narrative strategy. The book's *genre* is that of the pastoral idyll, and the patterns of satire, parody and apocalypse are ultimately subsumed into that form and mode. Its setting is that of an Irish Arcadia and its heroine, in accordance with the pastoral convention, is a shepherdess, living in a state of primal innocence with nature. In the book's last sentence, where the Philosopher returns to 'the country of the gods', that innocent pastoral world finally triumphs and Eden is restored. The book therefore fulfils Schiller's famous definition of the idyll as that literary form which 'presents the idea and description of an innocent and happy humanity':

A state such as this is not merely met with before the dawn of civilization; it is also the state to which civilization aspires, as to its last end, if only it obeys a determined tendency in its progress. The idea of a similar state, and the belief in the possible reality of this state, is the only thing that can reconcile man with all the evils to which he is exposed in the path of civilization. . . .[4]

Stephens, who perhaps never read Schiller, put forward a similar view in a letter:

I believe that everything the best mind of humanity really wishes for, and formulates the wish, must come to pass. So I look on certain abstract words such as 'love', 'honour', 'spirit' as prophetic words, having no concrete existence now, but to be forged in the future by the desire which has sounded them. Poems, too, are to me prophecies, and there will be a gay old world sometime.[5]

*The Crock of Gold* is written in this spirit of passionate desire. By an intense imagining the writer brings the 'gay old world' into figurative existence, and by the same process brings closer its actual possibility. Stephens's apocalypse is therefore at one with Schiller's concept of 'aspiration' and Blake's assertion that his own work was 'an Endeavour to Restore what the Ancients call'd the Golden Age'.[6] Stephens's work makes a similar act of faith in human possibility. He does not appeal for our belief in the actual existence of his gods and fairies but for the possibilities of love, innocence and energy which they symbolize.

A.E. believed in the objective existence of the Celtic gods and in the imminence of their return. Yeats's belief in them is notoriously problematical, but in his three 'apocalyptic' stories, 'Rosa Alchemica', 'The Tables of the Law' and 'The Adoration of the Magi', their return is treated without irony as a terrible and immediate threat to contemporary civilization. In this context the parodic element in *The Crock of Gold* becomes evident.

Some fifteen years before its publication Yeats and Russell, together with MacGregor Mathers, William Sharp ('Fiona MacLeod'), Maud Gonne and others, had been active in the founding of a cult of 'Celtic Paganism'. Convinced that the gods of the Tuatha de Danaan were about to return to Ireland they had attempted to set up a religion based on the old Celtic mysteries as interpreted in the light of Theosophy and Rosicrucianism. They had sought out a castle on an island in Lough Key, in County Sligo, which was to be their temple. They believed that a Celtic 'Avatar' or redeemer had already been born and was at hand—if he could be found—to preside over the movement. In a letter of February, 1896, Russell assured Yeats that

The gods have returned to Erin and have centred themselves in the sacred mountains and blow the fires through the country. They have been seen by several in vision, they will awaken the magical instinct everywhere, and the universal heart of the people will turn to the old druidic beliefs. . . . I believe profoundly that a new Avatar is about to appear. . . . It will be one of the kingly Avatars, who is at once ruler of men and magic sage.[7]

Yeats set himself to draw up a ritual for the proposed cult, and it is significant in the present context that the chief god was to be Aengus, symbolizing 'Spiritual Intelligence'. In *The Crock of Gold* Angus stands for 'the intellect spiritualized'. The attempt to establish the cult failed,[8] and when *The Crock of Gold* came to be written was little more than an exotic and perhaps bizarre memory. It seems certain that James Stephens had it in mind when he brought back Pan and Angus to Ireland, the comic landscape of his fantasy, and that his attitude towards them lacked the solemnity of his elders. He was the first of the Irish writers to treat the Celtic gods and heroes irreverently and is thus the forerunner of a burlesque tradition in Irish fiction that later includes Joyce, Eimar O'Duffy and Flann O'Brien. Parody of Yeats and Russell is not a central ingredient of *The Crock of Gold* but it provides, as we shall see, a delicate and playful flavour to the book's more essential concerns.

The element of satire in the book arises chiefly in the counterpoint of the rural idyll of endless freedom against the city with its prisons, laws and repressions. When the book was first published it was compared to Goldsmith's *Vicar of Wakefield*. The comparison is apt because Goldsmith was the first writer in English to effect a conjunction of traditional pastoral with the novel form. *The Vicar of Wakefield* draws much of its strength and poignancy from the contrast between the world of rural innocence with its peaceful seasonal patterns and the treacherous world of the towns with their pitfalls for the simple, their arbitrary laws and inhuman prisons. In *The Crock of Gold* a persistent argument goes on between the two worlds. It is at its most overt when the Philosopher is arrested by Policemen for a crime he did not commit, and at its most intense and desolating when, in Chapter XVI, he sits in darkness and listens to the stories of his two cellmates about their persecution by society and its laws. This conflict furnishes one aspect of the book's satirical syndrome: the contrast between the pastoral world where the motions and desires of man are given free and harmonious expression among the rhythms of nature, and the world of social man, where these aspirations are repressed and maimed by law and custom. The second, and no less important, function of the satire concerns Pan's mission to Ireland, a country where 'no people have done reverence' to him. This prong of the satiric intention is aimed at Ireland's traditional distrust of the passions, its Jansenist and Victorian suspicion of natural impulses. In this respect Stephens joins Moore, Yeats and Joyce as a critic of the conservative *mores* of contemporary Irish life. Together with the satire on law and justice, this criticism of society's attitude to the natural instincts finds expression in the allegorical pattern which traces the fortunes of Caitilin, the Philosopher and the Thin Woman through the book's narrative process.

## The Comic Idiom

*The Crock of Gold* is above all a comic novel. Though all of its fictive characters may stand for separate human faculties they must also put on flesh and become believable human personalities. To achieve this verisimilitude Stephens had to find a narrative idiom which would suspend disbelief and persuade the reader of a lived reality while, at the same time, making sure that the doctrinal implications of the fable would not drop altogether from sight.

He begins therefore with a narrative convention that is fabulous, proverbial, gnomic: 'In the centre of the pine-wood called Coilla Doraca there lived not long ago two Philosophers.'[9] The narrative voice assumes the privileges of the Irish 'seanchaí' (traditional story-teller) and places the action at a suitable distance in time and space, somewhere between myth and history, between Eliade's *illud tempus* and *hoc tempus*.[10] If the message is to be Blakean the setting will be radically Stephensian, a world which can accommodate not only Pan and Angus Og, but policemen, tinkers, leprechauns, resurrected heroes and arguments about lumps in the porridge. Magic, mystery and miracle are fused with the quotidian and the domestic: the Philosopher's ministry is, as we are told at the opening of Chapter II, to give advice to people 'on subjects too recondite for even those extremes of elucidation, the parish priest and the tavern'(13). The chief catalyst between the human and the numinous is the comic. The book, like *The Charwoman's Daughter*, employs the traditional comic plot: its heroine eludes the constraints of prudence and of parental sanction to achieve marriage with the youthful god, Angus Og. In doing so she not only transcends the dry morality of the Philosopher but becomes instrumental in his conversion to those values of joy, spontaneity and fertility which he had so strenuously distrusted. On the human level the book's rhetorical trend affirms these traditional comic values against the sterile constraints of established social *mores*. The book's *dramatis personae* are drawn from the comedy of humours: the naïve heroine, the bumbling policeman, the mischievous fairy, the droll countryman, the absent-minded philosopher plagued by his practical and shrewish wife—perhaps a deliberate echo of Socrates and Xanthippe. But here the comic action works itself out in consistent patterns of allegory and the comic ending passes on into happy apocalypse.

That the two Philosophers, despite their prodigious learning, do not know everything, is deftly suggested in the first chapter when it appears that they cannot account for the simultaneous birth of a boy and a girl to their wives. Logic is their thinking instrument and their home is a dark wood; the marvel of fertility is beyond them. By the end of the first chapter their children have discovered the sun. By the end of the second one of the Philosophers has died because he 'has attained to all the wisdom [he is] fitted to bear'(15). Before he goes his brother informs him of certain things that he has not mastered—'how to play the tambourine, nor how to be nice to your wife, nor how to get up first in the morning and cook the breakfast . . . how to smoke strong tobacco' or 'dance in the moonlight with a woman of the Shee'. For his own part he concludes that perhaps 'the ultimate end is gaiety and music and a dance of joy' (16). The brother is not deterred; but it is also true that the surviving Philosopher makes no attempt to put his own theories into practice. He continues to talk and cerebrate and infuriate his wife. His enlightenment and transformation form the main allegorical strand in the book's pattern; the flowering and development of Caitilin's womanhood form the next; the pilgrimage of the Thin Woman fills out the third. But as Caitilin's development precipitates all of the others—including those of the minor characters and that of Angus Og himself—it is best to begin with her role in the fable.

## Caitilin's Progress

Caitilin, like Mary Makebelieve, is introduced at the moment when her sexuality is beginning to announce itself. Like Blake's Thel she is a virginal shepherdess poised on the brink of experience. Unlike Thel she does not recoil from the reality of sex, nor, like Oothoon, is she delivered over to the forces of morality and convention. Instead, through the good offices of Pan and Angus, she is granted in the end a joyful progress to full womanhood.

From the outset she is seen as having an especial affinity with nature as she moves among the vegetation and the animals in a mood of 'warm thoughtlessness':

Indeed, everything in her quiet world loved this girl: but very slowly there was growing in her consciousness an unrest, a disquietude to which she had hitherto been a stranger. Sometimes an infinite weariness oppressed her to the earth. A thought was born in her mind and it had no name. It was growing and could not be expressed. She had no words wherewith to meet it, to exorcise or greet this stranger who, more and more insistently and pleadingly, tapped upon her doors and begged to be spoken to, admitted and caressed and nourished.(34)

This stranger, her instinctive desire for sexual fulfilment, approaches first through the half-heard music of Pan, then through the discernible melody of his pipes 'full of austerity and aloofness'(36), and finally through the apparition of the god himself. The process is subtly managed in its early gradations and it moves towards confrontation:

The upper part of his body was beautiful, but the lower part . . . She dared not look at him again. She would have risen and fled away but she feared he might pursue, and the thought of such a chase and the inevitable capture froze her blood.(37)

The skill with which Stephens has dramatized the girl's state of mind anchors the experience in the world of psychological reality. Simultaneously, of course, the moment is heightened by the presence of older, more archetypal versions of the situation, the fables of Pan and Syrinx, of Cupid and Psyche.

When Pan speaks to her Caitilin first takes refuge in the conventional response: 'I will do whatever you say if it is right.'(38) Pan dismisses the concept urging instead the Blakean imperative of desire: 'You must not do anything because it is right, but because it is your wish.' As he proceeds with his argument—half homily, half seduction—he refashions the Philosopher's earlier propositions on wisdom and love:

The name of the heights is Wisdom and the name of the depths is Love. How shall they come together and be fruitful if you do not plunge deeply and fearlessly? Wisdom is the spirit and the wings of the spirit, Love is the shaggy beast that goes down. Gallantly he dives, below thought, beyond Wisdom, to rise again as high above these as he had first descended.(39)

When Caitilin consents to go with him it is in response not to her intellect but her heart, 'because he was naked and unashamed'(40).

A consistent feature of Stephens's narrative strategy is the counterpoint of the solemn against the whimsical, the momentous against the commonplace, the cosmic against the domestic. Pan's wooing of Caitilin, accordingly, is followed by her father's comic embassy to the Philosopher for help in getting her back. Here, as the Philosopher weaves his way intricately towards a solution, and as Meehawl with a sort of droll patience tries to keep him to the point, the abduction is at once annotated and placed in the mundane perspective of kitchen comedy. Two kinds of discourse are played off against each other in humorous counterpoint while patterns of literary parody and social satire are fed into the structure. Meehawl's rustic idiom constantly picks up Synge's dramatic dialogue:

'Did you ever hear', said Meehawl, 'of the man that had the scalp of his head blown off by a gun, and they soldered the bottom of a tin dish to the top of his skull the way you could hear his brains ticking inside of it for all the world like a Waterby watch?'(42)[11]

Similarly the expectations of Yeats and Russell of a Celtic Avatar are gently mocked in the dialogue that follows. The Philosopher's assertion that Pan had never visited Ireland and that 'his coming intends no good to this country'(44) is an obvious comment on the sexual puritanism of contemporary Ireland which so many writers of the Revival had been consistently satirizing.

Having identified the abductor as Pan, the Philosopher explains to Meehawl that Pan has power over all grown people to make them 'fall in love with every person they meet, and commit assaults and things I wouldn't like to be telling you about'.

He resolves to send his two children to treat with the god and to tell him 'he isn't doing the decent thing'. If this ploy fails, the Celtic god, Angus Og, is to be their last resource:

'He'd make short work of him, I'm thinking.'
'He might surely; but he may take the girl for himself all the same.'
'Well, I'd sooner he had her than the other one, for he's one of ourselves anyhow, and the devil you know is better than the devil you don't know.'
'Angus Og is a god,' said the Philosopher severely.(45)

From this point forward the Philosopher and Caitilin are set upon parallel courses: both come under the sensual influence of Pan and both proceed, by different paths, to human completion under the influence of Angus Og, the 'intellect spiritualized'. The children's embassy to Pan having failed, the Philosopher sets out to invoke the aid of the Irish god. His encounter with Pan is provoked by the sight of Caitilin, naked and unashamed, in the fields by the Greek god's cave. His disputation with Pan is a battle of polarities in which he is defeated, comically, not by the god's logic but by the music of his pipes, which strike at his hitherto undeveloped sexual faculties:

'You leave out the new thing,' said the Philosopher. 'You leave out brains. I believe in mind above matter. Thought above emotion. Spirit above flesh.'
'Of course you do,' said Pan, and he reached for his oaten pipe.
The Philosopher ran to the opening of the passage and thrust Caitilin aside. 'Hussy,' said he fiercely to her, and he darted out.
As he went up the rugged path he could hear the pipes of Pan, calling and sobbing and making high merriment on the air.(61–2)

## The Philosopher's Progress

Chapter XI of Book Two takes the Philosopher from the cave of Pan to the dwelling of Angus Og, and as he proceeds a series of changes and recognitions takes place in his psyche. He begins with a wilful adherence to his previous ethical imperatives: ' "She does not deserve to be rescued," said the Philosopher, "but I will rescue her. Indeed," he thought a moment later, "she does not want to be rescued, and, *therefore*, I will rescue her." '(62) The servant of Urizen dies hard, but his three encounters on the journey guarantee the birth of the new man. Haunted by the naked beauty of Caitilin, and in obedience to an unprecedented impulse, he kisses a fat woman by the way. He offers sympathy to an old beggarwoman and is witness to her humiliation at the hands of settled society.[12] As yet he is unable to relieve her distress. Pan has, by irrigating his sexual instincts, aroused the capacity for sympathy; but the influence of Angus Og is necessary before that faculty can blossom into active and effective charity. Thirdly, he becomes involved with a tinker band who wish him to marry their woman and thus resolve their difficulties. The tinkers are refugees from Synge, problematically involved with a social institution alien to their freebooting way of life. The Philosopher refuses to be conscripted, escapes under cover of darkness, and soon finds himself bowing before the godhead of Angus. Here the two main allegorical strands meet again: at the Philosopher's request Angus proceeds to Pan's cave to claim Caitilin; the Philosopher, renewed by the Divine Imagination of Angus, sets out on his journey home.

The contention of the gods Pan and Angus for the love of Caitilin is, significantly, a trial not of strength but of weakness, of need. Caitilin had gone with Pan because he had been naked and alone. She chooses Angus because his need is greater. His plea is similar to that of Pan and recalls Pan's earlier complaint that 'in this country no people have done any reverence to me':

'I want you,' said Angus Og, 'because the world has forgotten me. In all my nation there is no remembrance of me. I, wandering the hills of my country, am lonely indeed. . . . Thought has snared my birds in his nets and sold them in the market-places.'(88)

It is hardly fanciful to detect in these sentences the voice of the Irish Literary Renaissance pleading for the values of poetry and imagination against the materialism and philistinism of the age. And as he proceeds Angus invokes the larger perspectives of Blake and his aspiration of human wholeness: 'Lo, I am sealed in the caves of nonentity until the head and the heart shall come together in fruitfulness, until Thought has wept for Love, and Emotion has purified herself to meet her lover. Tir-na-nÓg is the heart of a man and the head of a woman.'(88–9)[13] Union with a mortal woman rescues the god from non-entity. Caitilin becomes the bridgehead from which the Immortals can reconquer Ireland and re-establish Tir-na-nÓg. Analogously Caitilin has progressed from unthinking virginity through awakened sensuality to union with the Divine Imagination of Angus Og. The stage is being set for the final apocalyptic climax of the book's action.

The Philosopher's homeward journey is marked by a two-fold pattern. His state of well-being now issues in overt acts of humanity and loving-kindness, and each of these acts becomes the occasion for his message of regeneration. He offers to share his bread with a bearded man and his sons, and in the exchange of hospitality that follows he discovers that the man is Mac Cúl. He comforts the love-lorn girl and discovers that her lover is MacCulain. He proffers food to a boy and it is revealed that the boy is named MacCushin. To each of them—clearly versions of the Irish heroes, Fionn, Cú Chulain and Oisín—he delivers Angus's message that the 'Sleepers of Erinn' are about to awaken. But before the apocalypse can take place the allegory has a number of intricate strands to unwind.

The role of the sub-plot, from which the novel takes its name, does not become apparent until the Philosopher returns and is arrested by policemen for the alleged murder of his brother and sister-in-law. The leprechauns have given false evidence against him because, in helping Meehawl to recover his washboard, he had been unwittingly responsible for the loss of their crock of gold. The leprechauns are elementals, and therefore have no morality. When they lose their crock of gold they kidnap the Philosopher's children, but when the Thin Woman threatens them with her fairy relatives they give them back. When the children return their gold they try to make amends by ambushing the Policemen and rescuing the Philosopher on his way to prison. They are perhaps best seen as part of the novel's 'machinery'—a sort of earthy version of Pope's sylphs—and their function at this stage of the fable is twofold. They throw open the way for the Philosopher to submit deliberately to the law, and to deliver himself formally to the Policemen's custody. They provide the opportunity for the Thin Woman to undertake her pilgrimage to Angus Og by first performing the Blakean sacrament of the 'Forgiveness of Enemies':[14]

Before the Thin Woman could undertake the redemption of her husband by wrath, it was necessary that she should be purified by the performance of that sacrifice which is called the Forgiveness of Enemies, and this she did by embracing the Leprecauns of the Gort and in the presence of the sun and the wind remitting their crime against her husband. Thus she became free to devote her malice against the State of Punishment, while forgiving the individuals who had but acted in obedience to the pressure of their infernal environment, which pressure is Sin.[15]

The Philosopher is about to enter upon his final purgatorial experience. He is still the book's sturdy champion of the mind. From the story's outset he had dwelt in the darkness of Coilla Doraca, 'the Dark Woods', and there he had asserted the stamina and indomitability of the intellect over darkness, limitation, human perplexity. In the spiritual adventure of meeting the two gods his mind had been enriched by imagination and love. Now, more than ever, when the Policemen arrest him, he feels confident of the power of mind over matter, of innocence over the hostile world of law and custom. So, as he is borne through the darkness by the police, there is meaning as well as absurdity in his indefatigable monologues on ants, birds and policemen. In these the free mind refuses to be silenced by the truncheons of retributive justice. When, after his rescue and his stir-about, he resolves to give himself up, he does so in obedience to a conviction that is admirable, but which the fable's action is to reveal as mistaken:

'An innocent man', said he, 'cannot be oppressed, for he is fortified by his mind and his heart cheers him. It is only on a guilty person that the rigour of punishment can fall, for he punishes himself. That is what I think, that a man should always obey the law with his body and always disobey it with his mind. I have been arrested, the men of the law had me in their hands, and I will have to go back to them so that they may do whatever they have to do.'(131)

The humour with which the Philosopher's arrival at the police station is related, the confusion and delight of the policeman on duty, the hospitality of the Sergeant and of Shawn seeing him on the morrow, can easily deflect us from the serious implications of the action. What is being urged upon us is the conviction that the mind of man cannot, despite its best efforts and purest intentions, triumph over an organized system of social restraint and punitive justice. The Philosopher is permitted by his relieved and beaming captors to wander in the prison yard and 'smoke until he was black in the face'(134). There he finds himself mourning with the sweet pea on its wretched existence and congratulating the nasturtium 'on its two bright children'. Gradually the reality of imprisonment begins to oppress him: he finds himself exclaiming, 'Indeed, poor creatures! . . . ye also are in gaol'(135). And when he returns to his cell he is possessed of a blackness 'both within and without'. It is a poignant moment in the book when this sterling exponent of the free intellect finds himself asking: 'Can one's mind go to prison as well as one's body?'(136) It is as he faces this new and unnerving possibility that the two prisoners' stories are brilliantly interpolated.

Both prisoners had been clerks, obedient servants of society, but now they are thieves and outlaws. Misfortune had come to one through sickness, to the other through age. Both had been put out of their employment with no means of livelihood. The first had taken to the road because he had been afraid to face his starving wife and family, the other because he could no longer pay the rent. Both stories are rehearsed in total darkness, symbolic of the unredeemed city ruled over by 'the dark People of the Fomor'[16] later indicted in the 'Happy March' with which the book triumphantly ends. The stories serve to define the aridity and injustice of the urban world and to bring it into sharp contrast with the sunlit, fertile world of gods and fairies which the Philosopher has so recently vacated. They foreshadow for us the fate in store for the hero if the Thin Woman cannot enlist the help of the gods to effect his rescue. As the second prisoner falls silent the section ends:

When the morning came the Philosopher was taken on a car to the big City in order that he might be put on his trial and hanged. It was the custom.(147)

## The Thin Woman's Ordeal

Though the influence of Blake has been frequently invoked in discussing the novel so far the fable can be perfectly enjoyed without any reference to the English poet. The use of prose narrative frees Stephens from the intrusion of Blake's style; the comic idiom, the Irish setting and the *dramatis personae* give free play to the originality of Stephens's genius. And the relevant areas of Blake's thought have been so thoroughly absorbed by Stephens that they merge easily into the elaborate narrative pattern of the fantasy. Indeed the plea for sexual freedom and the primacy of impulse, the sense of polar tension between male and female, might be justly claimed as a foreshadowing of Lawrence rather than as a derivation from Blake.

But there is one episode in *The Crock of Gold* which would be hard to account for without formal reference to Blake's symbolic system, and that is the Thin Woman's encounter with the Three Absolutes in Book VI, Chapter XVII. This is the least successful phase of the novel. These three massive naked men who challenge the Thin Woman as she makes her way with her children to the cave of Angus are in every sense intruders. We have not met them before, we are not clear as to their intentions— the Thin Woman is hardly an object of spontaneous desire—and we feel the need to cast around for their backgrounds and identity.

Here immediately we recognize them as shadowy visitors from Blake. Hilary Pyle is clearly right in identifying them as the Three Britons who escaped after the last Battle of King Arthur as related in Blake's *Descriptive Catalogue* of 1809,[17] and in associating them further with three of Blake's Zoas, Urizen, Luvah and Tharmas. Her exegesis may, however, be taken a little further. Urizen, whom Stephens rightly associates with Thought and plausibly with Beauty, offers the Thin Woman immunity from 'all raging passions' and from the 'gross' demands of the flesh(163). On the fictional level the offer is a little incongruous. Lust has not been one of her besetting sins and she is anything but a sex object. We recall that when the Philosopher had urged her to approach Pan at the opening of Book II he had pointed out 'that her age, her appearance, and her tongue were sufficient guarantees of immunity against the machinations of either Pan or slander'(58). Her reply to Urizen is as bald and simple as Bartleby's: she chooses not to, and he cannot compel her. He acquiesces. The incident is not psychologically satisfying as fiction. As allegory it can be defended on the grounds that her married life has entered into a new phase of love and tenderness, and that she has already, by the 'Forgiveness of Sins', freed herself from the more predominant of her 'raging passions', anger.

Luvah, properly associated with Love and again plausibly with Strength, offers the Thin Woman peace and love under the protection of that strength. Her answer is that as a mother her 'strength cannot be increased', her love 'cannot be added to'(164). Tharmas, rightly identified with Lust and rather arbitrarily with Ugliness, offers her everything that is 'crude and riotous, all that is gross and without limit'. His appeal, perhaps because it is made to the side of her nature that she has most consistently denied, proves hardest for the Thin Woman to resist. Significantly it is 'the hands of the children' that 'withheld her while in woe she abased herself before him'. Her answer is twofold: that it is not lawful 'to turn again when the journey is commenced'(165), which can refer to the journey through life or the pilgrimage to Angus Og; and secondly that 'the torments of the mind may not be renounced for any easement of the body until the smoke that blinds us is blown away, and the tormenting flame has fitted us for that immortal ecstasy which is the bosom of God.' Like the other replies it is both cryptic and perfunctory and not strikingly to the point. None of the answers has the felicity or ingenuity found in the many folk tales where this sort of challenge is offered to the traveller. Taken as a whole, the incident can be seen as the Thin Woman's refusal to have her faculties separated. She must cling to her psychic integrity until she too has found Angus. He stands for the fourth Zoa, Los or Urthona: through and with him the other three are to be reunited to form the perfect human person.

## The Celtic Apocalypse

The books ends on a note of triumphant apocalypse in which the motifs of allegory, satire and literary parody are given a final orchestration. As they prepare for the 'Happy March' on the city to rescue the Philosopher—

'the Intellect of Man', Angus announces to Caitilin that there will be a second journey from which they will not return, 'for we will live among our people and be at peace':

'May the day come soon,' said she.
'When thy son is a man he will go before us on that journey,' said Angus, and Caitilin shivered with a great delight, knowing that a son would be born to her.(168)

George Russell's Avatar is clearly in the womb of time. Accordingly the return of the old Celtic gods is at hand. On their second visit to the city we presume that Dublin—like Blake's London—will be redeemed and transfigured. But for the moment, in accordance with the spirit of pastoral comedy, the celebratory close of the story will have its setting amid the peace of nature, in 'the country of the gods'.

As the dormant hosts of fairy Ireland descend upon the city, their song gathers together the entirety of the book's themes: the prison of urban society; the tyranny of Law, convention and morality; the slavery of the factory and the counting house; and the contrary values of freedom, spontaneity, sexual love and poetic imagination. The song's refrain ingeniously echoes lines from a poem by Yeats and one by A.E.: in 'The Hosting of the Sidhe' Yeats evokes 'Caoilte tossing his burning hair' and Niamh calling *'Away, come away'*,[18] while A.E.'s poem 'Content' ends

> Come away, O, come away;
> We will quench the heart's desire
> Past the gateways of the day
> In the rapture of the fire.[19]

Thus Stephens's victorious chant is at once a summary and a culmination to the book's rhetorical intention:

Come away! Come away! from the loom and the desk, from the shop where the carcasses are hung, from the place where raiment is sold and the place where it is sewn in darkness: O bad treachery! Is it for joy you sit in the broker's den, thou pale man? Has the attorney enchanted thee? . . . Come away! for the dance has begun lightly, the wind is sounding over the hill . . .(172)

The book's last flourish comes through the narrative voice where Blakean rhetoric, Irish myth, and a wry note of comedy are blended into the pattern, and the allegory enacts its last gesture:

And they took the Philosopher from his prison, even the Intellect of Man they took from the hands of the doctors and lawyers, from the sly priests, from the professors whose mouths are gorged with sawdust, and the merchants who sell blades of grass—the awful people of the Fomor . . . and then they returned again, dancing and singing, to the country of the gods . . .

# NOTES

First published in Augustine Martin, *James Stephens: A Critical Study* (Dublin: Gill and Macmillan, 1977).

1  The author's note on the flyleaf of a first edition of the book, quoted in Birgit Bramsback, *James Stephens: A Literary and Bibliographical Study* (Dublin: Hodges and Figgis, 1959), p. 134.
2  *The Secret Rose. Stories by W.B. Yeats*, edited by Phillip L. Marcus, Warwick Gould and Michael J. Sidnell (Ithaca and London: Cornell University Press, 1981 ), p. 139.
3  'Apocalyptic Structure in Yeats's *Secret Rose*', Chapter One of this volume.
4  Schiller, 'On Simple and Sentimental Poetry', *Essays Aesthetical and Philosophical*, 1875.
5  *Letters of James Stephens*, edited by Richard J. Finneran (London: Macmillan, 1974), p. 207.
6  'A Vision of The Last Judgement', pp. 71–2, *Blake: Complete Writings*, edited by Geoffrey Keynes (London: Oxford University Press, 1971), p. 605.
7  *Letters from A.E.*, edited by Alan Denson (London: Abelard-Schuman, 1961), p. 17.
8  For a full account of the cult of Celtic Paganism, see the chapter 'Search for Unity' in Richard Ellmann, *Yeats: The Man and the Masks* (New York: Norton, 2nd ed., 1978).
9  James Stephens, *The Crock of Gold* (London: Macmillan, 1912; London: Pan Books, 1965), p. 9. All future references to *The Crock of Gold* are to this edition and will be incorporated in the text.
10  Mircea Eliade, *Myths, Dreams and Mysteries* (London: Fontana, 1968), pp. 27–35.
11  The specific parody is of a passage in Act III of Synge's *Playboy*:

> JIMMY FARRELL: . . . I knew a party was kicked in the head by a red mare, and he went killing horses a great while, till he eat the insides of a clock and died after.

[J.M. Synge, *Collected Works Volume IV: Plays II* (London: Oxford University Press, 1968; Gerrards Cross, Bucks: Colin Smythe, 1982; Washington, D.C.: The Catholic University of America Press, 1982), p. 137.]
12  There is almost certainly an incidental parody of a poem by Padraic Colum here, 'An Old Woman of the Roads':

> *Stephens*: I wish to God I could get a cup of tea. . . . Me sitting down in my own little house, with the white tablecloth on the table, and the butter in the dish, and the strong, red tea in the teacup. . . . (70)

> *Colum*: O, to have a little house,
> To own the hearth and stool and all!
> The heaped up sods upon the fire,
> The pile of turf against the wall ! . . .

[Padraic Colum, *Wild Earth: A Book of Verse* (Dublin: Maunsel and Co., 1909), p. 15.]
13  It seems certain that Stephens has in mind Blake's lines in 'Jerusalem', *Plate 56*, line 16, referring to 'Non-Entity's dark wild' (*Blake: Collected Works*, ed. Keynes, p. 688), which was the destination of Thel when she recoiled from sexual fulfilment.
14  'Jerusalem', *Plate 49*, lines 72–5:

> Learn therefore, O Sisters, to distinguish the Eternal Human
> That walks about among the stones of fire in bliss & woe
> Alternate, from those States or Worlds in which the Spirit travels.
> This is the only means to Forgiveness of Enemies.

[*Blake: Collected Works*, ed. Keynes, p. 680.]
15  *The Crock of Gold*, Book VI, Chapter XVII, p. 148. In Blake's view such forgiveness was necessary for the Brotherhood of Man. Cf. 'Jerusalem', *Plate 96*, line 28: '. . . nor can Man exist but by Brotherhood'. [*Blake: Collected Works*, ed. Keynes, p. 743.]

16  The Fomor, or Fomorians, were the mythical Irish tribe, ruled over by Balor of the Evil Eye, who were defeated by the Tuatha de Danaan—the Shee, of whom Angus was one—at the Battle of Moytura. They can be seen as Stephens's Celtic equivalent of Blake's Urizen and his forces.

17  Hilary Pyle, *James Stephens: His Work and an Account of his Life* (London: Routledge and Kegan Paul, 1965), pp. 52–3.

18  'The Hosting of the Sidhe', *The Variorum Edition of the Poems of W.B. Yeats*, edited by Peter Allt and Russell K. Alspach (New York: Macmillan, 1957), p. 141. Also echoed is the refrain of Yeats's 'The Stolen Child':

> *Come away, O human child!*
> *To the waters and the wild*
> *With a faery, hand in hand . . . (Ibid.,* p. 87)

19  A.E., *Collected Poems* (London: Macmillan, 1913), p. 269.

# 11

# Fable and Fantasy

Since the rise of the novel in the eighteenth century, fiction has been predominantly a realistic, social art form, reflecting accurately, and often minutely, the conditions of life within a recognizable society. Its great practitioners, Jane Austen, Dickens and George Eliot in England, Balzac and Zola in France, rejoiced at the fidelity with which they rendered in imaginative prose the reflection of an actual world—its houses, streets, farmyards, factories, its mansions and its hovels, its private and public way of life. Fable and fantasy, the less realistic forms of prose fiction, have played very little part in the English tradition—though writers like Lewis Carroll, Kenneth Grahame, G.K. Chesterton, and more recently C.S. Lewis and J.R.R. Tolkien have held a place of special affection among British readers. The Irish nineteenth century tended to follow or parallel the English, with Edgeworth, the Banims, Carleton and George Moore adhering by and large to the realist form and idiom.

There was, however, a dimension of the strange, the magical, the miraculous, always at the margins of these Irish novels: a belief in a world of fairies, witches and ancient gods, a belief in the spiritual and the visionary, a sense of eternity surrounding and sometimes invading the world of time. As the Irish Literary Renaissance grew to a head towards the end of the last century this concern with the unseen world gave rise to a great body of writing—poetry, drama and fiction—which employed the methods of fable and fantasy to express its peculiar idea of life and reality. It is no accident that Yeats's first performed play was called *The Land of Heart's Desire* or that the 'Father of the Irish Renaissance' was one Standish James O'Grady whose histories and prose romances assumed that Cuchulain was a real man living at an identifiable time and place in Ireland's distant past.

Yeats and George Russell (A.E.) believed that the old Celtic gods were returning to Ireland to bring about a spiritual renewal in a world that had been polluted by industrialism, commerce, materialism—everything summed up in the post-Darwinian concept of scientific rationalism. Ireland had been spared these movements; ancient, mystical beliefs about nature and the spirit world survived among the people, and were coming to life again with the re-discovery of Irish myth and legend in folk-tale and manuscript. In a letter of 1896 A.E. confided to Yeats:

The gods have returned to Erin and have centred themselves in the sacred mountains and blow the fires through the country. They have been seen by several in vision, they will awaken the magical instinct everywhere, and the universal heart of the people will turn to the old druidic beliefs. I note through the country the increased faith in faery things. The bells are heard from the mounds and sounding through the hollows of the mountains. A purple sheen in the inner air, perceptible at times in the light of day, spreads itself over the mountains. All this I can add my own testimony to.[1]

The sincerity of A.E.'s belief is in no doubt—one has only to read his poetry or gaze at his pictures to share his sense of that mystical landscape. Yeats's stories in *The Secret Rose* look forward to a time when the spiritual forces of ancient Ireland will return in triumph to 'set up once more their temples of grey stone'. As Michael Robartes explains in 'Rosa Alchemica': 'Their reign has never ceased, but only waned in power a little, for the Sidhe still pass in every wind, and dance and play at hurley, but they cannot build their temples again till there have been martyrdoms and victories, and perhaps even that long-foretold battle in the Valley of the Black Pig.'[2]

These beliefs—for beliefs they were, not just whims or fancies—seem strange to us now. But there were all sorts of millennial doctrines in the air through the capitals of the world at the turn of the century, and heaven only knows what sort of weird prophecies will emerge as the year 2000 comes upon us. Theosophy, Rosicrucianism, Kabbalism, the Golden Dawn—the weird prophetic figure of Madame Blavatsky—pervaded the artistic salons of London, Paris and Dublin, gained especial authority here because of the surviving Irish interest and belief in the Sidhe. The fever passed in a decade or so, and even while it lasted many of our writers viewed it sceptically. Looking at a picture by A.E., John Synge wrote:

> Adieu, sweet Angus, Maeve and Fand,
> Ye plumed yet skinny Shee,
> That poets played with hand in hand
> To learn their ecstasy.
>
> We'll stretch in Red Dan Sally's ditch,
> And drink in Tubber fair,
> And poach with Red Dan Philly's bitch
> The badger and the hare.[3]

A generation later Louis MacNeice wrote:

> It's no go the Yogi-Man, it's no go Blavatsky,
> All we want is a bank balance and a bit of skirt in a taxi.[4]

But there is no doubt that the fairies and the ancient gods provided the Irish prose writer with a remarkable opportunity for experimental fiction, for breaking with the conventions of realism in pursuit of a purer sense of reality—or at the very least in pursuit of, imaginative worlds, versions of Tír-na-nÓg, where some of the deeper and livelier human themes could be rehearsed and where we might for a while contemplate life as it could be rather than life as it is.

The main figures in this tradition of symbolic narrative were James Stephens, Eimar O'Duffy, Flann O'Brien, Austin Clarke and Mervyn Wall, and of course James Joyce himself who created the most monumental work of visionary prose in *Finnegans Wake* and deployed fable, myth and fantasy with such brilliant effect in, for instance, the 'Cyclops' scene in *Ulysses*. But as Joyce has had an essay to himself in this series[5] I will merely note his contribution in the present context. I must also pass over writers whose main work is in different areas of literary creation—in realist fiction like Benedict Kiely, or in poetry and drama like Padraic Colum—who have performed vividly but occasionally in the fabulous or fantastic: Mary Lavin in 'A likely Story', Liam O'Flaherty in *The Dream of Aengus*, Tom MacIntyre in *The Charollais*, Seamus O'Kelly in *The Leprechaun of Kilmeen*, George Fitzmaurice in *The Crows of Mefistopheles*, Brendan Kennelly in *The Crooked Cross*, Bryan MacMahon in his radiant idyll *Children of the Rainbow*.

The first commanding figure therefore is James Stephens whose output involves six novels and three collections of short stories. Stephens is remarkable not only because of his readability and his perennial appeal to a wide audience, from children to adults, from academe to the common reader, but also for the many purposes served by his fictions—social commentary, mystical insight, philosophic discourse, prophecy, parody, satire. These themes and doctrines are not just tagged on to the fables but, for the most part, are deftly embodied in plots and characterizations of great ingenuity and freshness where the reader may find in the words of C.S. Lewis 'some of the finest heroic narrative, some of the most disciplined pathos, and some of the cleanest prose which our century has produced.'[6]

Stephens's *annus mirabilis*, his year of miracle, was 1912, when he published: his prose romance of Dublin, *The Charwoman's Daughter*; his first radical fantasy, *The Crock of Gold*; and his second volume of poetry, *The Hill of Vision*. He immediately became a best seller on both sides of the Atlantic, and *The Crock of Gold* has remained in print ever since—a distinction shared with few if any Irish works of fiction apart from Joyce's. The only rival I can think of in this respect is Somerville and Ross's *Irish R.M.* another book that has survived without the help of academe, finding, like *The Crock of Gold*, spontaneously, new readers in every generation.

*The Crock of Gold* has the typical Stephens blend and marriage of opposites: it is profound and funny, realistic and fabulous. Its cast of characters: the two crotchety Philosophers and their wives, Meehawl and his daughter, Caitilin, the Leprechauns of Gort na Cloca Mora, the policemen and the two gods, Pan and Angus Og, make up a bizarre and visionary milieu, and their adventures between the malign city and the country of the gods have all the ingredients of suspense, surprise and comic reversal that make for a narrative cliffhanger. Then in the narrative pauses, as when Caitilin wanders drowsily through the pastures with her sheep and goats, or when the Philosopher broods disconsolately in prison, there is an enchanting sense of atmosphere that woos the reader's mind towards the novel's governing themes. Finally there is the dialogue in which these themes are strenuously and divertingly argued. The god Pan, hairy and goat-legged, has come to Ireland and made off with Caitilin into the hills. Meehawl, her father, comes to the Philosopher who suggests that if all fails—and predictably it does—they can get Angus Og, the Irish god of love, to intervene on their behalf. Meehawl likes the idea:

> 'He'd make short work of him, I'm thinking.'
> 'He might surely; but he may take the girl for himself all the same.'
> 'Well, I'd sooner he had her than the other one, for he's one of ourselves anyhow, and the devil you know is better than the devil you don't know.'
> 'Angus Og is a god,' said the Philosopher severely.[7]

And so the two gods struggle for the love of Caitilin and for the mind of the Philosopher in the adventures that follow. It is of course a battle for the heart and mind of Ireland, a country where Victorian and Jansenist doctrines have subdued and enslaved the life-affirming values of Pan—erotic love and exuberance of the body—and outlawed the values of Angus, spiritual love and the poetic imagination. By the end of the book the battle has been won, and the fairy host sweeps down on the city to rescue the Philosopher, the Intellect of man, 'from the hands of the doctors and lawyers, from the sly priests, from the professors whose mouths are gorged with sawdust, and the merchants who sell blades of grass'.[8]

*The Crock of Gold* is not only a universal fable of the war between the spiritual and the material, between instinct and law, love and convention, vision and reason. It is also a shrewd satire on Victorian Ireland which has become, as it were, a missionary country for Pan and his cult of love, passion, joy, spontaneity, the holiness of the heart's affections and the truth of imagination. Stephens is to that extent a faithful adherent of the Literary Revival as pioneered by Yeats and Russell, as ordained from the dawn of English Romanticism, in the visionary projections of Blake and Shelley.

But Stephens was his own man in one important respect. Where the older generation tended to view the Celtic gods and heroes with awe and reverence Stephens saw them with a kind of affectionate irony that made them amenable to his purposes as a satirist, a commentator on society's ill and humanity's failures in justice, compassion and vision.

In *The Demi-Gods* for instance, published in 1914 (the year of *Dubliners)*, Stephens continued his fictional dialogue with eternity by bringing three angels with Irish names down on earth where they became part of the *entourage* of a tinker family, Patsy MacCann and his daughter Mary, with whom they travel the roads of Ireland. In the course of these wanderings they encounter a man called Brien O'Brien and the hero, Cuchulain, who is thrown out of heaven for stealing a three-penny piece, and who strips Mary MacCann of her clothes when he arrives naked on the Donnybrook Road. If Stephens outraged the spirit of O'Grady and Russell in making Cuchulain the first drag-artist in Irish fiction, he seems also to have provided an inspiration for some of the more experimental writers of the decade to follow.

Eimar O'Duffy's Cuchulain, when he comes on earth in *King Goshawk and the Birds,* goes one better than Stephens's hero by borrowing a body, that of a grocer's curate from Stoneybatter, one Robert Emmet Aloysius O'Kennedy. It is probably not a coincidence that O'Duffy situates his action in the area of Barney Kiernan's pub where the comic transformations of Joyce's 'Cyclops' episode take place. And it is certainly not a coincidence that O'Duffy's chief character is, like Stephens's, a Philosopher with a capital P.

*King Goshawk and the Birds* is a more radical *satire* than anything in Stephens, where the satire tends to take second place to the comic and prophetic. *King Goshawk* is the first volume of a trilogy that foresees a world where capitalism is altogether rampant, and where the ruthless wheat magnate, King Goshawk, has not only enslaved humanity by 'selling blades of grass' on a large scale, but also captured for his wife, Guzzulinda, all the song-birds of the earth. It is to make war on that capitalist tyranny that Cuchulain is brought back, but before the book's satire reaches out to its global significance it is deployed in the local cockpit of Dublin, Ireland's capital city, now that the foreigner has been driven out. O'Duffy had already written a bitter, sprawling novel, *The Wasted Island,* on the events leading up to the Easter Rising—he had taken the side of MacNeill against Pearse—and he was not impressed with the narrow puritanism of the new state.

On his first day, therefore, Cuchulain, shackled uncomfortably within the decrepit body of O'Kennedy, responds with heroic impetuosity to every sign of injustice, meanness and inhospitality that he encounters. The collision between heroic generosity and spontaneous passion on the one hand, and bourgeois caution and prudery on the other, makes for shrewd comedy and sharp social criticism. The hero, for instance, outrages the sensibilities of a Drumcondra girl by his overtures of heroic love: 'My desire is for two snowy mountains, rose-crowned, that are fenced about with thorns and barriers of ice.'[9] He is treated as a sex maniac when he tries to court a member of the local tennis club in similar vein, and hauled before the censor. Though the book was published two years before the Censorship of Publications Act it depicts a world where the Arts are embattled: the nude 'was a forbidden subject; and there had been a great holocaust of exciting works in this genre . . . two fifths of the world's literature had suffered the same fate. . . . The Old Testament had been reduced to a collection of scraps, somewhat resembling the Greek Anthology; and even the New Testament had been purged of the plainer-spoken words of Christ which were offensive to modern taste.'[10]

The ploy of bringing the hero into conjunction with the unheroic present—skilfully used by Denis Johnston in his play, *The Old Lady Says 'No'*—has its obvious satirical opportunities. Flann O'Brien, however, employs the device for imaginary exploits and squalid adventures in the comic and absurd in his strange fictional extravaganza, *At Swim-Two-Birds*.

The book came out within a year of Beckett's first absurdist novel, *Murphy*, and both fables—as if foreseeing the barbarism of Hitler's war— have autistic heroes who retreat from reality into their inner consciousness. Both works question the nature of language by a radical approach to cliché. Kavanagh is soon to do the same in his doctrine of 'the habitual, the banal'.[11] Both ride roughshod over the conventions of the novel form.

Not only does Flann O'Brien bring back Finn McCool to live in a Dublin pub in a milieu of assorted jocksers, but he assembles a Pooka, a Good Fairy, two cowboys, and the medieval Mad Sweeney within his narrative patterns. Their works and days are inset to the story of an undergraduate at University College Dublin who engages in spare-time literary activities of which they are the product. This technique of plot within plot, world within world, may well have been learned from James Stephens whom O'Brien openly admired. But the crabbed ingenuity of the humour is unique to O'Brien himself. Week after week through the war years that humour helped to keep Dublin sane, as it issued in *The Irish Times* under the pseudonym of Myles na Gopaleen.

The war itself prevented the publication of O'Brien's next and finest novel, a dark fantasy about earthly crime and eternal punishment called *The Third Policeman*. This masterpiece of comic macabre did not appear until 1967 when it made its author a sort of cult figure with connoisseurs of reflexive fiction. It was in *The Third Policeman* that O'Brien developed his 'atomic theory', that people who *rode* bicycles slowly *became* bicycles due to the interchange of atoms between man and vehicle. The theory becomes, in the novel, a sly mockery of Yeats and Joyce who based their late work on cyclical theories of human history. When O'Brien's hero wakes up in the afterlife he walks into a garda barracks and is greeted by the desk sergeant with the question, 'Is it about a bicycle?'[12] When the book's action has run its course we find the hero entering the same barracks and being greeted with the same question. His eternity is to be bound about a double wheel of fire.

If Stephens chose to bring the Gaelic heroes into a modern setting, Austin Clarke and after him, Mervyn Wall, chose to move modern Ireland back into the Middle Ages. Clarke's three prose romances, *The Bright Temptation* (1932), *The Singing-Men at Cashel* (1936), and *The Sun Dances at Easter* (1952) are all chapters in what Clarke called 'the drama of racial conscience.'[13] Though they are set in medieval Ireland, the world of Clarke's beloved Celtic Romanesque, these fictions—like Clarke's medieval lyrics—are relevant to contemporary Ireland where Clarke sees a neurotic terror of sexuality. There is the tormented anchorite, Malachi, in *The Singing Men at Cashel,* and his voyeur's obsession with the young queen; and that horrendous vision of Gleann Bolcan in Kerry and its guilt-ridden inhabitants who have been 'crazied by scruples of conscience'[14] to a hell of endless self-abuse. Fantasy or fable, for Clarke, became in effect, a bleaker form of psychological realism, a stage of history where the main tensions in modem Irish life could be profiled in their aboriginal simplicity. What was realist for Kiely and McGahern was mystic in the narrative of Clarke.

Mervyn Wall, who moves two of his novels into the same period and landscape, is more openly satirical in intention, more thoroughly comic in his method. The eponymous hero *of The Unfortunate Fursey* is a chubby little monk with a stammer, living as a lay brother at Clonmacnoise. When the devil and his army of evil spirits invade the monastery Fursey is the only monk who cannot pronounce the words of exorcism in time to repel their enchantments. The demons camp in his cell and in time he is cast out upon the roads by the abbot with Lucifer as his only friend and comforter. It is part of Wall's purpose that the devil is by far the most attractive figure in that medieval landscape. So much so that we tend to applaud when at the Synod of Cashel he brings off a deal that puts the Catholic clergy of Ireland in his bag for all time, while he muses bleakly that hell will soon resemble an annual general meeting of the Catholic Truth Society of Ireland. The Devil has undertaken as his side of the bargain to rid Ireland of the 'hideous sin of sex'—if the hierarchy agrees to turn a blind eye on the others—'simony, nepotism, drunkenness, perjury and murder.'[15]

The clergy are thrilled with their side of the bargain, and with Satan's summing up, in which he promises 'the clergy of this country wealth and the respect of their people for all time. When a stranger enters a village, he will not have to ask which is the priest's house. It will be easy of identification, for it will be the largest house there.'[16] This was 1946, and though time has reversed the position both as regards sex and priest's houses, the passage is grim witness to the spirit of the times, the sense of alienation felt by the writer in a society that banned his works and brought the weight of Church and State to bear on his every utterance.

In point of fact Mervyn Wall was one of the few Irish novelists never to be banned. There was no room for the sensual in his dry, cerebral humour, and the Censorship Board was after books that could be deemed 'indecent or obscene'. The mask of fantasy, however, enabled him to mock that system through the most wicked indirections. In *The Return of Fursey* he describes a Censor who arrives at Clonmacnoise to check out the library. Within three weeks he has committed to the flames many 'treasured manuscripts of secular and pagan origin . . . as well as four copies of the Old Testament, which he had denounced as being in general tendency indecent.'

One of his principal qualifications for the post of Censor was that each of his eyes moved independently of the other, a quality most useful in the detection of hidden meanings. Sometimes one eye would stop at a word which might reasonably be suspected of being improper, while the other eye would read on through the whole paragraph before stopping and travelling backwards along the way it had come, until the battery of both eyes was brought to bear on the suspect word. Few words, unless their consciences were absolutely clear, could stand up to such scrutiny. . . .'[17]

One could hardly find a more devastating image of sexual monomania then in this medieval Censor. And it is by going outside the conventions of realist fiction that the satiric vision of contemporary Irish society can be so sharply focused.

Mervyn Wall seems to be the last Irish writer to address himself seriously to this unserious mode of fiction. Benedict Kiely digressed brilliantly into it in *The Cards of the Gambler* where a folktale frames the destiny of a drunken Irish doctor. Tom MacIntyre's *The Charollais* looked like a brilliant sortie into the territory, but after its magical opening chapters it tended to lose impetus—and the author abandoned the form in favour of theatre and the short story. Brian Moore brought off one dashing *coup* in *The Great Victorian Collection,* but returned immediately to the realist idiom. Alf MacLochlainn has written a novella called *Out of Focus* (1977) which is described by one critic as 'four short reflections on Flann O'Brien's de Selby as dictated by Samuel Beckett.'[18] And there was Bernard Share's *Inish* in 1966, weird and startling in its ambition to monitor the quotidian chaos of an average Irishman's mind, but somehow yielding to the chaos that it had set out to dramatize. And there are the later experiments of Desmond Hogan who has made a big reputation in Britain for the manner in which he catches in refracted patterns the nightmare of Irish history within ostensibly realist fiction.

With Mervyn Wall, however, the radical adventure of fable and fantasy, the idiom of Stephens, O'Duffy and O'Brien, tends to fade from Irish writing. Perhaps it has been replaced by the more spectacular imaginings of science fiction—our modern form of quest romance wherein technology caters for the instinct once served by magic and miracle. Perhaps with the retreat not only of superstition but of religion itself, heroes, demons, fairies, gods and demi-gods have lost their hold on the Irish imagination and faded into the light of common day. I hope this is not the case. But even if it is we have still access to a unique body of fiction in the dark and the light fantastic to remind us of what we once had the impudence to imagine.

# NOTES

First published in *The Genius of Irish Prose*, edited by Augustine Martin (Dublin and Cork: The Mercier Press, in collaboration with Radio Telefis Éireann, 1985). The Thomas Davis Lectures Series, General Editor: Michael Littleton.

1  *Letters from A.E.*, edited by Alan Denson (London: Abelard-Schuman, 1961), p. 17.
2  W.B. Yeats, *Mythologies* (London: Macmillan, 1959), p. 281.
3  'The Passing of the Shee', *The Plays and Poems of J.M. Synge*, edited by T.R. Henn (London: Methuen, 1963), p. 295. [Editor's Note. The version of this poem in J.M. Synge, *Collected Works Volume I: Poems*, edited by Robin Skelton (London: Oxford University Press, 1962; Gerrards Cross, Bucks: Colin Smythe, 1982; Washington, D.C.: The Catholic University of America Press, 1982) contains the odd 'We'll search in Red Dan Sally's ditch' as its fifth line (p. 38) and so the Henn citation is preferred and retained.]
4  'Bagpipe Music', *The Collected Poems of Louis MacNeice*, edited by E.R. Dodds (London: Faber, 1966), p. 97.
5  The essay on Joyce in this Thomas Davis Lectures Series on Irish prose fiction was by Denis Donoghue.
6  C.S. Lewis, *On This and Other Worlds* (London: Collins, 1982), p.152.
7  James Stephens, *The Crock of Gold* (London: Pan Books, 1965), p. 45.
8  *Ibid.*, p. 173.
9  Eimar O'Duffy, *King Goshawk and the Birds* (London: Macmillan, 1926), p. 77.
10  *Ibid.*, p. 83.
11  'Canal Bank Walk', *The Complete Poems of Patrick Kavanagh*, edited by Peter Kavanagh (New York: Peter Kavanagh Hand Press, 1972; Newbridge: The Goldsmith Press, 1984), p. 294.
12  Flann O'Brien, *The Third Policeman* (London: Hart-Davis/MacGibbon, 1967), p. 54.
13  'Notes', Austin Clarke, *Later Poems* (Dublin: Dolmen Press, 1961), p. 90.
14  Austin Clarke, *The Bright Temptation* (1932; rev. ed. Dublin: Dolmen Press, 1965), p. 221.
15  Mervyn Wall, *The Unfortunate Fursey* (1946; rev. ed. Dublin: Helicon Press, 1965), p. 233.
16  *Ibid.*, pp. 233–4.
17  Mervyn Wall, *The Return of Fursey* (London: Pilot Press, 1949), pp. 82–3.
18  Robert Hogan, *Dictionary of Irish Literature* (Dublin: Gill and Macmillan, 1980), p. 412.

# 12

# A Skeleton Key to the Stories of Mary Lavin

Because of the curious position of Mary Lavin in the modern short story, this essay is in the nature of a rapid survey, a preface to criticism, rather than a formal critical essay. It attempts to examine briskly and consecutively (1) her technical and aesthetic approach to the form, (2) her fictional material and milieu, (3) the operation of her creative technique in a selected number of her stories, and (4) her dominant and recurring themes as exemplified in these and—more briefly—in other examples of her work. If the essay is in places unceremonious it is due to the space at my disposal and the wide, and critically uncharted extent of her work. (So far she has provoked only one critical article, 'The Girl at the Gaol Gate', a brief and somewhat rambling commentary on three or four of her stories in *A Review of English Literature*, Vol. 1 No. 2. April 1960.)[1] Consequently the present purpose is to blaze some sort of trail rather than to set up critical monuments by the wayside.

Before setting out I find it necessary to make clear a few basic convictions about the stories of Mary Lavin. The first is that she belongs to the thin front line of Irish short-story writers—to the company of O'Flaherty, O'Connor and O'Faolain. I have no idea how readily this rating of her work will be accepted because so far no body of criticism has grown up around her writings. The reason for this critical neglect, I feel, is almost wholly an extra-literary concern. An explanation of it would belong—to borrow a distinction from F.R. Leavis—more to the history of publicity than the history of literature. Finally I feel that she occupies a unique position in the Irish short story. Frank O'Connor has written that the Irish short story is in the nature of a separate art-form. If this remark is true—and it is as true as such remarks can ever be—then Mary Lavin is outside the tradition.

The form of short story she has evolved owes less to Irish models—George Moore, James Stephens, Daniel Corkery, Seamus O'Kelly,

O'Flaherty, O'Connor and O'Faolain—than to Turgenev, Chekhov, Katherine Mansfield and James Joyce, who was far more a European than a specifically Irish artist. As the present essay is largely a work of critical pioneering, one feels the need of plotting these basic coordinates.

Mary Lavin has written two novels, *The House in Clewe Street* (1945) and *Mary O'Grady* (1950), and six collections of short stories: *Tales from Bective Bridge* (1943), *The Long Ago* (1944), *The Becker Wives* (1946), *A Single Lady* (1951), *The Patriot Son* (1956) and *The Great Wave* (1961). The scope of this review forces me to ignore the two novels completely and regretfully to pass over her greatest single achievement, *The Becker Wives*, which in its conception is more a novella than a short story. It is such a richly structured work, raising questions of allegory and symbolism, that an adequate discussion of it would unbalance an essay of this kind. But as it has not yet received the attention it deserves I would like in passing to record the conviction that it is one of the finest works of fiction, long or short, to come out of modern Ireland.

Mary Lavin has provided us with only two comments that might be taken as guides to her creative method. The first, characteristically, is embodied in one of her short stories, a shrewdly self-critical piece entitled 'A Story with a Pattern'. The other occurs in the preface to her *Selected Stories* (1959), the only piece of formal literary criticism she has ever written. 'A Story with a Pattern' tells how she 'finds' herself at a party, being taken to task by a rather forthright guest for failing to supply her stories with the sort of plot and pattern which, he claims, the normal reader demands. Ruthlessly telescoped, the argument goes like this:

> 'Now your stories,' he said, 'are very thin. They have hardly any plot at all.'
> 'But don't you think. . . .?'
> 'And the endings,' he said. 'Your endings are very bad. They're not endings at all. Your stories just break off in the middle! Why is that, might I ask?'
> I'm afraid that I smiled superciliously.
> 'Life itself has very little plot,' I said. 'Life itself has a habit of breaking off in the middle.'[2]

Her self-appointed mentor disagrees. He is convinced that life is full of incidents that have 'a pattern as clear and well-marked as the pattern on this carpet.'[3] The author challenges him to tell such a story and he chooses one from an apparently infinite repertoire. It is the story of a man afflicted with club feet who spends his life in pursuit of money and power; he marries, but refuses to believe that his wife could love him for himself. He mistrusts her—unjustly—so much that when she becomes pregnant he savagely asserts that the unborn child is not his. In despair he demands proof, knowing that it cannot be furnished. That night his wife dies giving birth to a still-born child that has two clubbed feet.

This is obviously a story with a pattern, with a built-in scheme of dramatic irony and poetic justice. The man had demanded proof that the child was his and fate provided him not only with the proof but with the appropriate punishment for his disbelief.

The author does not deny the effectiveness of the story; but she sees no point in her writing it, because she would have to go back to her old methods again afterwards:

'Because I won't always be able to find stories like this to tell. This was only one incident. Life in general isn't rounded off like that at the edges; cut into neat shapes. Life is chaotic; its events are unrelated; its . . .'
'Please don't start that nonsense again,' he said, and he casually walked away.[4]

This story is the closest the author ever gets to an artistic manifesto. She does not deny the validity of the 'story with a pattern' but she is emphatic that it is not her sort of story. What is then? Is her aesthetic a simple negation of all pattern, her stories uncritical reflections of life's disorder? Her preface to the *Selected Stories* indicates a more positive stance:

I believe that it is in the short story that a writer distills the essence of his thought. I believe this because in the short story shape as well as matter is determined by the author's own character. Both are one. Short story writing—for me—is only looking closer than normal into the human heart. The vagaries and contrarieties there to be found have their own integral design.[5]

Everything here is highly relevant. It seems that Lavin's attitude does not entail any real repudiation of pattern in life or art. Life has its own pattern, a subtle pattern that inheres in 'vagaries and contrarieties' if one looks hard enough to find it. Hence she asserts that shape and matter are one. Form or pattern therefore must not be imposed from without, as the emphatic scheme of poetic justice was superimposed on the story about the club feet. That, as she tells the man at the party, would be—at least for her—'distorting the truth'.[6] Instead she feels it is her duty as a story teller to approach her living material with an intense and much more humble scrutiny; to find its intrinsic rhythms, choose its significant emphases and deploy them in a meaningful artistic sequence. If I have so far interpreted her position correctly the rest follows.

And it is here that devices of concentration, poetic association and above all implication are sometimes needed. To interpret these devices the reader must be sensitive, alert and above all willing to come forward and take the story into his mind and heart.

This is very forthright, even challenging. The reader is being put on his mettle; his intelligence and sensitivity are made to stand by; some of the onus is thrown on him if he is not to miss the story's point. The challenge might seem even righteously defensive if it were not for its peculiar truth and peculiar relevance to Miss Lavin's stories. But they do require in the reader this sensitivity and alertness. They do not deliver their impact in one flash of insight at the end, or through any internal progression of emphatic or cumulative incident; they seldom make use of dramatic tension or issue in dramatic resolution. They provide a minimum of kicks. But instead, if read attentively, they set up vibrations in the mind and the imagination which continue in the reader's mind long after the story has been put down. It is as if the author has so unerringly found the innate rhythms of her human material that the story goes on in the reader's mind and merges with his own experience.

Consequently—to instance crudely—one will get no value at all from the stories of Mary Lavin by grasping the expository material, rapidly skimming the middle and attending closely to the end. The reason is that she is not concerned with telling a 'story' but with mirroring life. Now it may be justly objected that the cursory method of reading I have instanced would be indefensible for any work of literature. Yet it will get one at least somewhere with stories like say 'Boule de Suif' or 'Twenty Grand' or 'A Lear of the Steppes' or 'Rain', just as it will be utterly useless with 'The Lady with the Dog', 'Marriage à La Mode', 'The Mountains Look Different', 'Uncle Wiggily in Connecticut' or 'The Dead'. Mary Lavin's stories, with a few exceptions such as 'A Small Bequest' or 'The Pastor of Six Mile Bush'— which are exceptions to her general method—belong overwhelmingly to the latter group. And while these are her literary ancestors and kindred, because she is an original and exploratory writer she has evolved from them an attack and an aesthetic of her own.

Let us test these general assertions against a selected number of her stories. To choose from the substantial body of her writing stories that are at once typical and especially meritorious would be a most difficult task. My idea, therefore, is to start with a series of pieces dealing with the same family, which she has written over twelve years of her career and through three volumes. They concern the Grimes family and, though they are not all typical of her best work, they are typical of her milieu and serve to point up her characteristic techniques and some of her central themes. In this sense they are satisfactory as the purpose here is not to dispense accolades but to examine significant aspects of a writer's art and artistic material. For the main body of the author's work is set against the background and amid the milieu of Irish middle-class existence—the small town with its shop-keepers, priests and farmers from the surrounding country-side. On the surface it is a drab, uneventful world where the chief occurrences are marriages, deaths and unspectacular scandals.

It is a world where outward, emphatic action scarcely exists, where human tensions are muted, where love, joy and desperation are subsumed into a common ethos of stoic respectability. But it is her especial genius to pierce beneath these colourless surfaces and wrest significance from the most outwardly commonplace situations. Hence it is altogether typical that the rather squalid saga of the Grimes family begins with an apparently insignificant visit to a disused graveyard where the mother of the family has been buried.

'A Visit to the Cemetery' appeared in her collection *A Single Lady* (1951) and it introduces Liddy and Alice Grimes, two daughters of the family who have come to visit their mother's grave. The cemetery has been closed for some time and it is a jungle of twisted grass and tottering headstones. Alice, the elder of the sisters, keeps expressing her disgust at the condition of the place and saying what a pity it is that her mother had not been buried in the bright new cemetery on the other side of the town. Having completed their devotions at the grave they are about to leave when Liddy, on seeing a dislodged bone, is suddenly struck by a horribly real sense of death. She gets a shuddering vision of her mother's body in the dank earth. Alice, the more pragmatical one, tries rather impatiently to console her.

> 'After all we must all die—we know that' she said.
> But Liddy was incorrigible.
> 'That's what I mean,' she said quietly.[7]

The desolate mood has completely taken hold of her:

> 'I can never believe that I won't go on feeling: feeling the cold and the damp—you know, even after—'(116)

The realization is borne in on Alice too; it seems almost as if death is reaching out at them from the dank earth. It is then that Alice makes the remark that magically transforms their mood and at the same time gives the story its shrewd ironical lift:

> 'Well, thanks be to goodness we won't be buried here, anyway!' she said impulsively.(117)

Liddy is shocked into curiosity. Alice rushes on to explain that their father will be the last to be buried there. As for themselves—

> 'there aren't any more plots to be got here now, thanks be to God, so our husbands will have to provide them—in the new cemetery—thanks be to God again!'(117)

Our husbands—it was an intoxicating thought! Like a flash Liddy's depression lifts and a whole new vista is opened up to her imagination.

The old cemetery with its dank emblems of decay loses its grip upon her as she rushes Alice out into the sunlight which has suddenly been switched on again. Now, by a natural but quietly hilarious association, the new cemetery becomes a symbol of life and marriage, a focus for all the romantic aspirations of young womanhood. The author, of course, makes no overt reference to this—but it is shrewdly planted in the dialogue.

'It must be lovely up there on an evening like this: we could walk around and read the names on the stones—they're all names we know: not like in this old place. I don't suppose—' she hesitated—'I wonder if—'(118)

The mood infects Alice. Why not walk out towards the new cemetery! So arm in arm they set off—towards marriage, death, destiny, towards whatever hazily formed images have taken shape in their imaginations—but before they go they take care to close the gate of the old graveyard behind them.

I feel that this story is a little masterpiece. If it were only for the accuracy with which the varying moods of the girls are caught in the descriptions and dialogue it would be masterly. But its genius is even more manifest in its rich suggestiveness, its specifically fabulous quality; and so its insights into life, love, human aspiration and human mortality take on the authority of a universal statement. And then there is the quality in Mary Lavin's stories to which I have referred already: their ability to set up vibrations in the mind, to capture the essential and characteristic rhythm of her chosen situation so that the reader's imagination can be carried forward in sympathetic resonance well beyond the limits of the story itself.

Thus at the end of 'A Visit to the Cemetery', not only can we see the girls walking around among the graves of the new cemetery—though it is not described—but we have a fair sense of what their future lives are to be like. Despite the strictures of the man at the party the story does not break off at the end; the whole point is that it goes on—at least for those who have picked up its imaginative frequency. This is surely the salient virtue of this type of story. 'Twenty Grand' brings us up short at the end—it exerts no forward pressure on the imagination. But in 'The Lady with the Dog', 'Hills Like White Elephants', 'The Dead' or 'Uncle Wiggily' the reader as it were falls into step with the imagined characters and moves forward with them well beyond the formal terminus of the action.

Finally 'A Visit to the Cemetery' has, as perhaps its most engaging quality, a complete absence of authorial comment; it is the most shameful case of literary eavesdropping. The transition of mood that changes a tombstone to a wedding cake is carried solely by dialogue and imagery. One could say quite accurately that it is all done with tombstones.

The next three stories in the Grimes saga occur in the author's next volume, *The Patriot Son*, published five years later in 1956. The first of the three 'An Old Boot' is a rather slight piece, important only in that it introduces another one of the Grimes sisters, Bedelia the eldest, who is to play a pivotal role in the future fortunes of the family. The father of the family, Matthias Grimes, has by now turned odd with the death of his wife and Bedelia is preparing to get her claws on the family business. In 'An Old Boot' we find her making crafty overtures to Daniel, the seedily eligible manager of the shop. In the midst of their furtive negotiations—no element of love seems to arise—they are rudely silenced by the clump of old mad Matthias Grimes's boot—'hot and smelly with the sweat of a living foot'[8]—on the ceiling above. But though their tepid intimacies are momentarily suspended, the reader has no doubt as to who shall be in control when the old man dies. Therefore at the beginning of the next story in the sequence, 'Frail Vessel', we find that the father has died and that Bedelia and Daniel—well in control of the business—are preparing for their marriage of convenience.

Apart from being a fine sample of the story-teller's art, 'Frail Vessel' enacts a central theme in the author's consciousness, and its two chief actors, Bedelia and Liddy—the younger sister of 'A Visit to the Cemetery'—represents two recurrent and crucial types in her stories. Cold Bedelia, practical, inflexibly determined, is summed up in the author's phrase, 'a conniving woman'; Liddy is the opposite—warm, whimsical, romantic, outwardly frail. Liddy is the frail vessel of the title and against her is levelled all the very formidable artillery of Bedelia's ruthless connivance.

The first confrontation takes place when Liddy interrupts Bedelia's marriage preparations with a sudden request for permission to marry an unsuccessful solicitor, Alfonsus O'Brien, who has recently come to town. Bedelia, though deeply suspicious of O'Brien and secretly livid that Liddy should be so obviously in love, gives her consent for purely selfish reasons—the chief one is that she foresees certain embarrassments in having Liddy around the house when Daniel moves into her bedroom. But afterwards, when both of them are married, she regrets her generosity, not because Liddy and her husband are wretchedly poor but because she realizes how useful Liddy would be to her, now that she is heavy with child. So by a series of calculated and unscrupulous financial manoeuvres she breaks up the marriage, sends O'Brien packing and leaves Liddy no choice but to return to live with herself and Daniel. It is here that the muted irony of the story begins to accumulate. Too late Bedelia discovers that Liddy too is pregnant; instead of a dependent handmaid she has an added encumbrance on her hands. Worse still she realizes that Liddy is still in love with her worthless husband; her secret store of happiness is still undamaged. Bedelia's carefully laid plans for power and patronage have blown up in her face and in a burst of thwarted malice she tries again to destroy Liddy's inner serenity:

> 'Do you know what I think?' she cried. 'I think you've seen the last of him— do you hear me—the last of him!'
> But she couldn't make out whether Liddy had heard or not. Certainly her reply, which came in a whisper, was absolutely inexplicable.
> 'Even so!' Liddy whispered. 'Even so!'[9]

This theme, the indestructibility of human love, given generously, is a constant energizing principle in Miss Lavin's stories. It occurs in 'The Will' where the love of Sally, who married beneath her, survives all the pressures of her respectable and uncomprehending family; in 'A Happy Death' where the dying man salvages from a lifetime of oppressive shrewishness an image of early love that irradiates his end; in 'A Tragedy' where the act of surrender to conjugal love is proof against the corroding and malicious influence of a sister-serpent beneath the same roof. The converse position is equally dominant and articulate. Failure to give oneself generously in love carries its own punishment—that limbo of the affections inhabited, for instance, by Elgar in 'The Convert' who neither marries Naida Paston whom he loves nor loves Mamie Sully whom he marries; or Rose Darker in 'A Gentle Soul' who through sheer pusillanimity twice betrays the man she loves, once in life and once after his death; or Brede in 'Bridal Sheets' who through some inscrutable meanness of spirit allows her hidden finery to stand between her and complete surrender to her husband's love, even after she has died.

(It seems to be a conviction of the author's that people, even when given a second chance, will behave exactly as they did before. Both Rose Darker and Brede reject their second chances to make amends: one by refusing to give the evidence that will vindicate her dead lover's character, the other by refusing the body of her dead husband the bridal sheets that she had never shown him in life.)

If 'Frail Vessel' establishes the impregnability of romantic love, the next story in the sequence dramatizes the destructive and self-destroying power of connivance as it operates in the soul of Bedelia. In 'The Little Prince' Bedelia sets about removing her younger brother Tom from the field of her activities. Tom is gentle but feckless and Bedelia has little difficulty in forcing him to emigrate. But Tom's very impracticality takes its revenge on her because he departs without claiming his share in the business and he never writes to let her know of his address. Her scrupulous husband Daniel lodges Tom's shares of the profits to his—Tom's—account in the bank every week, and as the years pass it grows into a substantial sum—an ever-present and maddening reminder to Bedelia of both her ruth-lessness and lack of foresight. (In Mary Lavin's stories, as in life, extreme craftiness in some things is often accompanied by obtuseness in others.)

As time passes Bedelia becomes obsessed by anxiety—partly familial, mostly financial—about Tom's fate till eventually word reaches them from America that an old tramp called Tom Grimes is dying in a New York hospital. In desperation Bedelia and Daniel set out to identify him. During the voyage the author introduces a characteristic device, obliquely underlining the central theme. Bedelia takes up with a widow on the ship, a woman who is transporting the corpse of her husband for burial to America. The body in the hold becomes an almost obscene symbol of human chicanery. An Englishman remarks to Daniel as he watches the two women pacing the deck:

'I must say she looks a cold fish to me,' he said. I bet she has some shrewd motive for taking the poor stiff back to the States. Look at the face of her: I can't stand a conniving woman!'[10]

It was with a shock that Daniel realized that the other had mistaken Bedelia for the owner of the corpse.

The voyage continues and so does Bedelia's equivocal remorse while the corpse in the hold is 'like a shuttle, rattled backwards and forwards with each uneasy movement of the water.' This macabre and inexorable motion brings Bedelia to New York and to the unresolved crises of her anxieties. Because there she fails to recognize Tom's corpse; she is brought up against the grey stonewall that she has been unconsciously raising between herself and her brother:

She looked again into the dead man's face. But if it was her brother, something had sundered them, something had severed the bonds of blood, and she knew him not. And if it was I who was lying there, she thought, he would not know me. It signified nothing that they might once have sprung from the same womb. Now, in this fateful moment, they were strangers.

By her actions, by the whole crafty pressure of her life Bedelia has renounced the right to recognize her own flesh and blood; and so, fittingly, she is punished. And the mind of the reader acquiesces because the punishment is as much a part of the integral pattern of her life as were her grey ambiguous crimes. The biblical 'she knew him not' is justified. (I can find no such justification for the cliché 'this fateful moment' which arises from a stylistic carelessness of which the author is sometimes guilty.)[11]

In Mary Lavin's scheme of things you cannot violate the ties of love, in any of its forms, without involving yourself in unhappiness. This has nothing to do with any doctrinaire invocation of poetic justice; it is the relentless working out of all organic human sequence.

I shall not dwell on the last story of the series 'Loving Memory' chiefly because I find it especially problematical. I find it difficult to judge as an independent work in its genre because it seems to set out to explain why the Grimes family turned out as it did. It tells how the father Matthias Grimes first married their mother Alicia, a rather supernal young woman—a sort of reincarnation of Flora of *The Becker Wives*—and lived with her in an intense, exclusive, lifelong relationship with scarcely a thought for the children. It tells how Alicia died young and how Matthias, imprisoned even more rigorously within her memory, haunts her grave and slips slowly into madness. In it, one finds it difficult to be sure whether the author is committed to writing a fresh short story or to extending and rationalizing the Grimes saga. So, even though it contains some of her most energetic writing—her energy seems to increase not only in control but in intensity with each new volume—I shall pass it over; in any case we have had enough of the Grimeses for the moment.

However, taken together with 'A Visit to the Cemetery' and 'The Little Prince', it raises a broader issue in the author's work as a whole— her virtual obsession with the theme of death. These three stories deal specifically with the power of the dead over the living and to them might be added at least three other stories involving this theme, 'A Gentle Soul', 'The Convert' and 'Lemonade.' Perhaps it is significant that the theme has had a strange attraction for many of the great short story writers; one recalls at random Chekhov's 'Easter Eve', Joyce's 'The Dead' and Katherine Mansfield's 'The Stranger', all piercing and memorable tales. In Mary Lavin's stories it is difficult to generalize on its significance except to note that with one exception—'A Visit to the Cemetery'— the memory of the dead person acts so as to paralyse or impair the grip of the living upon living reality. Matthias Grimes, Bedelia, Rose Darker, Mad Mary and Elgar are all in different ways trapped within their memories. But the exception is so forceful as to reduce the validity of this generalization; Alice and Liddy are quite emphatically projected towards the future and the business of living by their epiphany in the graveyard.

This fixation of memory is only one of the many instances of the author's preoccupation with death; the theme looms large throughout the body of her work. Even a glance at the titles establishes its pervasive presence in the author's mind—'The Green Grave and The Black Grave', 'The Cemetery in the Demesne' and 'The Will' might be added to the titles already cited. An investigation of its provenance and causes would be unlikely to yield much of critical value—in fact it could be explained better in terms of sociology and Irish sociology in particular. But it ties up in a strange way with another stream of the author's sensibility which is likely to yield more specifically critical dividends.

In her work there is a whole range of characters who recoil from the more fullblooded implications of life and settle for a cool cloistered compromise; over against them stands an equal rank of figures who are characterized by their energetic commitment to the hot realities of living. Several of her stories enact the conflict between these two basic life attitudes and it is especially significant that in one of her very earliest stories 'Love is for Lovers' the tension is quite clearly epitomized. Here Matthew, a character of the first type, is almost tempted from his ordered, emotionally tepid existence by a stiflingly full-blooded widow, Mrs Cooligan, but he retreats quite deliberately into the cool cloister of his bachelorhood. As it is an early story the author presents the issues less subtly than in her subsequent work and the contrast is quite aggressively deliberate:

Life was hot and pulsing and it brought out a sweat on the forehead. He didn't know anything about marriage, but it must be close and pulsing also. . . . Life was nauseating to him. Death was cool and fragrant. Of course, he had a long way to go yet before its green shade lengthened to reach him. But in the meantime, he could keep away from the hot rays of life, as he had always done before he got familiar with Rita.[12]

Surely this is the death wish presented in a most assertive, not to say unnerving form. If it cropped up only in one early and rather clumsy story, one might dismiss it as a transitory if curious tangent of the author's creative imagination. But it re-emerges inexorably though more subtly through her later work: in the contrast between Miss Holland and her fellow lodgers; in the contrast between the prim and pathetic spinster and her father in 'A Single Lady'; in Daniel's rejection of the little servant girl in 'Posy'—where even the heroine's nickname is redolent of the life principle; in the disparity between the vigorous and sweating Magenta and the two pallid old maids; and more subtly in the contrast between Mamie Sully and Naida Paston in the two stories in which they appear. This persistent dichotomy could be expanded and developed. There is little doubt that the author is on the side of life despite the fact that many of its protagonists in her work are little short of repellent—Mamie Sully, Annie Bowles, Rita Cooligan—and many of its deniers are sympathetically, almost tenderly evoked—Naida Paston, Miss Holland, Matthew and Daniel. Again it is difficult to be sure whether the author is, however unconsciously, presenting the death wish as something central in the human condition or merely posing the question of its peculiar relevance to Ireland. It is sufficient here to note that the psychological tensions which surround it are a constant principle of energy in her creative consciousness.

In centring this critique around the Grimes saga I have been forced to exclude, except for passing mention, several areas of the author's work which would have made incomparably more exciting material for criticism. There would have been much more colour and liveliness in stories like 'My Vocation' or 'The Yellow Beret' which are set against a Dublin background; again there are stories like 'The Haymaking', 'Brigid' and that powerful and grievous story 'Assigh' which exploit the ethos of agrarian society; finally it has been necessary to bypass that handful of stories set in Synge and O'Flaherty country, the western sea-board, stories like 'The Green Grave and The Black Grave' and 'The Great Wave' with its rich biblical implications. But for all their colour and excitement these stories are really on the periphery of her artistic vision. The centre of her focus is the 'vagaries and contrarieties' of the human heart as seen in its small-town habitat. This is her objective correlative and it is on this murky prism that she concentrates the strongest creative light; it is here that her human concern is most sustained and urgent. Out of this material she builds not only the Grimes cycle but her only other related sequence of stories—those featuring Naida Paston, Elgar and Mamie Sully—'The Convert', 'Limbo' and 'The Mouse', though in the last of these for some inscrutable reason she gives the character new names.

Outside of this small-town ethos Mary Lavin has written accomplished and powerful stories but it is within it, one feels, that she is most consistently close to the hard core of the human predicament. 'The Great Wave' is more exotic and spectacular, more overwhelming in its symbolic overtones than, say, 'Frail Vessel', but it is also more remote from the authentic problems of living. With all its lyrical splendour it is really no more than an illuminated capital on the parchment of life. It is in the tedious and unadorned script of the Grimes history that life's meaning is to be read. It is the final proof of Lavin's integrity as an artist that she has pursued this squalid chronicle with such relentless and minute concern and forced it to yield up its hidden and unexpected riches.

# NOTES

First published in *Studies*, Vol. LII, Winter 1963.

1   [Editor's note. The article was by Frank O'Connor and was reprinted as Chapter Eleven, 'The Girl at the Gaol Gate', in O'Connor, *The Lonely Voice: A Study of the Short Story* (London: Macmillan, 1963). Martin developed his critique of O'Connor's treatment of Lavin as a short story writer when he went on to review *The Lonely Voice* for *Studies*.]

2   Mary Lavin, *In a Café*, selected by Elizabeth Walsh Peavoy (Dublin: Town House, 1995), p. 205.

3   *Ibid.*, p. 207.

4   *Ibid.*, pp. 225–6.

5   'Preface', Mary Lavin, *Selected Stories* (New York: Macmillan, 1959).

6   'A Story with a Pattern', Mary Lavin, *In a Café*, p. 207.

7   *The Stories of Mary Lavin*, Volume One (London: Constable, 1964), p. 116. Further references to 'A Visit to the Cemetery' are from this volume and will be incorporated in the text.

8   Mary Lavin, *The Patriot Son and Other Stories* (London: Michael Joseph, 1956), p. 73.

9   *The Stories of Mary Lavin*, Volume One, p. 19.

10  *The Stories of Mary Lavin*, Volume One, p. 321.

11  [Editor's note. Martin is quoting from the original version of 'The Little Prince' in Mary Lavin, *The Patriot Son and Other Stories*, p. 251. The phrase to which he objects is omitted from the version in the 1964 *Stories of Mary Lavin*, Volume One, which reads: 'Now they were strangers.' (p. 329)]

12  Mary Lavin, *Tales from Bective Bridge* (London: Michael Joseph, 1945), p. 121.

# Section Four

## *Selected Reviews*

# Selected Reviews

FRANCIS STUART
## The Pillar of Cloud and Redemption
*New Island Books, 1994*

The publication of these two handsome paperbacks — the cover designs by Jon Berkeley are strikingly apt — presents yet a new generation with the opportunity of experiencing and judging a writer who has been a major enigma since he published his first postwar novel, *The Pillar of Cloud,* two years after the Second World War, which he had endured by choice, in Berlin. Hugo Hamilton, himself of Irish-German parentage, attests in a brilliant preface to the novel its relevance to his own development as a writer. Beginning his own career in the seventies, Hamilton found Stuart an 'inspiring writer' who taught him 'how impossible it is to be false in fiction'.

I read Stuart for the first time in the fifties, probably before Hamilton was born, and Stuart is still writing his curious brand of fictional truth. In those days I had to go to the National Library to find his books; and was especially puzzled by the variety of their themes. Alongside those fine early novels such as *The Coloured Dome* were pamphlets like *Nationality and Culture, Racing for Pleasure and Profit in Ireland* and *Mystics and Mysticism,* this last for the Catholic Truth Society. Yet there was a weird consistency. The novels were attempting to portray life as a gambler's throw wherein the hero can only achieve vision if he plays for the big stakes. His heroes—surely the most wilful and didactic in all fiction—tend to goad his heroines over some threshold of pain and danger into prophetic insight.

We therefore can see a logic in Stuart's adventure to Germany in 1941 to take up a lectureship at the University of Berlin and his refusal to leave till the war was over. The inner impulse towards fear and suffering certainly met its monstrous mirror image in the concentration camps and the blitzed German town pictured in *The Pillar of Cloud*. If Stuart's achievement as a novelist is to be judged, it is in this extraordinary book, where the energy of the fable and the strength of the characterization win the aesthetic struggle against Stuart's importunate didacticism.

The novel is most notable, perhaps, for its haunting evocation of a defeated city: its darkness, cold, hunger and poverty, the stench of humiliation amid the ration books and food queues, the weary insolence of the occupying bureaucracy. The hero, Dominic Malone, befriends two fugitive sisters, Halka whom he loves and the consumptive Lisette whom he finally insists on marrying. While giving scandal by sharing a room with both, he makes love to neither. In the Stuart cosmos it is somehow wrong to do what is either sensible or gratifying.

The early phases of the novel are rather static, sustained by the vividness of the scene-setting and the strange psychic atmosphere which makes people act upon skewed yet plausible impulses. We endure, however, and to a great extent enjoy, the pictures of those strange *dramatis personae* which he assembles: the sensitive interrogator, Captain Renier, with whom Malone discusses the French writers 'who brought back with them from the concentration camps the words of life'; the prophet of apocalypse whom he interviews in a Zurich hotel; the Rumanian, Petrov, who believes that pain can 'bear fruit' in literature; the patient sensualist Descoux; their landlady, Frau Arnheim, whose bourgeois façade makes her refreshingly impenetrable to the metaphysical chat which makes up most of the book's dialogue.

But in spite of Malone's invincible goodness and inveterate celebration— delivered in dialogue, monologue, seminar, sermon, tutorial, aria—and despite the improbable degree to which he imposes his wisdom on others, especially the women, the novel has a haunting fascination. The sheer force of its honesty carries it through.

*Redemption* attempts to transport the psychic drama of the war back to Ireland in the person of Ezra Arrigho—you get marvellous results if you try decoding the name—who finds himself at the centre of a provincial town drama in which a servant girl is murdered by an acquaintance of his, a most un-Polonius-like fishmonger named Kavanagh. Again the sense of atmosphere is powerful, when fitfully evoked, the prose clean and elegant. But the novel is fatally disabled by the faults so narrowly evaded in *The Pillar of Cloud*.

Henry James has memorably asserted: 'What is event but the illustration of character, what is character but the determination of event?' In *Redemption* there is virtually no organic relation between character and event. The murder itself seems altogether arbitrary. It is foreshadowed by a succession of quasi-biblical meals at which Arrigho blathers on about the evils of wartime Europe which his audience had the spiritual misfortune to escape. And it is followed by an equal succession of symposia about the nature of guilt, redemption and apocalypse.

Arrigho's audience, surely the most patient ever assembled in a novel, comprises a Christlike priest, Father Mellowes, his virginal sister Romilly, the fiancé from whom the Arrigho doctrine deftly separates her, the hero's own wife who learns late in the novel that he has been back in Ireland for two years without letting her know. After the murder, Arrigho—having pulled off a betting coup at the dog-track—manages to assemble most of these disciples under the same roof to break bread with him and hear his teachings. Their motivation lies entirely in his will. But we cannot accept that such a charmless Prospero could persuade his fictional companions to act with such heroic docility. He has all the earnestness of Dominic Malone without a trace of his courtesy and innocence.

The two novels dramatize the problematic of Stuart's fiction. His chosen form is that most hazardous of enterprises, the *roman à thèse*. This requires an organic relationship, or at least a dramatic tension between story and message. It works as a brilliant balancing act with *The Pillar of Cloud* and again with *Black List, Section H* because of that book's autobiographical momentum. If we compare all three with *Manna from Heaven,* his late wife Madeleine's exquisite, unadorned memoir, we have the material for further seminars on the mystery of life, prophecy and literary genre.

*The Irish Times*
10 December 1994.


EDNA O'BRIEN
**Time and Tide**
*Viking, 1992*

I think it was Frank Tuohy who asserted that, while Joyce had expressed the drama of Irish male sexuality in Stephen Dedalus, we had to wait for Edna O'Brien to express in fiction the inner world of Nora Barnacle. He was referring, of course, to O'Brien's magical Country Girls trilogy. The sense of longing and challenge, disappointment and remorse, of emergent sexuality and religious taboo, the struggle with 'motherland and mother church and mother'—Desmond O'Grady's phrase—which irradiated those early novels is as relevant to their originary milieu as it was when they were published.

Opinion on the novels that followed has been mixed, and looking back on it, let's admit that it has been mixed up. The author has been blamed because the experience in such subsequent novels as *Casualties of Peace* and *August is a Wicked Month* had an air of the factitious; or of having been too recently lived for the sea-change into art to work its mystery; or—in one odd version—of having been lived hastily in order to provide grist to a mill that was running out of raw material. Critics in search of grist to their own mills, considerably downstream, then tended to argue that O'Brien's return to the pre-reflective experience of *A Pagan Place* and *Night* somehow lacked the 'spontaneity' of the trilogy, being self-conscious and overworked. Her short stories, on the other hand, have been justly and universally acclaimed.

But though she has never lacked champions, less still readers, there remains a genuine sense that the world of literature has not been gener-ous to Edna O'Brien. Ireland, its clerisy as much as its clergy, has been grudging, and at times positively vindictive, in response to her great and honourable achievement. Perhaps it is the rage of Caliban at seeing his own face in the mirror. Ireland was somehow personally hurt by her witness, and has taken its share of petty revenge. It has not forgiven the intimate chronicler of its shortcomings for being a woman; the feminists, because she was never quite their kind of woman, have offered little support. It has been all too easy to summon spurious 'literary' strictures to mask a more atavistic sense of rage or grievance. Which is why *Time and Tide* is *so* important and timely; no critical subterfuge can threaten the invulnerable brilliance of this new novel.

*Time and Tide,* in a prologue, begins at the point where the story ends, and there is an eternal cycle implicit in its structure. Its theme is O'Brien's obsessive theme, love's painful mystery. The heroine, Nell, sits in her London kitchen listening to the ungracious noise being made by the second of her two sons, Tristan, as he packs to leave home. He is going to join a 'black scowl of a girl' called Penny, who is pregnant—or so she claims—by his elder brother, Paddy. Paddy, who in his turn had almost broken his mother's heart, has been lost in the famous collision of a pleasure boat with a dredger on the Thames.

The novel's keynote is struck in a quotation copied out by the heroine in a doctor's waiting room:

'In the morning of life the son tears himself loose from the Mother, from the domestic hearth, to rise through battles to his destined heights. Always he imagines his worst enemy in front of him, yet he carries the enemy within himself, a deadly longing for the abyss, a longing to drown in his own source, to be sucked down into the realm of the Mothers . . .'

From this cockpit of guilt, power, broken and humiliated love, the heroine's memory ranges hungrily over the landscape of event that has brought her to this pass. It is a desperate narrative, negotiating between the plain vivid prose and dialogue of her early work, the drug-driven phantasmagoria of middle life when the earth seems to open beneath the heroine's feet, and those reveries, piercing in their clarity and grasp, through which she periodically reviews her appalling destiny.

Some of the material is familiar in the same sense that *Ulysses* subsumes into its maw all of Joyce's earlier fictions—and is subsumed in turn into *Finnegans Wake*. So O'Brien's novel proper opens conventionally with a visit by the heroine, with her husband and two children, to the family farm in Ireland. There is a parody of the expulsion from Eden in the inevitable row with her mother over the religious upbringing of the children. The father, an obscene Jehovah, pursues her to the gate:

'Little shite . . . and you always were . . . always . . . from the minute you were born.' A death blow there and then.

The event is echoed in painful symmetry as the first book ends. Nell's obnoxious husband has combined with the new Irish *au pair* Rita—characterized with some touches of wicked detail—to estrange the children from her, and force her from their London house. Having won custody in court Nell is pursued with insults from the law courts by the demented *au pair* who

ran back, helter-skelter, as if the malediction had to be put somewhere safely and she herself, batlike in her black attire, the custodian of this spurious curse.

In our last unexpected glimpse of the same Rita we find her cursing outside a ruined church with an even fiercer energy.

The centre of the novel balances the idyllic with the threatening in an increasingly precarious equilibrium. The scenes with the mother and children, tender, funny and intimate, slowly give way before the inner uncertainties of the heroine, torn by guilt for her parents and by the erotic needs of her own volatile, bohemian impulses. Her lovers are inexplicably awful, chosen as if to trigger the self-destructive urge that never ceases to pulsate through her strange metabolism.

The chaos that ensues when she picks up a piece of casual trade called Boris is matched only by the horrors of her eldest son's disintegration when he abandons her for the drug culture. There are few more powerful passages in modern fiction than when Nell tries to negotiate for his survival with a group of spaced-out hippies in the hot daylight of a London street. The valiancy with which she battles for his health—so intrinsic to her own—is matched in turn with the blackness of soul that envelops her as she prowls the riverside waiting in vain for his body to be retrieved from the depths.

As the novel ends, its heroine faces again the ordeal of survival. In an earlier incarnation, as Cait Brady of *The Country Girls,* she had faced defeat and disappointment with the words:

I came out of the kitchen and took two aspirins with my tea. It was almost certain that I wouldn't sleep that night.

'Almost' is a good word there; even at nineteen she is learning something of love's attrition on the heart and nerves. Nell, who has lived longer, who has lost parents, lovers and children, all, ends her last reverie:

'You can bear it', the silence said, because that is all there is, this now that then, this present that past, this life this death, and the involuntary shudder that keeps reminding us we are alive.

*Time and Tide* is the most inclusive of Edna O'Brien's fictions, not just in the technical resource of its narrative or the range and empathy of its characterizations, but for the intensity of its spiritual concern, its deep intellectual seriousness. I judge it her masterpiece.

*Irish Literary Supplement,*
Spring 1993.

AIDAN MATHEWS
## Lipstick on the Host
*Secker & Warburg, 1992*

If there is a literary renaissance under way among the post-Kinsellar generation of Irish writers, Aidan Mathews is its most many-sided embodiment. He has carried off most of the prizes, with his three plays, two books of poetry, and three volumes of prose, and he goes from strength to strength. With *Lipstick on the Host* he confirms that he is making a world, and it is a world of words—of language, if you like, but he is closer to Wilde, Joyce and Burgess than to their post-structuralist descendants. Yet he is a master of characterization, his proliferating cast varied and memorably differentiated.

His fictional personae, nevertheless, all seem to speak the same crazy dialogue, think the same daft monologue, spin themselves in the same word-driven reverie. And how can they tread the boards of a certifiably commonplace world while being themselves, give or take a twitch, all engagingly certifiable? Is it their obsession with verbal conceits that enables their grip on sanity; or is that propensity the prime symptom of their mental vertigo?

In 'Elephant Bread and the Last Battle', the second story of this volume, the boy hero, on holidays to the French Riviera, meets a weird word-mate in a classmate of his father's. The two immediately evolve a verbal code—the retarded adult is 'dear boy', the precious child, 'old man':

'I always have to say *deux Cokes*,' he said, 'because I never know whether it's masculine or feminine, *un* or *une*.'
'Dear boy,' I said, 'that is something for you and your conscience.'

When the adult determines to smuggle the boy across the border into Italy it happens in a riot of Mathewspeak:

'Hop in,' he said. 'In less time than it takes to say the names of all the countries in the world, I'll have you in the oldest one of all. Then you can tell your great-grandchildren you were smuggled into the land of Giotto, Garibaldi, the Emperor Claudius, the Empress Claudia Cardinale. And Hannibal can eat his heart out. *Andiamo*.'

I can imagine the delight of a research student in the third millennium at discovering the story was written in the same year as *The Silence of the Lambs*—no offence, of course, dear boy, to Hannibal of the Elephants.

In the title story, a witty, sexy Catholic schoolteacher of forty falls in love with a Protestant gynaecologist. When she asks the school chaplain whether it is okay to receive the Anglican eucharist he equivocates, suggesting it might be worth one-third of the Romish sacrament. She accuses him of making it seem 'like Coke and Pepsi'. Her sexual need is betrayed to us in many ways, not least when she suggests to her senior class that Milton uses his 'lovely, long Latin words' in *Paradise Lost* as a 'compensation for no sex,' as a 'kind of cunnilingus'.

Afterwards, regretting the possible consequences of her slip she reflects that you 'can show them pictures of the electric chair or a baby eating blue-bottles in a back-street in Bangladesh, but you can't tell them that people receive each other like Holy Communion.' Later, reflecting on the richness of her newfound love, she feels certain 'that the theologians and the pornographers only know the half of it, like the two families who have fifty per cent of the secret formula for Coca-Cola.'

But Mathews knows the all of it, and tells the all of it. Not since Joyce has there been such a profound exposition of the Catholic conscience as in these fictions in which the word is so poignantly made flesh. He has an Augustinian apprehension of the things that flesh is heir to, its birth between urine and faeces, its glory and humiliation between sexual joy and bodily decrepitude, its pride and degradation. But he has none of the great African's Manichaeism. In fact some of the more shocking moments in the book are those that find grace and sanctity in the places of excrement.

The appalling tension and consequence of a long-delayed bowel movement makes up the action in 'Train Tracks', the opening story, in which Mathews revives that clever, saintly child, Timmy, whom we had met in his first volume, *Adventures in a Bathyscope*. Still haunted by the Nazi newsreels to which he had been exposed too young by his father, he is sent, with sphincter muscles in spasm, to a family in Germany. When he eventually produces a turd of humiliating grossness, the cistern refuses to flush it down the spotless German toilet.

He uses a section of a toy railway track to break it up, but, failing in his frenzied effort to get the toy clean, he hurls it into a neighbour's garden. At dinner next evening:

Herr Sterm walks back in. He says nothing. He's holding the train track. Why had he thrown his identification label into the toilet on the train? . . . And why had the Allied bombers not bombed the train tracks leading to Auschwitz?

As he cringes before the accusations and watches Herr Sterm beat his own blameless son with the soiled train track the sweat forces his glasses to slip down the bridge of his nose 'until the half of his field of vision is a blur, the other half is sharper than italics.'

The blur is filmic, the italics are the writer's stylus. The cruelties of the Holocaust have always loomed large in Mathews's poetry, less as a racial thing than as register of what human-kind is capable of when drunk on authority. Before patriarchy became a boring buzz-word, Mathews was writing obsessively of fathers, not least in an early story of that name.

The two biblical fables in the present volume explore this theme as it collides with the doctrine of love that a certain inexplicable Jesus seems to be preaching all over Palestine. Inexplicable because he is seen in one story through the eyes of the donkey who carried him on Palm Sunday, in the other—with exquisitely painful comedy—through those of the Paschal lamb as it awaits its death in a crate before the Last Supper. The lamb can't make head or tale (stet) of the Master's parable of good shepherds and lost sheep in the upper room; while the Roman soldiers in the room below sing triumphalist songs about the tarts of Carthage and 'the cunts of Cappadocia'. This is one of the most unsettling narratives I've ever read.

All of these stories are carried on the zany, inexhaustible current of words that is the characteristic idiom of the volume. But this idiom is nowhere as mad and brilliant as in the second long narrative in the book, 'Moonlight the Chambermaid', in which a sophistical, half-senile old priest is asked by a distinctly odd couple to baptize their second child, as yet not quite born. The priest inquires from Al, the husband, as to how the father is keeping, and is told, 'He enjoys poor health.' When the priest murmurs sympathy, 'No need', said Al. 'The verb was enjoy.' It's quite relentless, as is the Mathews theme: Al's wife, by his own account, is 'Very hormonal. Still filled with the Holy Spirit.' And here is Al, not the worst of fathers, thinking of his impending baldness and the destiny of his three-year-old daughter:

Aoife would be out buying brassières by then, filling them with facial cleansers for the girlfriends at McDonald's, or squatting at night over a doll's mirror to watch how the inside of her lips darkened with blood on the second day of her period. The sun would breed in her, the moon bleed in her. She would do metalwork and algebra, and eat turtle-soup for a dare at a waterfront restaurant in Lanzarote.

It is all odd, relevant, euphuistic, hilarious, heartbreaking. At the centre there is a profound moral seriousness, the sense of an 'infinitely gentle, infinitely suffering thing.' That thing is the human compassion that always, somehow, manages to hang in, without ever really getting a look in, but which manages to survive by the desperate expediencies of its wits and its wit. Aidan Mathews is one of its latterday witnesses.

*Irish Literary Supplement*,
Fall 1993.

SEAMUS HEANEY
## Death of a Naturalist
*Faber & Faber 1966*

Not every poet seeks and finds himself in his first volume. Even the greatest of the moderns have struck attitudes in their early work that have lived to embarrass them with the coming of wisdom. But Seamus Heaney seems to have come to maturity at a single stride. In the first of these poems he states his condition and the body of poems that follows is a rich, varied confirmation of that stance. Poetry is a task like farming, a task that must be faced with the puritan virtues of courage, industry and skill. The business of living and making is, for Seamus Heaney, rather a craft than an art.

In his mind's eye he sees his father 'Stooping in rhythm through potato drills' and salutes that rude expertise:

> The coarse boot nestled on the lug, the shaft
> Against the inside knee was levered firmly.

He recalls the 'curt cuts' of his grandfather's spade cutting turf,

> Nicking and slicing neatly, heaving sods
> Over his shoulder, going down and down
> For the good turf. Digging.

He sees his mother at the churn 'set up rhythms/that slugged and thumped for hours' or again his father ploughing, 'His shoulders globed like a full sail strung/Between the shafts and the furrow'. This is not facile nostalgia or modish whoring after poetical archetypes, nor is it primarily an exercise in piety. It is a manysided expression of the author's concept of human vocation: he cannot be as good a farmer as his father, but he can make poems with a comparable skill:

> Between my finger and my thumb
> The squat pen rests.
> I'll dig with it.

Just as craft must be mastered so must experience, and the encounter is no less terrifying for the courage with which it is faced. Young Heaney's farm was a vivid paradigm of the world: as a child he is sickened by the 'early purges': he sees kittens dumped in a bucket, their paws making 'a frail metal sound' as they are 'slung on the snout/Of the pump and the water pumped in'. He watches as the farm labourer 'trapped big rats, snared rabbits, shot crows' or 'with a sickening tug, pulled old hens' necks'. But he survives it—'on well-run farms pests have to be kept down'.

When the gross, spawning frogs, 'the great slime kings', invade the flax-dam his nursery notions about procreation are brutally revised. When he sees a rat on a bridge he fights down panic and faces the rodent, examining him with 'thrilled care'—

> He clockworked aimlessly a while,
> Stopped, back bunched and glistening,
> Ears plastered down on his knobbed skull,
> Insidiously listening.

The rat trains all its poison on him but the young poet 'stared him out', forces it to retreat and then crosses the bridge. The poem is correctly entitled 'An Advancement of Learning'. And Seamus Heaney's poems carry a message that many of his Irish contemporaries might well heed: before learning to write you must first learn to live. And he is such a marvellous poet that only fools can fail to heed him.

*Studies*,
Winter 1966

JOHN MONTAGUE
**The Dead Kingdom**
*Wake Forest University Press, 1984.*

When in his introduction to *The Faber Book of Irish Verse* John Montague praised Seamus Heaney's 'homage to the earth goddess' he was, however unwittingly, defining the difference between himself and Heaney, between himself and so many other Irish poets with whom he has accidental affinities. Montague's commerce is not with goddesses but with people. He leans toward fiction rather than myth. The bedrock of his art is the personal rather than the archetypal, and *The Dead Kingdom*, so full of living—and dying—human shapes and voices, crowns that emphasis. It reminds us too that its author, as a young man, proved himself in the short story form.

This tendency showed itself from the start. In one of his finest early poems, 'Like Dolmens Round my Childhood, the Old People'. The mysterious old characters proved far more interesting than the dolmens. Where a myth-maker would have sought to intensify their mystery, Montague's determination was to find their personality. Maggie Owens was 'reputed a witch, all I could find/Was her lonely need to deride.' And in a later poem, 'The Wild Dog Rose', the poet goes back to confront the sinister 'Cailleach' and discover her all too human in her loneliness and fear.

Of course, another side of his imagination goes constantly whoring after the 'Formorian fierceness' of strange gods, and there are some elegant invocations of the Babylonian 'Guardian', of Gautama, Dis, Ceres and Cúchulainn in the present volume. But they are consigned to the shades by the real mother and father, the wife, the Montagues and the Carneys, the cousin Brendan who make up the *dramatis personae* of this vivid, companionable suite of lyrics. These characters live as in the stream of live narrative fiction. This sense of human particularity, what Philip Larkin termed the sense 'of a real girl in a real place', puts Montague in a tradition that comes down from his beloved Goldsmith through Wordsworth to moments in Eliot like that of the clerk and typist (which owes much to Goldsmith), Yeats's 'Upon a Dying Lady,' and some unforgettable passages in Kavanagh's 'The Great Hunger'.

*The Dead Kingdom* opens with the poet being called from the shore at Roche's Point to the phone by his wife on the death of his mother in Tyrone: 'the Strangeness of Evelyn/weeping for someone/she has never known/—her child's grandmother.' While Kinsella's 'Downstream' had lunged downwards into darkness, Montague's first movement, 'Upstream', proceeds through sunlight, upwards, like the salmon, to origins and endings. The car journey takes them over the Irish Midlands where emotional and political innocence is epitomized—as it was twenty years ago in his 'Auschwitz, Mon Amour'—by the memory of wartime neutrality in the South, armed engagement in Ulster:

> . . . a solitary childhood,
> our divided allegiances;
> a mock and a real war:
> spitfire and Messerschmitt
> twinned in fire, Shermans
> lumbering through our hedges,
> ungainly as dinosaurs, while
> the South marched its toy
> soldiers along the sideline.

In the book's third section 'The Black Pig', its quality of lyric narrative becomes more insistent. The names of lake and townland come alive with significance, ancestral, topical, familial—the ominous 'Black Pig's Dyke', the 'sandbagged/barracks of Rosslea', 'our homely Ulster swollen/to a Plain of Blood'. Yet all this fierceness is to be tamed and domesticated in the last two movements in which the mother and father take over the stage. Caught in that sensual music these names give off a gentler melody:

> Pomeroy, Fintona—
> placenames that sigh
> like a pressed melodeon
> across this forgotten
> Northern landscape.

To register this family romance, poems from earlier volumes are deployed in perspective, and the narrative unfolds of a father who emigrated to Brooklyn in the twenties; a mother who arrived on his landlady's doorstep years later—'just in time for the Depression'—with two grown sons; a child, John, born but unwanted in New York, sent home to fosterage with his father's people in Garvaghey; the mystery of these relationships and re-unions rendered in lyrics of unexampled precision and tenderness.

With the excessive privacy of *The Great Cloak* serving as a fulcrum, *The Dead Kingdom* balances the achievement of *The Rough Field*, turning the innner layers of that landscape outwards. In *The Dead Kingdom* history, myth, politics and prophecy yield to the humbler mystery of the heart's affections. In a real sense John Montague has got it together in this book.

*Irish Literary Supplement*,
Fall 1984

# Section Five

## *The Poet as Witness*

# – 13 –

# The Rediscovery of Austin Clarke

By far the most exciting event on the Irish literary scene in the last ten years has been the rediscovery of Austin Clarke. To speak of any kind of 'discovery' in the case of a poet who has been steadily producing over a period of almost fifty years, and who has some thirty serious books to his credit, may seem unnecessarily dramatic. In the case of Clarke, however, it hardly does justice to the facts. He has had a curious history, an interaction of critical neglect and authorial intransigence seldom equalled in modern times. The situation is perhaps best revealed by going back for a moment to the year 1956, and to the comments of Donald Davie, the distinguished English critic, who was then lecturing at Trinity College, Dublin. An apparently unsuspecting Englishman, he was presented with a volume of Irish poems for review, a mere booklet, 'flimsy and fugitive' in form, published by 'a small press' and running 'every risk of being overlooked'.[1] Davie's review of the book is a dramatic blend of recognition and alarm. His critical insight told him immediately that this handful of poems, *Ancient Lights* by Austin Clarke was the work of a unique poetic craftsman. He realized, furthermore, that Clarke had a message not only for a limited—and apparently indifferent—Irish public, but for the whole republic of letters; and that the extraordinary manner of the publication—'is this inevitable, or perverse policy'?—might prevent this message from ever being delivered. To Donald Davie it 'should be taken up into the tradition of English poetry wherever it is written';[2] it was poetry so technically adventurous that it 'could be a momentous innovation in the whole tradition of Anglo-American verse', poetry which demanded 'the fullest treatment which the best modern criticism can give'. This outspoken praise by a perceptive and disinterested foreign critic marks the period when readers of poetry in Ireland were beginning to turn again in guilty recognition to the forgotten but relentless genius of Austin Clarke.

Writers react differently to neglect; Irish writers in general do not tolerate it. Wilde, Shaw, Yeats, Stephens, O'Casey and Behan were not self-effacing men; it is unthinkable that they would have allowed the world to ignore them, even if the world had been that way inclined. But Austin Clarke reacted differently: if his countrymen did not want his poems he would not tout them; in fact he would make them a little harder to come by; he would bring them out privately, in severely limited editions 'on a small press' and in forms 'flimsy and fugitive'. If the public could not be bothered he would be at pains not to bother them. So, throughout his middle period, from the appearance of *Night and Morning* (1938) to *The Horse-Eaters* (1960), he published all his original poetic work under the imprint of his own Bridge Press, Templeogue, Dublin. It is strange to think that some of the finest lyrics and satires, not only of modern Ireland but of modern times, made their appearance in this obscure and unpretentious manner in a city where Patrick Kavanagh dominated the poetic skyline on the strength of two very slender, if very distinguished, volumes of verse. Ten years ago Kavanagh was regarded as Ireland's leading poet, just as surely as Austin Clarke is now considered to have taken his place. These matters may seem more irrelevant and extrinsic than in fact they are, because to understand Austin Clarke's poetry one must understand a little of his history. More strenuously than any Irishman of his generation he took up the tormented dialogue between 'sow' and 'farrow' where Joyce left it down. If Robert Frost 'had a lover's quarrel with the world', Clarke has had for the past fifty years a most angry lover's quarrel with his country. This quarrel is woven into the fabric of every poem he wrote, transfigured but still trenchantly articulate. Therefore, in following the broad path of his poetic development it will be helpful, even necessary, from time to time to mention some of the biographical events which helped to shape it.

Austin Clarke was a writer of the Celtic Twilight, and it was his tragedy that he embraced its enthusiasms when the movement was on the point of flickering out. He belonged, like his fellow poet Padraic Colum, to that younger generation of Celtic Twilight writers who inherited the tradition from Yeats, A.E. and Stephens. He caught their enthusiasms for Irish folklore, legend and mythology. With a greater dedication and tenacity than any of them he adopted the ideal of an indigenous Irish art, and he has never since abandoned that ideal. When Yeats set sail for Byzantium and Stephens followed A.E. into the upper air of the Vedas, Austin Clarke remained among the legends and traditions of ancient and medieval Ireland. But though he writes overwhelmingly of the past he remains the most modern of our poets: for him the past is used as a drawbridge across which he can make the most unexpected and ruthless raids upon the present. In the words of his fellow-poet Robert Farren he has remained 'a literary separatist', a deliberate 'builder of Irish culture'.[3] This limitation he imposed consciously on himself, and though he has paid dearly for it both in his pocket and his reputation, he has never abandoned it. It is only by dint of sheer, irresistible merit that he has finally transcended it, and has begun to achieve an international reputation. And this has not only vindicated his own merit, it has also vindicated the aesthetic principle upon which it is built: the notion of an Irish poetry drawing its strength and standards from native sources; a poetry and an art that is not provincial, not just an echo of English art; a poetry which achieves universality by being faithful to its own vision rather than by imitating any foreign model, fashion or trend. This doctrine of Irishness— already enunciated in the criticism of Thomas MacDonagh and Daniel Corkery—underlies everything that Austin Clarke has written, even his most destructive satires; and it gives a certain ironical significance to his growing extra-national celebrity. And whatever we think of it as a basis for literature in the present age, we must recognize it as the master pattern of Clarke's literary achievement.

His first book, *The Vengeance of Fionn*, a re-telling of the Irish heroic tale of Diarmuid and Grainne, appeared in 1917, and is perhaps his only work which was in full and timely sympathy with the temper of its era. It was a natural, even a modish gesture on the part of a young poet emerging into that literary ethos. The country had risen in arms the previous year, and it was natural to look to the past for heroic parallels. The revolutionary gesture had, in fact, justified decades of heroic redaction by such writers as O'Grady, Ferguson, Yeats, Lady Gregory, A.E. and Colum. It launched James Stephens on a whole series of mythological reconstructions. Austin Clarke's first book must be seen against this background. But, and this is important, it must not be absorbed or obscured by it. That has been his fate for too long. It has been too easy to look on Clarke as a mere sedulous follower of tradition, as one who was doing in a minor way what Yeats was doing greatly. 'The Vengeance of Fionn' may not be a great poem, but it is a great deal better than Yeats's 'Wanderings of Oisin'. It exhibits a far greater scholarship. Austin Clarke understood the Irish originals, which Yeats did not, and he is far more faithful to the spirit and idiom of the old tale. But more important, his poem has a firmer sense of reality, a sharper and more definite use of language, a more compelling power to create a world than the soft, dreamy, Italianate texture of Yeats's saga. Note, for instance, the precision with which Clarke evokes the landscape and the weather in this rather breathless extract:

> So on a gusty day
> From bare stone mountains where the kittiwakes
> Scudded and screamed beneath the clouds of grey
> Sea-rain or tossed above the long black lakes
> Whitening in the gale, at fall of night
> Across the boglands under mountain tops
> That huddled darkly in the cold, wet light
> Of westward rivers, through loud leaves and drops
> Whirling from tattered trees the Fenians came
> Into Rath Grainne.[4]

The faults of this are obvious enough, though they are not serious: it is overloaded with adjectives and adverbs; its headlong iambic rush lacks metrical variety; the word 'scudded' betrays, perhaps, a rather too active Tennysonian influence. Yet, we can believe in these rain-soaked warriors because the poet has placed them in a real, recognizable world. It is not a 'romantic' rendering of epic experience, and to the contemporary eye it contrasts favourably with the blurred and swooning pre-Raphaelitism in which Yeats drenched his narrative. Austin Clarke's human figures and their passions are also real. The heroine Grainne awakes from her bridal bed 'in sweating heat', and when her husband grows impatient for the hunt she pulls him 'on her hot breasts until he slept'(5–6). How different she is from Yeats's Niamh, that radiant assemblage of 'citron colour' and 'stormy sunset' who 'wavered' in 'white vesture', 'glimmering crimson' and 'pearl-pale shell'.[5] Diarmuid too is in sharp contrast to the dreamy hero-poet, Oisin: his love for 'Grainne, the golden, the beautiful'(17) has all the intensity of warrior passion, but the hero is unusually conscious of beauty's transience, and his vision is well conveyed in the crude, earthy sensuousness of Clarke's language:

> Tell that the clay of age could never creep
> Coldly around my heart nor did I sit
> Mumbling at a turf fire half blind with rheum
> And maybe groping feebly in the gloom
> Finger the leather breasts of a dumb hag
> That once, O Gods, was the white Grainne.(10)

Quite clearly this is not the voice of a mere follower of tradition. In 1917 this note of sexual frankness was new in Irish poetry; a similar candour does not fully emerge in the poetry of Yeats for another decade, to foreshadow the great poet's fury at the thought of old age. In Austin Clarke it sprang from two sources: from the primitive demands of the original tale, and from a strong antecedent bias in the poet's sensibility. Sexual candour is just as prominent in Clarke's latest work as it was then, though it has now come under a sterner formal discipline. His next three books embody epic redactions: *The Fires of Baal* (1921) concerns a biblical theme, *The Sword of the West* (1921) and *The Cattledrive in Connaught* (1925) form part of an uncompleted plan to re-tell the *Táin*. In all three the same tone of erotic frankness persists. In the biblical tale he writes

> Of Nubian eunuchs, their naked paramours
> And men, lust-maddened, taken in strange sin[6]

and so on. So much so that he seems—if we are to judge by his autobiography—to have disquieted the authorities of University College Dublin, where he was employed as an assistant lecturer. When he added to his misdemeanours by contracting a secular marriage, his appointment was not renewed. This was the first, perhaps, of the series of blows which have helped to build up Clarke's bitterness with his country's Establishment. He attributed the move to clerical influence, and it may be significant that his anticlericalist feeling finds expression almost immediately in his writings. Finally it was largely responsible for his going to England in 1922 where he remained for twelve years, living mostly by his pen.

This removal cost him a great deal. In his fascinating autobiography, *Twice Round the Black Church* (1962), he recalls that when he left, Dublin seemed to be on the brink of a new literary movement, with Yeats and A.E. as high priests in residence:

I did so with regret for, despite the emotional havoc of the Civil War and its immediate miseries, the Irish Free State was just beginning and hopes for a small independent literature with its own standards of criticism were astir.[7]

But he remained true to his vocation as a cultural separatist, and his creative imagination remained at home, moving up in history from the heroic to the medieval age. The heroic consciousness died in Irish literature in 1925 with *The Cattledrive in Connaught*. James Stephens, who had undertaken in prose the same task that Austin Clarke had attempted in verse, abandoned his enterprise after two volumes— *Deirdre* (1923), *In The Land of Youth* (1924)—and followed Clarke into exile. The 'terrible beauty' which the Rising had awakened was effectively demolished in the ugly bitterness of the Civil War. From that point on, in the hands of men like Joyce, Eimar O'Duffy, Darrell Figgis and Flann O'Brien, the Gaelic hero became a figure of fun. But Clarke did not turn his back on Irish material as, in effect, Stephens did. Instead he sought for and found a new frontier on Ireland's past, a territory which in his hands was to become subtly germane to her present. The discovery not only consolidated the literary but, in the same gesture, released the religious separatist in him:

One night I lay listening to the dreamiest sound in the world, the sound of our soft Irish rain in the trees between my window and the locked church. . . . For some months I had been thinking over our forgotten medieval Ireland when we almost had a religion of our own and had been searching for some image which would bring me other images. . . . In that inner silence, the image for which I had been groping came into my mind:

> Rainfall
> Was quiet as the turning of books
> In the holy schools at dawn.[8]

With this superlative evocation Austin Clarke opens his magic casement on the past, makes his imaginative leap across the centuries into Ireland of the Celtic Romanesque, what Padraic Colum has called 'the country native to his mind'. For the next thirty years the world of medieval monasticism is to dominate his mind and his work, forming the material and the background for seven plays, three prose romances and two tremendous volumes of verse, *Pilgrimage* (1929) and *Night and Morning* (1938). Why does he allow himself to become so dominated by this medieval world? Obviously if we can answer this question we shall come near the heart of this poet's curious and individual mystery.

The most obvious reason is that implied in his tendency towards separatism: a deeply religious man, he found himself repelled by the Victorian and Jansenistic version of Catholicism in which he was reared, and later, by what seemed to him an excessive clericalism in present-day Irish society. In a private letter to the present writer he states simply:

I wish we had a small church here as in Brittany, but we seem to have taken over, since the establishment of the Republic, the imperial and evangelical spirit of the British race.

This desire for national uniqueness in religion as well as art, accounts for some of his involvement in this particular era of the past. We shall see, in dealing with his more recent satires, how it accounts also for some of his dissatisfaction with the present. A second reason is that the scholar and the artist in him fell in love with the period. This monastic society, it will be remembered, produced a superb flourishing of native art: the chaste and intricate splendour of manuscript illumination as it survives, say, in the *Book of Kells*; the finesse and cunning of the metal-work as instanced in the Tara Brooch or the Ardagh Chalice; above all there was the delicate proportion of the Celtic-Romanesque architecture, as exemplified in Cormac's Chapel, still standing on the Rock of Cashel. (Cormac Mac Cuilleanain, the great ninth-century King-Bishop of Cashel, his celebrated bride Gormlai, and the exquisite chapel to which he gave his name, all loom large in Clarke's mind and work.) Here was a native religion[9] producing an indigenous art. What more perfect model could one hope to find for a modern movement to found a small national literature?

But there is a third motive, I believe, a reason which runs counter to the two already mentioned and which exemplifies the curious complexity, even ambivalence, of Austin Clarke's thought. At his deepest level he is a religious poet, and his most fundamental concern is for what he calls 'the drama of racial conscience'.[10] The phrase, which he uses in the notes to his *Later Poems* (1963),[11] seems to me to betray Clarke's underlying and perhaps unconscious intention in re-building this monastic world. He is not just trying to conjure up a perfect society—as he has often been accused of doing—and the proof of the matter is that the world he creates is, in fact, a dramatically imperfect society. It has its perfect side, the peaceful monasteries, the beauty of metal-work and art, of prayer and chant, but against them he is at pains to contrast frequent and startling manifestations of evil. Take that passage in *The Singing-Men at Cashel* when Cormac and Gormlai visit the famous monastic settlement at Glendalough. Surely here, one would think, was Clarke's vision of an ideal world: the scholarly king walking around the holy schools discoursing on theology and art with the churchmen; the young queen Gormlai spellbound before an illuminated page composed by 'holy men who had a hand in heaven' as she 'perceived the inner richness of religion and the murmur of Europe was about her'.[12] Here, epitomized, is the perfect society based on learning, chastity and grace—a small cenobitic church following its own native genius. And so, for a moment, it remains. Then as the young queen—still in her virginal state—waits alone outside the chapel, she is confronted by the obscene figure of the anchorite Malachi who has been tempted from his penances to spy on her with 'terrible eyes glittering'.[13] Austin Clarke is determined to impress this frightening creature on our minds, and he does so by means of relentless physical description and priapic symbolism. This tormented hermit, driven by sexual obsession and religious taboo, is the product of the same austere discipline as Cormac Mac Cuileanen who is in most respects Clarke's perfect man. Religious aberrations such as this occur frequently in these prose romances. In *The Bright Temptation* (1932) we are given a horrifying picture of Gleann Bolcan in Kerry, and its guilt-ridden inhabitants who have been 'crazied by scruples of conscience'[14] over the threshold of sanity to a condition of endless self-abuse. No bleaker vision can be imagined than this landscape of lost souls, broken beneath the fervours of his ideal religion. Quite clearly the poet has a purpose beyond romantic reconstruction of the past; and that purpose, I suggest, is suddenly revealed in his reference to the 'moral rigour which forbids passion in Ireland'[15]—something more than a striking use of the present graphic: it is clearly a submerged but deliberate comment on present-day Ireland, a passing gloss on the 'drama of racial conscience'. So also his mythological Young Woman of Beare in his poem of that name, digresses from her meditations on the flesh and the spirit to warn her counterparts of today to 'keep from [the] dance-hall'(166), 'obey the mission' and 'be modest in your clothes'(168). Obviously the poet is examining, from his own peculiar stance, the moral and religious structure of Ireland using history as his stalking-horse. The 'drama of racial conscience' is restlessly in progress.

It is easy, therefore, to see why this medieval stage appealed so strongly to him; there the drama raged in its full simplicity. His Romanesque world is one of Manichean extremes—extremes of austerity and sensuality, of learning and ignorance, of saintliness and profanity, of religious discipline and civic anarchy. These are the issues which have always exercised Austin Clarke's mind, and by dramatizing them in a remote, yet relevant, period of history he attempts to clarify them for himself. These are the issues which he sees momentously at work in modern Ireland complicated and intensified, perhaps, by the accretions of modern living. Again by viewing the basic principles at work on the medieval stage he can clarify them and point their relevance to the present scene. As will be seen with increasing emphasis, the poet's view of Ireland's spiritual condition is astringent and progressively satirical. This tendency was perhaps given new impetus when Ireland's newly-constituted censorship board banned successively these three romances. It was an especially bitter blow for a writer like Austin Clarke, who wrote about Ireland and for Ireland, to be thus partitioned from the only readers who could fully comprehend his message. It was their sexual outspokenness, of course, which got them banned and the decision merely served to confirm the poet in his growing distrust for Irish institutions, civil or religious. So in his 1938 volume, *Night and Morning*, we find him striking back with a devastating quatrain:

> Burn Ovid with the rest. Lovers will find
> A hedge-school for themselves and learn by heart
> All that the clergy banish from the mind,
> When hands are joined and head bows in the dark.[16]

This astringent little piece was one of his first excursions into overt satire: in the later volumes the satirical mode dominates. But in the lyric poetry of his middle period—*Pilgrimage* (1929), *Night and Morning* (1938)— he uses the historical objective correlative for a more personal and anguished dialogue. These two volumes contain his most intense and moving poems; in them is portrayed the search of an individual soul for clarity and peace. They reveal Austin Clarke as wrenched between the opposing demands of the flesh and spirit, of religious prohibition and intellectual freedom, between the dark legacy of the Fall and the alternative gaiety of paganism towards which the artist and the humanist in him incline.[17] These tensions are most clearly dramatized in the curious figure of Anier MacConglinne, the renegade clerical student who is the hero of his first poetic play, *The Son of Learning* (1927) and who sustains the hilarious sub-plot in *The Singing-Men at Cashel*. This wayward, irreverent culdee[18] is surely Clarke's 'alter ego'—a man who has thrown off the discipline of the Church, yet retains his clerical habit,[19] and finds himself irresistibly drawn to shrine and monastery; not always, be it said, with pious intent. In a dramatic lyric entitled 'The Straying Student' from the 1938 collection, this key character makes his final appearance. In it we see the student being tempted from the dull pieties of his youth by the pagan muse of poetry. The poem is worth dwelling on at length because it not only renders the cardinal tensions of Clarke's dilemma, but also because it exemplifies most of those technical innovations which impressed Donald Davie so forcibly.

Because these innovations derive from the metrical forms of classical Irish poetry, many have been inclined to regard them as incomprehensible to readers who cannot read Gaelic. Such a view is quite absurd. The technical problem that Austin Clarke sought to solve was the same that all modern poets face in dealing with the shortage of rhyme and the rigidity of metre in English poetry. In solving these problems he drew on his knowledge of the elaborate technical patterns of Irish prosody and it is his particular triumph that he has accommodated a number of these Gaelic devices to the traditional prosodic convention of English verse. This was not new: it had been done successfully but sporadically by Larminie, MacDonagh, Stephens and Farren. But Clarke is the only one who has made it his habitual method, formed it into the basis of a personal style and used it to point a new horizon for English poetic technique. Whether his example will be followed to any significant extent remains to be seen. It is already bearing fruit among Ireland's younger practitioners, and I hope to show in a moment that at least one good English poet has not ignored its possibilities.

In his notes to *Later Poems* he states his principles. The first is the extended use of assonance both in the place of rhyme and to reinforce the tonic word at the end of the line 'by a vowel-rhyme in the middle of the next line'.[20] This, he claims, 'takes the clapper from the bell of rhyme', and it can be seen in the first two lines quoted below where 'Inishmore' in the second is supported by 'holy' and 'blowing' in the first. More exciting and radical is his approach to the problem of double-rhyme:

'The natural lack of double-rhymes in English leads to an avoidance of words of more than one syllable at the end of the lyric line, except in blank alternation with rhyme. A movement constant in Continental languages is absent. But by cross-rhymes or vowel-rhyming, separately, one or more of the syllables of longer words, on or off accent, the difficulty may be turned: lovely and neglected words are advanced to the tonic place and divide their echoes.'[21] I shall take the liberty of pointing out some examples of the method in the following stanzas; the theme of the student's spiritual conflict speaks, in general, for itself:

> On a holy day when sails were blowing southward,
> A bishop sang the Mass at Inishmore,
> Men took one side, their wives were on the other
> But I heard the woman coming from the shore:
> And wild in despair my parents cried aloud
> For they saw the vision draw me to the doorway.[22]

A reader, coming unexpectedly on this stanza, is, I suggest, surprised by an unusual sense of melody and counterpoint which cannot be accounted for by rhyme or the more conventional euphonies of English verse. This music has been elaborately wrought. The pivotal device is the correspondence of the end-words in lines two, four and six. This is the pattern which, with intricate supporting echoes, remains constant throughout the poem. Thus the echo is from 'Inishmore' to 'shore' to 'doorway'. The tonic 'o' sound moves back along the word; the cruder clapper of rhyme has been deftly muted. On this basic framework the poet is free to spin an infinity of variations. Each line in this particular stanza has its own internal assonance: 'holy'/'blowing', 'sang'/'Mass', 'side'/'wives', 'woman'/'coming' (assonance on the accent, taking the place of double-rhyme), 'despair'/'parents' (a simultaneous cross-assonance on and off the accent where the words 'divide their echoes'). It is a characteristic mark of Celtic design, whether in lettering or metal-work, to have inter-weaving, serpentine patterns—the same motif of snake or bird constantly re-emerging and intertwining on brooch or manuscript. The same effect is paralleled in the interweave of vowel and consonant in Irish classical poetry and the same delicate effect of submerged melody is everywhere in the poetry of Austin Clarke. One has to search to find how a given effect has been achieved: here, for instance, the second syllable of 'doorway' is not thrown away—it is picked up by 'parents' and 'despair' in the previous line and again a word has 'divided its echoes'. Similarly 'southward' is picked up by 'aloud' as 'other' is by 'coming' and 'woman'.

I have analysed this stanza far beyond the point of pedantry in order to alert the reader to similar designs in the succeeding stanzas and indeed throughout Austin Clarke's work. In the third the student, having put the

religious restraints of childhood behind him, abandons himself to the
pagan ecstasy of the muse:

> I learned the prouder counsel of her throat,
> My mind was growing bold as light in Greece;
> And when in sleep her stirring limbs were shown,
> I blessed the noonday rock that knew no tree:
> And for an hour the mountain was her throne,
> Although her eyes were bright with mockery.(189)

Even if one were unaware of the internal felicities—which are considerable—
the chiselled perfection of the verse would indicate the hand of a master
craftsman. Now the student recalls how he was sent down from the Irish
seminary at Salamanca, the wonder of art having superseded the rigour
of theology:

> They say I was sent back from Salamanca
> And failed in logic, but I wrote her praise
> Nine times upon a college wall in France.
> She laid her hand at darkfall on my page
> That I might read the heavens in a glance
> And I knew every star the Moors have named.

In this—surely one of the most splendid stanzas in Irish poetry—he
manages an extra correspondence on the first, third and fifth lines; the
recurrent, submerged vocalic echo begins in 'say' and winds its serpentine
course until it emerges finally—like the snake's head—in 'named' at the
end. Semantically, too, the language is busily engaged. Note the calculated
vagueness of 'they say' and 'a college wall in France'—how the whole
world of ecclesiastical discipline is subtly elided from his consciousness,
and the usurping influence of artistic wonder is faded in. But with savage
irony the last stanza reveals that the student's triumph over the stifling
restraints of Catholicism is far from perfect; the legacy of an Irish
religious upbringing is not so easily dissipated. Will he be able to retain
his hold on the enchanted vision, will his great shameless pagan mistress
remain faithful?

> Awake or in my sleep, I have no peace now,
> Before the ball is struck, my breath has gone,
> And yet I tremble lest she may deceive me
> And leave me in this land, where every woman's son
> Must carry his own coffin and believe,
> In dread, all that the clergy teach the young.

Here, poised, is the dilemma which haunts Austin Clarke, and which makes
the poems of this middle period such painful reading: it is comparatively
easy for him to reject the Faith with his reason; not so easy to exorcise its
terror and its ardour from his soul. Here too the mask of the dramatic lyric

is torn off and the poet speaks of his own personal anguish. Even if the images of damnation—which haunt Clarke as they haunted Joyce—can be kept at bay during his waking hours, he is defenceless against them in his sleep. *Night and Morning* is bristling with nightmarish intimations of religious dread: references to 'The soul/That wakes me now at night',[23] the 'body's heat, anger of vein/[that] Bring madness in our sleep'.[24] And again, in a splendid and moving poem named 'Summer Lightning', he seems to see these terrible dreams as a possible threat to sanity:

> When sleep has shot the bolt and bar,
> And reason fails at midnight,
> Dreading that every thought at last
> Must stand in our own light
> Forever, sinning without end:
> I pity, in their pride
> And agony of wrong, the men
> In whom God's likeness died.(191)

Everywhere we find this sense of 'sinning without end', a load of irrational guilt which dogs him despite the humanistic reassurances of his reason. One must read *Twice Round the Black Church* to realize what a disastrous version of Catholicism he received both in his home and from a series of encounters with strange priests. A morbid terror of the flesh was thrust upon him and a concomitant certainty of damnation. It is fair to state that what the young Austin Clarke received and rejected was not a Catholic education, but an unusually pestilent mixture of Victorian and Jansenist prejudice, reinforced by contemporary, pseudo-medical superstitions about the dangers—especially to sanity—of self-abuse. It is also fair to say that such an education was not untypical of its time and place, though few responded to it with the acute sensitivity of the young Austin Clarke. So, in a poem such as 'Tenebrae' he protests, with especial reference to the anointing at Confirmation, against the burden of the Christian mysteries:

> O when the forehead is too young,
> Those centuries of mortal anguish,
> Dabbed by a consecrated thumb
> That crumbles into dust, will bring
> Despair with all that we can know;
> And there is nothing left to sing,
> Remembering our innocence.(183)

This sacramental mystery has, in Austin Clarke's view, unseated the reason, stultified the voice of logic, replaced childhood innocence with unmerited guilt; it has glorified the Christian notion of humility at the expense of human dignity:

Before the truth was hid in torment,
With nothing but his mortal pride,
I dreamed of every joy on earth
And shamed the angel at my side.[25]

Along with happiness, freedom of intellect has been abolished by 'the misery of common faith';[26] 'the holy rage of argument' has been stilled:

All saints have had their day at last,
But thought still lives in pain.[27]

To Austin Clarke

. . . pride and intellect
Were cast below, when God revealed
A heaven for this earth.[28]

Everywhere liturgical imagery and diction are deployed to register an anti-devotional message:

. . . yet who dare pray
If all in reason should be lost,
The agony of man betrayed
At every station of the cross?[29]

Here the traditional meaning of the Catholic ceremony is tellingly reversed.

*Night and Morning* (1938), from which most of these quotations have been taken, was the first of the Tower Press Booklets, published from his own Bridge Press, Templeogue. It may not be wholly coincidental that two years previously Yeats had edited *The Oxford Book of Modern Verse* and had brutally and inexplicably excluded Clarke. It was a totally unjust decision considering that he included no less than seventeen of Gogarty's light and rather facile lyrics.[30] It was enough to embitter the meekest writer, and Clarke with his extreme sensitivity must have felt it acutely. It was to be the last time he would expose himself unarmed before his countrymen. From that point on he retires into his tent, not to sulk, but to sharpen the weapons of satire. Since then he has held Ireland at spear-point.

*Ancient Lights* (1955) is a transitional volume: in it one can see the poet in movement from the region of personal anguish to that of public satire. The satire which is almost exclusively anti-clericalist conveys, with all its trenchancy and bitterness, a sense of spiritual release. The catharsis for which he had looked in vain has somehow been achieved; the frowning circle of fiends has been exorcised, and he can now turn his pitiless vision outwards upon his countrymen. In the great title poem 'Ancient Lights' the accumulated load of guilt and suffering is stated and purged in eloquent catharsis; it deals with the childhood agony of a bad confession, an obsessional theme already treated at length in his autobiography[31] and in at least one earlier poem 'Repentance':

> For I had made a bad confession
> Once, feared to name in ugly box
> The growing pains of flesh.(186)

In 'Ancient Lights' the painful scene is re-enacted with all its attendant shame, the youngster squirming under the priest's over-zealous inquisition:

> . . .Did I
> Take pleasure, when alone—how much—
> In a bad thought, immodest look
> Or worse, unnecessary touch?(199)

A touch of levity—characteristic of the later Austin Clarke—enters in the middle of the next stanza as the young boy tries to answer evasively, but the omnipresent horror re-establishes itself before it ends. Note too how the increase of flexibility and colloquialism smoothly manages the transitions:

> Closeted in the confessional,
> I put on flesh, so many years
> Were added to my own, attempted
> In vain to keep Dominican
> As much i' the dark as I was, mixing
> Whispered replies with his low words;
> Then shuddered past the crucifix,
> The feet so hammered, daubed-on blood-drip,
> Black with lip-scrimmage of the damned.

One of the constant marvels of Clarke's poetry is his gift of compression. Here a vast range of psychological experience, of mood, physical circumstance and event is conveyed in a single stanza. The tight, crabbed, elliptical constriction of the syntax reflects the dark confinement of the confessional as well as the clenched tension of the little boy's mind.

Now the poem moves to catharsis. Leaving the church one evening, the youngster finds his morbid guilt lifted by a sudden epiphany in which he becomes piercingly aware of nature's beneficence: in this quasi-mystical moment

> . . . the air opened
> On purpose. Nature read in a flutter
> An evening lesson above my head.

And later, when he is forced to take shelter from the rain in the doorway of the Protestant Black Church, his private symbol for anti-Protestant bigotry among other things, he finds himself suddenly free:

There, walled by heresy, my fears
Were solved. I had absolved myself:
Feast-day effulgence, as though I gained
For life a plenary indulgence.(200)

At this stage it is unnecessary to indicate the contribution made by the
quiet internal cadences ('solved'/'absolved', 'effulgence'/'indulgence');
more important, perhaps, is the sacramental imagery in which the entire
experience is rendered, and which continues less overtly in the final,
magnificent stanza:

The sun came out, new smoke flew up,
The gutters of the Black Church rang
With services. Waste water mocked
The ballcocks: down-pipes sparrowing,
And all around the spires of Dublin
Such swallowing in the air, such cowling
To keep high offices pure: I heard
From shore to shore, the iron gratings
Take half our heavens with a roar.(200–1)

This is the stanza with which Donald Davie, in his review, was most
powerfully impressed—'There are few poets now writing in English who
are capable of such a stanza, so continually inventive in detail yet so
sure of the total effect, so strenuous and surprising in diction yet running
so free, so much at ease yet so tightly organized.'[32] Again it is worth pausing
to examine the detail that has contributed to produce such a rich finality
of utterance. The prosody is Austin Clarke at his simplest: unrhymed
iambic dimeter reinforced by a flexible assonantal correspondence, on
and off the accent. Hence 'up' is answered by 'gutters', 'mocked' by
'ballcocks', 'around' by 'cowling', 'shore' by 'roar'; 'sparrowing' seeks
an extra and strenuous echo in 'swallowing'. The freedom of movement
which this simple pattern permits could not be achieved with conventional rhyme and end-stop. But the metrics are insignificant beside the
remarkable use of language and symbol. The simple descriptive impact
of the poem, the freshness with which it describes the sun coming out
after a cloud-burst, is so arresting that one might overlook the inner,
psychological process which it triggers and parallels. In its simplest terms
the young man who had been burdened with religious fear, 'walled by
heresy', is suddenly absolved and exalted by the—perhaps numinous—
experience of a tremendous rain-shower. Thus, when the 'gutters of the
Black Church rang/With services', the word 'services' carries a double
connotation—there are the religious services going on in the church and
being echoed over the city under 'spires' and 'cowlings'. (An essay might
be written on the associative potency of 'cowling' in the context. Most

obviously there is the monastic cowl beneath which the monk shelters, representing the indoor world of observance which the poet is running from, a world which in turn resists the miraculous outdoor 'services' of nature. Secondly the chimney cowl turns in the gale, in a sense frustrating the cleansing process of rain and wind; keeps the 'high offices' of ecclesiastical worship 'pure' by keeping out the elemental influence of nature. One assumes an irony on 'pure'.) On the other hand there are the services of nature, the rain and sun which with their 'feast-day effulgence' take on a sacramental significance. The young man in his moment of heightened perception sees in them nature's—and God's?—act of forgiveness. The rain-shower not only releases him from guilt, it removes the whole fear of damnation from his soul—thus the 'iron gratings', in more than one sense, 'take half our heavens with a roar'(201). In these 'iron gratings' the gates of hell as well as the vengeance of heaven are reduced to manageable form.

This powerful poem with its theme of spiritual release projects Austin Clarke into a new phase of creativity, and this phase is reflected in the poems which accompany it in the volume. These poems, mostly satires on modern Ireland, reveal that the poet has abandoned his objective correlative, and withdrawn from the medieval landscape. Now he confronts his experience in the first person, and grapples fiercely with the living scene around him. Indeed so minutely does he at times take issue with the events and values which surround him that some of the occasional satires are virtually incomprehensible to foreigners. Even Irish critics of a younger generation have echoed the complaint which Donald Davie embodied in his final comment on what he regards as 'the final paradox of the collection: that while it goes out of its way to be provincial in its presentation and range of subject matter, intrinsically—in technique—it is entirely purged of provincialism, and should be taken up into the tradition of English poetry wherever it is written.'[33] The paradox of Davie's own statement is that despite its generosity and right-mindedness it applies to Clarke's subject-matter the one word which is, perhaps, anathema. Austin Clarke's whole ambition has been to destroy the notion of provincialism in Irish art. His poetry is not provincial because Ireland is not a province; his is a metropolitan art, his style arduously built from native models, his material deliberately and exclusively Irish; his Catholicism even refuses to be called Roman—in so far as he can be categorized, he is a medieval Irish heretic. This is his importance: that he has refused to compromise with any facile notion of 'universality', and that by the sheer force of his genius he is succeeding. It may seem a perverse and eccentric attitude, but it must be recognized for what it is: a deliberate and consistent aesthetic doctrine. Yet it is encouraging to see that he has been persuaded to supply notes to his most recent publications so that now poems on such events as the assault of some Jehovah's Witnesses in Killaloe, the visit of a Papal Legate, a pronouncement by a theologian on birth-control, the erection and deposition of various religious and patriotic statues, can now be enjoyed in clarity by foreign readers. But the parochialism of his themes must not be over-stressed, especially as local experience can yield such a poignantly universal poem as 'The Envy of Poor Lovers' which I quote in full without gloss or comment:

> Pity poor lovers who may not do what they please
> With their kisses under a hedge, before a raindrop
> Unhouses it; and astir from wretched centuries,
> Bramble and briar remind them of the saints.
>
> Her envy is the curtain seen at night-time,
> Happy position that could change her name.
> His envy—clasp of the married whose thoughts can be alike,
> Whose nature flows without the blame or shame.
>
> Lying in the grass as if it were a sin
> To move, they hold each other's breath, tremble,
> Ready to share that ancient dread—-kisses begin
> Again—of Ireland keeping company with them.
>
> Think, children, of institutions mured above
> Your ignorance, where every look is veiled,
> State-paid to snatch away the folly of poor lovers
> For whom, it seems, the sacraments have failed.(205)

This is a perfect example of his delicate, scarcely audible vowel-rhyming, finely modulated to the tender contemplative quiet of the theme.

Though Austin Clarke was producing verse as fresh and alert as this in the fifties, he had still failed to attract the attention of the Irish reading public. It was too easy to dismiss him as an unquiet ghost wandered in from the mists of the Celtic Twilight to trouble the living scene. Kavanagh stood out in striking and exuberant contrast. Here was the voice of the real Ireland, a voice straight from the soil, speaking with the weight and urgency of a powerful social message. It was, and still is, impossible to ignore the earthy and searing power of *The Great Hunger*; and if Kavanagh had shown stamina commensurate with his genius, Clarke's achievement might have remained permanently in his shadow. But this is not to say that Clarke was totally eclipsed. He had always a following of perceptive and dedicated readers. Robert Farren, in *The Course of Irish Verse* (1948) lamented the fact that in Ireland 'he is almost solely a poet's poet (though that's not a title to be despised); while in England the very vanguard neglects his work'.[34] Yet, undeterred, Farren granted him twenty pages in his relatively small book. Two years later Benedict Kiely in his survey of *Modern Irish Fiction* (1950) stated unequivocally that 'Mr Clarke is today the greatest living Irish poet and one of the few writers still living in Ireland who could be described as a beneficent, encouraging influence'.[35] In 1956 Donald Davie saluted his achievement in terms already glanced at, and the publication of his *Later Poems* was described by the English critic, Charles Tomlinson, in *Poetry* (Chicago), as 'the literary event of 1961'. By 1963 Douglas Sealy, in a long and thorough essay in *The Dubliner* (Jan/Feb 1963), already referred to, asserted that Austin Clarke, in his middle period, 'had produced the richest verse of any Irishman of our age, not excepting Yeats.'[36] These statements might be taken as representing the rising graph of the poet's reputation over the past twelve years or so. The verdict, of course, is not unanimous. At least one Irish critic Basil Payne, himself a fine poet, in reviewing Kavanagh's *Collected Poems* (1964), declares Kavanagh to be 'Ireland's best living poet' while the English critic, A. Alvarez, in an otherwise tepid review of the same volume, regarded Kavanagh as 'the best poet that Ireland now has'.

The change in Austin Clarke's fortunes came when the Dolmen Press brought out *Later Poems* in 1961, incorporating in one volume the fugitive canon of the Tower Press Booklets. *Collected Plays* (1963) made available his eleven remarkable verse plays. But the event that confirmed his stature was the publication of a new book of poems, *Flight to Africa* (1963), at the age of sixty-seven. The volume exhibits such exuberance, variety and innovation that his junior poetic colleague John Montague was moved to describe Austin Clarke as Ireland's youngest poet. Clarke himself seems mildly astonished at this new access of creativity, as he states in the notes:

All the poems in this book, with the exception of three, are due, indirectly, to the patronage of a leading American University, which enabled me to visit Mount Parnassus. Shortly after my return, I experienced for ten weeks a continual, voluptuous state of mind during which the various pieces arrived with such joyful ease that I suspected some to be Greek gifts.[37]

From a technical point of view it is impossible to imagine how such highly wrought verse could have been the product of 'joyful ease'. If we discount the possibility of their being Greek gifts, we can only conclude that the poet has at last won complete mastery over his medium, that he made his own style. His 'Song of the Books', a free translation of a most intricate nineteenth-century Gaelic poem, is a staggering tour-de-force in that it follows the pattern of the original stroke by stroke. It exhibits the poet's style at its most adventurous and flexible; quite clearly the style itself is inimitable, but it offers rich possibilities for adaptation. Here is the first stanza, where the poet describes a storm on the coast of Kerry:

South-westerly gale fiddled in rigging;
Furled canvasses in foam-clap, twigged
The pulley-blocks. Billows were bigger.
    The clouds fell out.
In Madmen's Glen, snipe hit the grasses,
Rains in Tralee had towned their phantoms
While rocks were thrumming in the passes.
    Below a shout
Was whisper and among the boulders
    The frightened trout
Were hiding from the beaten coldness.
    Soon every snout
Was gone. The noises of new shingle
Along the coast had swept the Kingdom
Of Kerry, league by league, from Dingle
    In whirlabout.(310)

This could not for a moment be mistaken for the work of any other poet; even the eccentricities, gleeful but functional, are uniquely his own. It is unnecessary to labour or particularize the extraordinary verbal cunning of the texture, the skill with which each of the four movements within the stanza is supported on its own assonance, the sense of symmetry and wholeness which the reiterated spinal rhyme—'out', 'shout', 'trout', 'snout', 'whirlabout'—contributes. But the inventiveness of the language, the constant sense of wonder which each new echo triggers, the startling kinetic vigour of the verbs, the concreteness and particularity of the details—nautical, meteorological and natural—the total effect of thrilling contrapuntal vibration can only be accounted for by genius. And this stanzaic pattern is sustained without irregularity or monotony for an additional eighteen stanzas.

The kinetic power of Austin Clarke's language springs largely from his genius in coining new verbs; in everything he writes there is an energetic and muscular sense of movement, due chiefly to these verbal coinages. The reader observes people who 'unfobbed/The time', listens to 'the flood unclay the trees', sees from a plane the 'upsnowing' of the waves, or in a church a coffin 'trestled in the gloom'. The device is even more effective in his humorous pieces. In 'Guinness Was Bad For Me' Clarke hilariously traces the movements of an indefatigable and picaresque drunk who, night after night, went 'street-lamping towards his home in drizzle', 'ballasting by Westland Row'(278–9). Having thus frequently 'trousered' back to his wife in Dublin he goes to London's West End where he 'neoned from Square to Circus'; finally he comes home to Ireland by boat 'night-tumbling' and ends a thoroughly untidy existence being 'barbiturated in the big Asylum'(280). Less cruelly he images—

> Young wives unzipple near our Bridge,
> Suburbed, soon to be bigger again.[38]

and in a passage such as follows where he conveys, in less than seven lines, a comic impression of the Irish War of Independence, the Civil War, and the subsequent compromise with piosity and commercialism. The idiosyncrasy of the language is, of course, a function of the satire:

> Once they were heroes, each a lad
> On his own. They fought the tammed
> And shantered British, then they crammed
> Machine-guns, shot at each other from tombs,
> Old abbeys. Now in smoking-rooms
> Hallowers sign, the half-lost drink:
> Horse-killers, knights who of old salaamed
> Mahoun.[39]

But the ranging valiancy of his language carries its own hazard and sends the poet swerving into obscurity in the three final lines of this fragment. I think I follow his meaning, but I'm not sure. Here, for the record, is my interpretation. These men who fought with such verve have become craw-thumpers, 'Hallowers' who 'sign' i.e. make the sign of the Cross ostentatiously, in smoking-rooms while their less prosperous countrymen, 'the half-lost', for whom piety holds less comfort, take refuge in drink. These are the gallant fighters, 'knights', who once fought a holy war—'salaamed Mahoun'—with the zeal of the Moslem; now, cynically, they export Irish horses for slaughter to the Continent (an activity which in driving Clarke to articulate fury has presented him with a number of fine satires). I have not much confidence in this piece of exegesis; there is too much conjecture in it. If it is approximately accurate then the allusions make too much of a demand on the reader; from any point of view the reference to 'Mahoun' is too far-fetched to elicit a precise response. I believe that the poet's desire for concentration has carried him beyond normal communication. He is a difficult poet and his obscurity has been a primary obstacle in his slow progress towards recognition.

But if the semantic obscurity remains, the spiritual anguish which had previously accompanied it has, to a great extent, lifted. There is still pain, but, as we have already glimpsed, it is other people who suffer. Clarke has set himself up as the scourge of the Irish establishment, lay and clerical. There is hardly a movement on the landscape but feels the sting of his distinguished whiplash. The clergy are castigated for building new churches and seminaries, for neglecting their religious duties, for staffing State-run homes—voluntary—for unmarried mothers, for their social teaching, for surrounding the poet's house at Templeogue with religious convents, for going on foreign missions, for encouraging the erection of statues and grottoes, for their educational practices, even for their celibacy. Technically these poems are as great as anything he has done, but in them he has, in a sense, forsaken the great themes for the lesser. What in the past he had attacked frontally and totally he now attacks piecemeal, in its more trivial and vulnerable manifestations. If we seek for a consistency in his religious and clericalist themes, we must return to his stated distrust of over-organization and evangelism. Thus he makes savage fun of a well-known Irish-American cardinal visiting Ireland and rushing through a headlong schedule of civic gestures:

> Accept a learned gown, freedom
> Of ancient city, so many kissing
> His ring—God love him!—almost missed
> The waiting liner: that day in Cork
> Had hardly time for knife and fork.[40]

But at times one feels that the poet's anger is out of proportion to the provocation. We are perhaps more amused than sympathetic when he is awakened from sleep to the realization that

> The Fathers of the Holy Ghost had bought
> A bigger bell.[41]

In 'Loss of Strength,' a powerful poem from his 1957 collection, *Too Great a Vine*, he bitterly recalls the invasion of Continental orders which the Normans brought with them to supersede the native monasticism as 'The arch sprang wide for their Cistercians'(216) and national uniqueness was lost. Now it goes on:

> But time goes back. Monks, whom we praise now,
> Take down a castle, stone by stone,
> To make an abbey . . .

while the bulk of his exasperation is summed up in two lines from 'The Flock at Dawn'—*The Horse-Eaters* (1960)—when he tries to

> Forget that morning faith like the milk supplied
> In bottles comes to us now with clatter and jolt.(226)

Not since Voltaire has there been such a pungent and obsessive anti-clericalist.

His attack on the lay establishment is even more broadly based. The politicians are chastised for their subservience to the clergy, for the horse-trade, for neglecting the poor, for rebuilding the Abbey Theatre to a new design, for their neglect of Ireland's patriot dead, for censorship—even obscurely for providing hydro-electric power by harnessing the rivers and developing the bogs. These attacks are in the main brilliantly and woundingly launched, but many of them seem to contradict each other; others—to those who know the facts—are grossly unfair. The reader finds himself searching for the poet's satiric norm, the standard by which all of these charges can be judged consistent and meaningful. In 'A Simple Tale', for instance, he indicts the social system that fails to find employment for an Irish labourer, Pat Rourke, who is subsequently brought to court for neglecting his children, the children being ordered to Industrial Schools. It is a sad story, resulting at base from Ireland's failure to provide work for its citizens. But when an Irish statesman goes to Africa to open up trade with that continent, he is vigorously mocked; and when the Government develop the Shannon and the bogs they are accused abstrusely of violence to nature. The move to attract German industrialists to set up factories here is equally condemned. One is therefore inclined to ask Clarke how *he* would solve the employment problem that produces tragedies like that of Pat Rourke. Again when the Abbey Theatre was almost irremediably damaged in a fire he opposes bitterly the decision to rebuild it as a well-equipped modern theatre, on the grounds that the old one was good enough for Yeats, Synge and Lady Gregory. Surely there is not another theatre person in Ireland—or outside it—who would agree either with the opinion or the reasoning that led to it.

I dwell on these points, not in an attempt to refute the poet's arguments but to draw attention to a specifically poetic concern—the distinction between satire and controversy. Surely true satire is incontrovertible, something that does not for a moment admit the possibility of disagreement. The true satirist, surely, embodies in his work an authority of utterance that enforces at least temporary acquiescence. The chief reason for this is that the great satirist applies himself to the more permanent and universal human failings. When Yeats attacked the reluctant patron of the Gallery, his own imitators, or the critics of Synge's *Playboy*, he lifted the theme in every case beyond the situation which occasioned it and produced satires on meanness, emulation and envy respectively. There is no such thing as a strictly occasional poem: to be a poem at all it must transcend its occasion. It is not poetically important whether Pope's Atticus is an accurate description of Addison. It is an accurate portrait of a recurrent human type and as such it will always be enjoyed even by those who know nothing of its contemporary relevance. That Pope appreciated the distinction is evident in the final couplet:

Who but must laugh, if such a man there be?
Who would not weep, if Atticus were he? (*Essay on Criticism*)

In other words the reader may decide for himself whether these charges apply to Addison, but he can have little doubt that they may be laid at the generic door of man. In this sense the portrait is incontrovertible. But too often Clarke writes controversy instead of satire. The moment a reader can stop for a moment and allow himself the thought: 'Yes, that's all very well, but there's another side to this story', the satirist has lost his hold on him; he has abdicated his satiric authority. One can frequently do this with Austin Clarke. Instead of pitching on the universal truth of a situation, he is likely to take up one side of a highly debatable issue and lavish his precious gifts in making a case for it. And so the incomparable brilliance of the writing is vitiated by the weakness of the argument.

Part of the problem is that Clarke has always existed on the fringe rather than the centre of society; in the strict sense his views are eccentric. And contrary to common prejudice the satirist ought to stand at the centre of society; his norm should be that which society recognizes without necessarily following. Dryden was a normal man of his time, Swift and Pope represented the accepted standards of the English Enlightenment; even Voltaire represented a whole submerged body of opinion in contemporary France, a substantial iceberg of which he and his fellow *philosophes* were but the visible peaks. But Austin Clarke, because of his highly personal and aggrieved vision, is almost totally out of sympathy with the received standards of his society. Strictly speaking he represents no-one beyond himself. Nor does he seem anxious to change his position. When questioned on his poetic practice by the late Robert Frost, Austin Clarke declared: 'I load myself with chains and try to get out of them.'[42] And there is, in his work, something of the frustrated anchorite, even of the spoiled priest. Indeed he expresses a good deal of his own predicament when he writes

They say I was sent back from Salamanca
And failed in logic . . .[43]

A sense of personal wrong has driven him to judge certain types of people—clerics, politicians—and their motives by standards so harsh that they seem to contradict both the humanitarian and the logician in him.

But it would be totally unjust to suggest that the bulk of his satire is squandered on unworthy themes. In such a poem as 'Street Game' his true satiric authority emerges, backed by the most formidable technique in modern English verse. The scene is the Dublin slums, but the theme is a universal one:

> . . . Last week I saw a marching band,
> Small Protestants in grey clothes, well-fed pairs
> Led by a Bible teacher, heard the noise
> Of boot-heel metal by bread-shop, sweet-shop, dairy,
> Scrap, turf, wood, coal-blocks. Suddenly Catholic joylets
> Darted from alleys, raggedy cherubs that dared them:
> 'Luk, feckin' bastards, swaddlers, feckin' bastards!'
> Too well they knew the words their mothers, fathers,
> Used. Silent, the foundlings marched along the street-path
> With clink of boot-heel metal. We have cast
> Them out. Devotion, come to the man-hole at last,
> Bawls: 'Feckin' bastards, swaddlers, feckin' bastards!'(256)

The specific charge of the satire is against the Catholicism of Dublin slum dwellers and their failure in charity. The charge cannot be denied: Dublin 'joylets'—what an inspired coinage!—will behave like this. But the poem transcends its local origins and finds its larger validity in the universal human weakness of bigotry and discrimination. The horror and the pity of it is not that it happened one day in Dublin, but that it happens every day in every city in the world where there are differences of race, religion or even class. On the technical side there is no doubt that his flexible pattern of vowel-rhymes give the lines a melody and a sense of fluid freedom impossible within the limits of traditional English prosody.

I am not certain that Austin Clarke is a great poet; that is a matter which must be left to more confident critics and then left to time. But I have no doubt that he is a great writer of verse, the greatest poetic crafts-man alive in the English-speaking world. It is as a technical innovator that he holds such relevance for the present decade. By his life-time of arduous experimentation with language and prosody he has found a new way out of the blind alley of rhyme, laid a highway across the desert of free verse. His example in the use of assonantal patterns, which I have tried to elucidate, could renew the apparatus of Anglo-American verse for a century to come. This achievement is even greater than his more insular apostolate of making viable a national poetic culture. It remains to be seen whether this life's work will bear fruit in the decades ahead. What is immediately important is that it be recognized now for the massive challenge it presents. In certain areas of contemporary English poetry I believe Clarke's example is already bearing fruit. In most of the suspected cases it is too soon for one to be certain that the 'influence' is not coincidental. But in one case, for reasons which will be immediately obvious, I have no doubt at all. I was amused and delighted to read a fine essay by Bernard Bergonzi[44] on the poetry of Donald Davie, in which he discussed stanzas like these from Davie's excellent poem 'New York in August':

Clammy, electric, torrid,
The nights bring no relief
At the latitude of Madrid.
Never the stir of a leaf.

Any night, as we went
Back, the children asleep,
To our bed in a loaned apartment,
Although I thought a deep. . .

Bergonzi made learned and altogether valid references to Pound, Joyce and William Carlos Williams; but I knew where that trick with 'torrid'/ 'Madrid' and 'went'/'apartment' came from. It is to be hoped that others as sensitive as he shall, in the years ahead, come to learn from the same master.

# NOTES

First published in *Studies*, Volume LIV, Winter 1965.

1 Donald Davie, review of Austin Clarke, *Ancient Lights: Poems and Satires* (Dublin: The Bridge Press), in *Irish Writing*, Number 34 (Spring 1956), p. 57.
2 *Ibid.*, p. 58.
3 Robert Farren, *The Course of Irish Verse* (London: Sheed and Ward, 1948), p. 150.
4 Austin Clarke, *Collected Poems*, edited by Liam Miller (Dublin: Dolmen Press, 1974; London: Oxford University Press, 1974), p. 4. [Editor's Note. For consistency and ease of reference, all citations of Austin Clarke's poetry are made from this edition, unless otherwise noted.]
5 *The Variorum Edition of the Poems of W.B. Yeats*, edited by Peter Allt and Russell K. Alspach (New York: Macmillan, 1957), pp. 3–4.
6 The lines in *Collected Poems* read:

> Of Nubian eunuchs, holding their black toys,
> And men, lust-maddened, taken in strange sin . . . (p. 52)

7 Austin Clarke, *Twice Round the Black Church* (London: Routledge and Kegan Paul, 1962; Dublin: Moytura Press, 1990), Chapter 10, p. 93.
8 *Ibid.*, Chapter 13, p. 140.
9 The 'uniqueness' of this Irish church can be easily over-stressed. Fr. Francis Shaw, Professor of Early and Medieval Irish at University College Dublin, takes up the question in *Studies*, Volume LII (Summer 1963), and concludes that the Early Irish Christians 'become holy not by being odd, but by being orthodox, not by being Celtic, but by being Catholic.'
10 Douglas Sealy, in a perceptive essay in *The Dubliner* (January/February 1963), has already pointed to this motivating theme in Austin Clarke's consciousness.
11 Austin Clarke, *Later Poems* (Dublin: Dolmen Press, 1961), p. 90.
12 Austin Clarke, *The Singing-Men at Cashel* (London: George Allen and Unwin, 1936), p. 98.
13 *Ibid.*, p. 108.
14 Austin Clarke, *The Bright Temptation* (1932; rev. ed. Dublin: Dolmen Press, 1965), p. 221.

15  *Ibid.*, p. 221.
16  'Penal Law', Austin Clarke, *Collected Poems*, p. 189.
17  In *Twice Round the Black Church*, Chapter 10, p. 102, he records how he 'yielded to the Celtic Paganism of our literary revival . . .'.
18  'Culdee', from Gaelic 'céile Dé', 'lover of God'.
19  See p. 32 of *Twice Round the Black Church* for Austin Clarke's amusing adventures in his 'wide-brimmed black hat and grave suit':
    'I am used to being mistaken for a priest, and so I am no longer embarrassed by the respect paid to my cloth.'
20  Austin Clarke, *Later Poems*, p. 89.
21  *Ibid.*, p. 89.
22  'The Straying Student', Austin Clarke, *Collected Poems*, p. 188.
23  'Repentance', *ibid.*, p. 186.
24  'No Recompense', *ibid.*, p. 190.
25  'Mortal Pride', *ibid.*, p. 182.
26  'The Jewels', *ibid.*, p. 192.
27  'Night and Morning', *ibid.*, pp. 181–2.
28  'Martha Blake', *ibid.*, p. 185.
29  'Tenebrae', *ibid.*, p. 183.
30  See *The Oxford Book of Modern Verse 1892–1935*, chosen by W.B. Yeats (Oxford at the Clarendon Press, 1936).
31  Austin Clarke, *Twice Round the Black Church*, Chapter 12, pp. 124–39.
32  Donald Davie, review of Austin Clarke, *Ancient Lights*, in *Irish Writing*, Number 34 (Spring 1956), p. 58.
33  *Ibid.*, p. 58.
34  Robert Farren, *The Course of Irish Verse*, p. 147.
35  Benedict Kiely, *Modern Irish Fiction* (Dublin: Golden Eagle Books, 1950).
36  Three valuable essays on Austin Clarke are also to be found in *The Celtic Cross: Studies in Irish Culture and Literature*, edited by Ray B. Browne, William John Roscelli and Richard Loftus (Purdue University Studies, 1964; reprinted New York: Arno Press, 1970): George Brandon Saul, 'The Poetry of Austin Clarke'; Maurice Harmon, 'The Later Poetry of Austin Clarke', William John Roscelli, 'The Private Pilgrimage of Austin Clarke'.
37  Austin Clarke, *Flight to Africa and Other Poems* (Dublin: Dolmen Press, 1963), p. 125.
38  'Midnight in Templeogue', Austin Clarke, *Collected Poems*, p. 281.
39  'Flight to Africa', *ibid.*, p. 254.
40  'Irish-American Dignitary', *ibid.*, p. 221.
41  'An Early Start', *ibid.*, p. 203.
42  'Notes', Austin Clarke, *Later Poems* (Dublin: Dolmen Press, 1961), p. 89.
43  'The Straying Student', Austin Clarke, *Collected Poems*, p. 189.
44  In *The Critical Quarterly*, Volume 4, Number 4 (Winter 1962).

# 14

# That Childhood Country: Extracts from a Biography of Patrick Kavanagh

I was sent to school at four. I didn't want to go, for I had heard stories of Miss Cassidy, the principal teacher, and the assistant, Miss Moore. Once I had caught a glimpse of Miss Cassidy walking to her school, and I didn't ever want to see her again. She had a bundle of yellow canes, with crooks on them, under her arm, and she looked like a girl that could use them for all they were worth. . . .

'Miss Moore,' George Maguire said once, 'she could cut cowld iron with her tongue.' George was my friend; he put nicknames on the teachers and advised me not to go to school. He called Miss Cassidy 'Sally' and Miss Moore 'Cutty'.[1]

One of my sisters dragged me into the school. I was wearing the pink bib.[2]

On his first day young Kavanagh fell foul of the system, and seems never to have recovered from its effects. A little girl spilled ink over him and Miss Cassidy sent him out to wash his hands. Failing to see the bucket of water placed outside the door for such purposes, he wandered off and got lost, throwing school and parish into turmoil until he was found sitting in a cranny beneath a nearby bridge. Even when he had graduated from the pink bib to trousers, his progress never seems to have matched his intelligence. In the family Commonplace Book his sister Lucy records that 'at Kednaminsha school he gave much trouble by disobedience'.[3] His own account records little educational gain apart from the passive absorption of poetry, songs and hymns.

The characterization of his two teachers in Chapter Three of *The Green Fool* is unusually curt and perfunctory for Kavanagh's autobiographical style. In the first place Miss Cassidy—'Miss Sally' because of the sally rods she wielded—is given her actual name in the book, probably because there were none of her relatives living in the neighbourhood when the book was published. Her assistant, Miss Agnew—whose family is still prominent in nearby Co. Louth—is called Miss Moore because of her passion for Moore's Melodies which, as singing mistress, she implanted in the poet's memory.

The fact that Miss Cassidy used her bundle of canes to such cruel effect may have motivated Kavanagh to portray her with these crude brush strokes: 'a big woman with a heavy, coarse face . . .' who wore in winter 'heavy hob-nailed boots of my father's making'.[4] When she put a nickname on Patrick, and his father accosted her about it in the roadway, she 'went down on her two knees in the gutter and cried for mercy'.[5] Miss Agnew, by contrast 'thin and wiry',[6] escapes with less criticism but no real credit.

Patrick thought himself a 'bright pupil' yet he was regularly administered seven or eight slaps on each hand 'and on top of that maybe a bonus of a box on the ear or—it is quite true—an ungracious kick on the behind.'[7] Barbarous as this sounds to modern sensibility it was typical enough of Irish primary education around 1910, and for some decades later. Kavanagh records that Miss Cassidy liked Kavanagh's father because he never protested against corporal punishment at school. The poet's only serious reproach against his father is that the latter not only condoned these beatings in the school but inflicted similar punishment on his elder son at home. In retrospect Patrick, according to Peter, 'took a more caustic view of their relationship, objecting to those beatings as psychologically damaging and unworthy of a father'.[8] Perhaps this is why his recollection of his teachers is so unrelentingly hostile.

The objective facts about the teachers suggest that they were not just conscientious and efficient within the norms of the time, but in some respects outstanding. Though neither had been to teacher training college, Miss Cassidy in 1903 had won the coveted 'Carlyle and Blake Premium', awarded 'for the special recognition of distinguished merit shown by teachers as school-keepers'.[9] The Department of Education records show that Kednaminsha School under their regime was rated highly for efficiency, attendance, the state of preparation of the pupils, all the measurable criteria that school inspectors record in their reports. The recollections of former pupils still living give a picture of a strict insistence on reading aloud, learning by rote, handwriting, catechism, poetry recitation, singing, sacred and profane. It is entirely typical of the period that self-expression was encouraged only within the stereotype of conventional essays and that the spirit of inquiry was directed only along the most orthodox channels.

The evidence of Patrick's copybooks reveal Miss Cassidy as a conscientious but pedantic teacher of English. When her pupil rises to a purple passage on 'the blazen orb just sinking below the horizon' as 'the golden strata of clouds appear on the Western sky' she offers no applause, uninterestingly corrects 'blazen' to 'blazing'. She evinces a consistent dislike for the subjunctive mood, as if reining him back with her corrections from any thoughts on how things might be, to how things are. Yet the exercises she sets him in formal grammar are comprehensive, intelligently performed and corrected. The passages she sets him for transcription and precis on 'rule', 'knighthood' and 'sensibility' as well as those introducing 'new words'—'The English House of Commons is the prototype of all assemblies that meet to govern nations'—are shrewdly aimed at the moral sensibility of the future citizen. Patrick's essays are therefore more remarkable for their elegance and correctness than for their originality. Yet a hint of the future nature poet flashes out of his essay on 'Gardens':

The vegetable garden possesses a hidden beauty. No-one can see this beauty except a lover of nature. He can see beauty in everything. He can see the finger of God even in a nettle.

While Miss Cassidy lodged locally during the working week—she went home to Tiercorck, Co. Meath, for weekends and vacations—and walked to school, Miss Agnew lived five miles away at Courtbane and cycled to Kednaminsha every morning, in all weathers. She came from a family of teachers, could play the harmonium and had a fine singing voice. She had charge of the junior classes and taught singing throughout the school. The door between the two classrooms was kept open, so that the activities of the several grades continued simultaneously. This method, universal throughout the small schools of rural Ireland down to the 1960s, meant that the brighter of the younger pupils had learned in advance much of what they were later to be taught in the senior classes. Young Kavanagh with his bright intelligence, retentive memory and the store of precocious knowledge gleaned from his father's conversation over the workbench, had probably exhausted the school's potential well before his final year.

Patrick was not promoted to the sixth grade, though he claims in *The Green Fool* that he was, locating himself among the 'play-boys . . . inscribing with pen-knives our names or initials'[10] on their desks in the back row. In fact his companions here are those unpromoted scholars who were doomed to spend their last two years in the fifth class.

There is a sense of lost opportunities in a valedictory remark by the ageing Miss Cassidy on the occasion of another pupil of hers going on to secondary school:

'Oh, Patrick,' she said with all the pathos and sympathy of a sick woman, 'if *you* could get to high school you'd leave them all far behind.' She spoke her heart to mine for a half-hour. I cannot remember the actual words she said. She spoke brokenly, appealingly, wistfully.[11]

The poet does not recall being moved by her words, but feeling instinctually that 'in the chinks between her cracked speech there was the intuitive wisdom of a woman' and that she believed in him.

The advances of his imaginative growth which he attributes directly to his schooling derive from a number of epiphanies, moral and poetic: a little girl who confessed to a meal of 'praties and gravy' when the rest of the class lied to the teacher about their dinners of 'potatoes, meat and vegetables'; he thought her honesty 'a pearl of great price . . . so pitiful, so beautiful';[12] the hymn with which the school always ended, 'Hail, Queen of Heaven'—'I am sure that Queen has prayed for me and has guided my wanderings';[13] a moment when during a geography lesson he heard a girl in the next room recite Mangan's 'Vision of Connacht in the Thirteenth Century'—when he felt 'rapt to that golden time in which poets are born'.[14] From this moment of rapture, we gather, he entered upon his life-long romance with poetry.

*Tarry Flynn,* Kavanagh's autobiographical novel, opens with these sentences:

'Where the devil did I put me cap? Did any of you see my cap?' Tarry Flynn was standing on a stool searching on the top of the dresser. He lifted an old school book that lay in the dust of the dresser-top and temporarily suspending the search for his cap was taking a quick glance at the tattered pages.[15]

This gesture when the young farmer forgets his cares to lose himself in a school text, the only books he actually owned in those early years, is entirely typical both of Tarry and his creator. The two competing English text-books of the period were the *Royal Reader* series issued in six volumes by Nelson in 1872, and later the *School and College Series* edited by that prominent literary Jesuit, friend of Yeats and A.E., Father Thomas A. Finlay, which were launched in 1878. The literary content of both series was, as his younger brother Peter was to witness, far richer than that of the English primers prescribed by the new state after 1922. They contained extracts from the great masters of literature, Shakespeare to Tennyson, which formed the basis for exercises in recitation, comprehension, grammar and vocabulary. The last generation of pupils taught from these text-books could produce from memory passages of remarkable length from Swift, Pope, Goldsmith, Burke, Wordsworth, Scott or Cowper, which, they might ruefully claim, the national teachers had 'beaten into them'.

Kednaminsha school used both series and it is likely that Patrick Kavanagh would have handled every volume, seeing that most of his siblings worked their way through the school's six grades. In *The Green Fool* he mentions as special early enthusiasms Longfellow's 'My Lost Youth', Tennyson's 'Locksley Hall', Scott's 'Lady of the Lake' and Pope's ubiquitous 'Essay in Criticism'—excerpts from all of which appear in Finlay's texts. In the Advanced Book of his series there are two less hackneyed pieces invoked by the hero of *Tarry Flynn* in his more meditative moments. Two lines from 'The Night' by Adelaide Proctor occur in Chapter Seven:

> He began to hum a poem that was in one of his school books.
>
> Oh the summer night has a smile of light
> As she sits on her sapphire throne.[16]

More dramatically at the opening of Chapter Eight the hero reads five lines from 'Under Violets' by Oliver Wendell Holmes and the narrative goes on to confide that the 'bottom of the page which contained this poem was encrusted with dried cow-dung and the pages were stuck together in the same way. Tarry shoved the old book between the rafters and the galvanized roof of the horse stable, and completed the buttoning of his trousers.'[17] Another less usual poem from this Advanced Book in the series, 'The Midnight Mail' by Samuel K. Cowan, gets a passing reference in an article written by Kavanagh for the *RTV Guide* (10 June 1966). Eliza Cook who is mentioned in Tarry Flynn's book of phrenology was represented in most junior schoolbooks including the Royal Reader series down to the 1950s.

The importance of these school readers to the poet's developing imagination would be hard to exaggerate. Not only were they the chief intellectual furniture of his mind but they probably confirmed him in his taste for anthologies. These he devoured and committed to memory. There is a well-vouched anecdote of John F. Kennedy's presidential tour of Ireland in 1963. The usual group of literati, John Ryan, Anthony Cronin, John Jordan among them, were in McDaid's pub, listening to one of Kennedy's speeches over the air. When he came to mention the Irish-American poet John Boyle O'Reilly, the company, never having heard of O'Reilly, looked at each other blankly. The voice of Kavanagh, who didn't bother to look up, intoned 'He's in t'Oxford Book'. Anthony Cronin recalls that:

He had an enormous love for the Irish sub-culture represented by schoolbook poems and ballads and some of the poems in the schoolbooks he had airs to and would sing: 'The Burial of Sir John Moore', 'Lord Ullin's Daughter', and Richard Dalton Williams's 'From a Munster Vale They Brought Her'. He had a perfect ear and was delighted to sing in the right company and on the right occasion.[18]

But while echoes of this childhood reading are to be sensed in Kavanagh's early lyrics, it is a measure of his independence that the nature poetry of his maturity owes little or nothing to the nature poetry of Collins, Coleridge, Keats or Tennyson, all of whom figure in these anthologies. And when he came to adapt Pope to his satiric purposes in 'The Paddiad' he avoided the heroic couplet so favoured by the schoolbooks and settled for blind rhymes and jazzy tetrameters:

> Hypodermics sourpiss loaded
> Are squirted at our foolish poet.[19]

His affection for the sonnet, however, may well have been triggered by Finlay's witty account of the form in his essay 'Various Kinds of Poetry' in the Sixth Reader (1902). Before presenting the pupil with Wordsworth's 'Scorn not the Sonnet', the editor prints a comic specimen of the form by a J.P. Collier, which exemplifies the rules of sonnet composition as it proceeds:

> These rhymes, said I, I never can complete,
>     And found the second quatrain half-way done!
> If now the triplets had but all their feet
>     These first two quatrains pretty well might run.

There can be little doubt that a detail in the Jesuit's essay 'What is Poetry?', in the same volume, provided the inspiration for Kavanagh's self-defining sonnet, 'Primrose'. In it Finlay defines the poetic faculty as an ability to 'discern the beauty of things around us and above us', citing the examples of Robert Burns who turns up a daisy with his ploughshare and exclaims:

> Wee modest, crimson tipped flower,
> Thou'st met me in an evil hour;
> For I maun crush amang the staure
> Thy slender stem.

Finlay uses this example to assert that the 'poet is, therefore, a seer—a seer of the beautiful', and goes on:

But he is more than this. He is able not only to see the beautiful as the actual world shows it—blurred, disfigured, and in many ways imperfect; he is also able to form in his mind an image or picture of what it would be without the imperfections and disfigurements. He is able to create for himself the form of beauty which corresponds to its perfect idea, to form as it is said, the ideal of that beauty.

Twenty years after reading that passage, Kavanagh wrote 'Primrose' almost to its prescription:

> Upon a bank I sat, a child made seer
> Of one small primrose flowering in my mind.
> Better than wealth it is, said I, to find
> One small page of Truth's manuscript made clear.
> I looked at Christ transfigured without fear—
> The light was very beautiful and kind,
> And where the Holy Ghost in flame had signed
> I read it through the lenses of a tear.
> And then my sight grew dim, I could not see
> The primrose that had lighted me to Heaven,
> And there was but the shadow of a tree
> Ghostly among the stars. The years that pass
> Like tired soldiers nevermore have given
> Moments to see wonders in the grass.[20]

Notwithstanding a possible intervention by Wordsworth's 'splendour in the grass' in the last line, the poem evinces the Christian mysticism—suggested in Finlay's prescription—that characterizes Kavanagh's most intense lyrics throughout his career. Published in *The Dublin Magazine* (October 1936) in the first year of his Dublin exile, it records a moment when only the remembered childhood epiphany can console him for present deprivation and lost innocence—what Eamon Grennan[21] was to characterize as 'the poet as Exile from Eden', Kavanagh's first significant poetic phase. The recovery of that lost vision was to be the great adventure of his third phase, exemplified in the life-affirming lyrics of *Come Dance with Kitty Stobling* (1960).

But the omnipresence of the Holy Ghost as source of created beauty and poetic inspiration is obviously derived from the intensity with which Catholic doctrine was taught and received in that enclosed homogeneous community. Whereas most of his schoolmates, as they grew up, seem to have taken religion easily enough as part of their mental stock-in-trade, Kavanagh—in some ways akin to the young James Joyce—took its doctrines with intense seriousness, especially the cult of Mary, the Virgin Mother, and the allied mystery of the Incarnation, the Word made Flesh.

The Catholicism that dominated the life of the Inniskeen of Kavanagh's childhood was a product of the 'Devotional Revolution' set in train by the first Vatican Council under Pope Pius IX who, among other daring strokes, consecrated the entire world to the Sacred Heart. His dispensation enjoined strict, weekly attendance at Mass, encouraged frequent confession and communion, instilled a strong sense of 'mortal sin'. Under Cardinal Paul Cullen the Irish church embraced this devotional and regimented version of religious faith and practice. Yearly or biannual 'missions' or retreats were organized in the parishes to which priests from the preaching orders—Passionist, Redemptorist, Dominican—would come to reinforce the faith of the people with exhortations and menaces, on the practice of the virtues (especially chastity) and the consequences of sin, including the impending reality of external punishment for those who did not adhere to the practices of the one true church.

This mental universe had much in common with that of the young James Joyce, but with significant differences. It was of course more primitive, less intellectual, ultimately less threatening. Kavanagh's account of the Mission in *Tarry Flynn* reveals brilliantly how much of the religious solemnity was deflected by the people in their rural scepticism, superstition and material self-interest. The mission, like the courthouse, catered to a sense of the theatrical, which was reinforced by pagan traditions that still, in Kavanagh's schooldays, defied the authority of the official church. There is no more vivid example of its operation, of the psychic atmosphere of the region and Kavanagh's place in it, than Chapter Six of *The Green Fool* in which a neighbour, Paddy Corbett, calls at the house to take young Patrick and his mother on the annual 'unofficial' pilgrimage to Lady Well.

A thunderstorm breaks as the party is about to set out:

Paddy Corbett, though a man of much physical courage, was afraid of lightning and ghosts. He crouched in a corner of our kitchen, praying: 'O Holy Mother of God, protect us.' My father kept working away at the boots right in front of the window, a dangerous place. I looked out watching the beautiful shapes and colours of the electrified elements.

'That was anchor lightning that time,' I said.

'Christ of Almighty, d'ye hear that fella?' Corbett exclaimed from his safe place behind the dresser.

'Fork,' I cried exultantly.

Holy Mary, save us from the bloody fool that is tempting God,' cried Corbett. I continued naming the lightning flashes as they signed themselves in radiant letters in the darkened page of sky, and each time Corbett groaned.

At the bottom of our garden the limb of a tall poplar crashed.

'The house is split in two,' Corbett shouted.

'You're a woeful coward,' my father said to him.

'It's right to fear God,' my mother said.[22]

While not losing sight of the semi-fictional nature of the narrative we can sense an authentic variety of metaphysical response to the lightning. Patrick and his father share the scientific view of the phenomenon, the son adding a poetic dimension to his father's stoical commonsense, as nature— not the Holy Ghost this time—makes its signature on the sky. Corbett, the less enlightened neighbour, reacts with peasant superstition. The mother, quietly holding the middle ground, sensibly composes the differences.

A similar range of attitudes towards the human and the divine are revealed as the pilgrims approach the holy well:

All the vicinity of the Well was packed with pilgrims. Like the mediaeval pilgrims very probably; some were going round on their bare knees making the stations, some others were doing a bit of courting under the pilgrim cloak. There was a rowdy element, too, pegging clods at the prayers and shouting. A few knots of men were arguing politics. I overheard two fellows making a deal over a horse.[23]

As they wait for the waters of the well to rise, the narrative voice explains:

There were no priests or monks or any official religious there. The priests didn't like the Well and tried to discourage the pilgrimages. They said it was a pagan well from which the old Fianians drank in the savage heroic days. The peasant folk didn't mind the priests. They believed that Saint Bridget washed her feet in it, and not Finn MacCoole.[24]

As the chapter concludes with the author's own homely reflections on the day's outing and its various significance, we get a pretty definitive glimpse of his relation to the community, the culture, the universe:

Our Lady was a real lady and human, she was not displeased, I knew, because some who pilgrimed in Her [*sic*] name were doubters and some cynics and a lot [of] vulgar sightseers. She is kind and no doubt she enjoyed the comic twists in the pageant round Lady Well.[25]

Patrick's schooldays which had begun at the age of four in June 1909 ended in June 1918 towards the end of his fourteenth year. He had made his First Confession and Communion at the age of six, recalling in adult life that his sins had not 'weighed heavily on my soul'. He seems to have been confirmed in June 1913—Confirmation occurred in three-year cycles—because he was permitted to stand as god-father for his sister Celia in 1913 and again for his only brother Peter in 1916. For this role Confirmation is prerequisite. While at school he also acted, with no great skill, as altar-boy for at least one of the priests, Father McElroy. In *The Green Fool* he records, ruefully, how years later, at Mass in Drumeatton, a Latin response came automatically to his lips:

The priest turned round. '*Dominus vobiscum,*' he murmured.
'*Et cum spiritu tuo,*' I answered involuntarily, remembering my Mass-serving days.
'Ye should be a priest,' a fellow remarked.
'Would you go to hell,' I said.[26]

While a priestly sense of the poet's vocation was to characterize his mature life, his young manhood was shadowed by an enforced celibacy endured and maintained by the pressure of family loyalty, social convention and religious precept. The theme of unwanted celibacy, stoically borne, becomes an obsessive concern in his poetry and fiction, receiving its most poignant orchestration in his long poem, 'The Great Hunger'. Yet the sexual side of Kavanagh's life from the beginning is altogether mysterious, accessible only by means of secondary sources. The privacy with which he conducted his love life in later years is matched only by the reticence of his surviving friends, most of whom insist that they don't actually know.

For the early Monaghan years the situation of his two young men, Tarry and Eusebius, in *Tarry Flynn* seems, in the light of other evidence, to fit their creator—'both more than twenty-seven in those enthusiastic years of nineteen hundred and thirty-five, yet neither had as much as kissed a girl.'[27] In school the catechism which was 'hammered into' the pupils in preparation for Confirmation had this to say about lust:

What is lust?
It is the desire of committing the sin of the flesh.
May one be guilty of the sin without committing the foul action?
Yes: the filthy sin is committed not only in the action: but also when one looks to, listens to, looks or thinks with pleasure on anything that may excite it.

Recalling this definition of sexual sin in *Collected Pruse* he declares this reference to the 'foul act' heretical, deploring that 'disease in the body of Irish society' for which 'the young priests sent out by Maynooth are not free from blame.'[28] On the other hand he and his friends seem to have had no doubt as to the facts of life, and their reaction to a sexual pervert they meet in the roadway seems to have been far less anguished than that of young Joyce a generation earlier. The strange man asks them for a pin to secure 'his immodest trousers':

Then he rose and accompanied us along the road. He gave us beans and explained how he had fallen into McGeogh's garden. When Larry left us to run home with his school-bag, the man with the torn trousers did. . . .

What exactly he did is not described—any more than in Joyce's 'An Encounter'—but the narrator reckons that it is worth 'a year in gaol'. The children 'make a great laugh about the business'. The girls wonder whether they should tell it to the priest, but they decide not to, on the grounds that there were too many people inclined 'to confess everybody's sins but their own'.[29]

Thus, a typical child of his time and place, strangely innocent yet curiously street-wise, backward in terms of the great world yet possessing a coherent universe of his own, Patrick Kavanagh completed the only formal schooling he was ever to receive at the age of fourteen in Inniskeen on 15 June 1918.

Patrick Kavanagh was ten years of age when a sequence of enormous changes came upon the world, Ireland, his own community at Inniskeen. The Great War sent tremors through the land, subtly changing patterns of thought and life that impinged gradually on the consciousness of the young poet. His growth to awareness ran parallel to a national awakening, not just the return of patriotic atavisms—expressed in the Easter Rising, the War of Independence, and the Civil War—but a slow stirring of modernism in a world that had been almost medieval in its essential rhythms. This sense of modernism took mundane as well as elaborate forms.

At the outbreak of the Great War his father acted with his customary shrewdness, immediately ordering supplies of coal, flour, leather, cobbler's spriggs and rivets, before the prices soared. A period of plenty came to the Inniskeen countryside, enabling the Kavanaghs to rent, on the eleven month system, an acre of land on the neighbouring Rocksavage Estate which they used to grow potatoes and turnips. The progress of the war was keenly followed by the Kavanagh household and endlessly discussed with its daily visitors. There were 'village statesmen [who] talked with looks profound.' The informed intelligence of James Kavanagh continued to dominate conversation, expanding the political horizons of his eldest son.

A new map of Europe appeared on the classroom wall at school affording Patrick some moments of glory as he demonstrated, in the presence of inspectors, his precocious knowledge of the conflict, the terminology of war, the name of 'every general on both sides'.[30] On a visit to the Dundalk egg-and-butter market he witnessed, moved and puzzled, the soldiers of the town's garrison marching off to the Front to the cheers, tears and recriminations of the local people. Inniskeen itself, because no-one there felt the requisite poverty or patriotism, seems to have produced no cannon fodder for the generals.

At the age of ten Patrick, for all his knowledge of the European conflict, was probably less conscious of certain local events that were to have especial significance for County Monaghan. The Bill granting Home Rule to Ireland was at last signed into law by King George V, at the insistence of Asquith's Liberal Government, on 18 September, 1914. The measure was bitterly opposed by the Protestant Unionists who had already formed the Ulster Volunteers to resist it in arms. The nationalists had responded by founding the Irish Volunteers—who were to rise two years later in the Rebellion of Easter 1916. The outbreak of the Great War brought about a postponement of Home Rule with the proviso that a number of northern counties might be partitioned off from the new state in order to accommodate the Northern Unionists who equated Home Rule with 'Rome Rule'.

Monaghan, with its large Protestant minority, was one of the frontier counties; and when partition was finally introduced, seven eventful years later, that Unionist minority in Monaghan was to find itself uneasily part of the Irish Free State. By 1914, however, the Ulster Volunteers were well organised in Co. Monaghan and heavily armed. After the Larne gun-running adventure of 25 April, 1914, it is estimated that there were at least 650 rifles in the hands of their units throughout Monaghan. The Irish Volunteers were inaugurated in Monaghan at a meeting convened by Thomas Toal, a passionate Home Ruler and Chairman of the County Council, in January 1914. Units were rapidly formed all over the county, one at Inniskeen. By June of that year it is estimated there were 5,000 men organized into active units throughout the county. By comparison with their Unionist opponents—who enjoyed the tacit approval of the police—they were comparatively ill-armed, possessing by the end of 1914 about 250 assorted rifles and virtually no ammunition. The old hostility between the Ancient Order of Hibernians and the Orange Order—which had hitherto expressed itself in faction fights with stones and cudgels—had nevertheless been given a more ominous turn, and would probably have resulted in significant violence were it not for the outbreak of World War One.

The issue of conscription, ironically, served to defuse the tension. The more conservative branches and members of the Volunteers followed John Redmond and his Irish Party in their support for the British war effort. When Eoin MacNeill, Chief-of-Staff of the Irish Volunteers, announced their anti-recruitment campaign he was condemned by the Monaghan Ancient Order of Hibernians on 27 October, 1914. The Inniskeen Branch of the Irish Volunteers supported this line, passing, on 27 December 1914, a strongly worded resolution to Eoin MacNeill condemning him for creating 'disunion in the ranks of the Volunteers'.[31] The majority of branches in Co. Monaghan supported this view, and apart from occasional disorder at recruiting meetings, an uneasy peace persisted in the region up to the Rising of 1916.

The Easter Rising of 1916, and the traumatic sequel in which its leaders were summarily tried and executed, occurred when Patrick Kavanagh was aged twelve, still too young in his rural backwater to be directly affected. Then Redmond's Party which still represented Ireland at Westminster was challenged and defeated by Sinn Féin, now the political arm of the Volunteers, in the General Election of December 1918. On the constitutional level the elected candidates refused to sit in Westminster. On the revolutionary level the secret Irish Republican Brotherhood which had infiltrated the Volunteers and masterminded the 1916 Rising was busily organizing cells or circles throughout the country, and this activity had its appeal both to idealist and hooligan alike among the rural youth. Kavanagh, now aged fourteen, was coming to a new sense of political awareness.

A chapter of *The Green Fool* entitled 'Patriotism' finds him a fascinated eye-witness to the new politics in action. It is the General Election of 1918 and he is watching the Ancient Order of Hibernians, righteous champions of the old Parliamentary Party—and veterans of many a faction-fight with the Orangemen—confronting the forces of Sinn Féin. The Hibernians are bearing aloft a banner with St Patrick on one side and St Colmcille on the other and wielding 'thick ash-plants, and blackthorns with knobs on them as big as horse-chestnuts: they held the sticks by the wrong end for walking with, but the right end for a fight.'[32]

Opposing them was a 'younger and less savagely determined-looking body of men . . . with hurleys on their shoulders', the Sinn Féiners. The fixing of the votes by the republican returning officers—'they were bringing supporters for the cause from the graveyard'[33]—and the pitched battle in the street that followed, were probably typical of the scene throughout the country, Ireland's new men prevailing in both encounters.

Though his father was a 'supporter of the old order', Patrick recalls that he himself 'fought hard during those hectic and glorious days expounding all I knew of the Sinn Féin policy'[34] though being often told that he didn't count because he was too young to vote. He was conscious that it 'was more than a mere election', that it was 'the battle of youth and the New Ireland versus the old men and the old servitude'.[35] Later in the year Kavanagh and a friend attempted to join the IRA guerilla unit being formed in the parish but were turned down because of their youth. Yet, in the wisdom of hindsight, Kavanagh judged this period, despite its 'loud glory and movement', among the 'lost years'[36] of his life.

Then came the declaration of an Irish Republic by the Sinn Féin Parliament at the Mansion House, Dublin, in January 1919, followed immediately by the War of Independence. This bloody period, involving the notorious Black-and-Tans, ended with the Anglo-Irish Treaty concluded on the Irish side by Arthur Griffith and Michael Collins in December 1921. Kavanagh, therefore, had just turned eighteen when the Irish Free State—together with the partitioned six counties of Northern Ireland—came painfully into being.

Co. Monaghan was specially affected. The Protestant population continued to regard the Royal Irish Constabulary as the true custodians of law and order, while the Catholic nationalists increasingly gave their allegiance to the newly formed, plain-clothes republican police with their Sinn Féin courts of justice. When arms raids were carried out by the RIC and the military, Protestants were suspected—often correctly—of passing information to the Crown authorities. After a series of thwarted raids and ambushes, the Monaghan Volunteers determined upon a calamitous plan to surprise the houses of Loyalists throughout the county with a view to seizing their privately held arms. On 31 August 1920 scores of houses were attacked. The raiders suffered almost as many casualties as they inflicted—at least four of their number were killed—few arms were taken, and a chain of bitter reprisals was the inevitable consequence.

Even more divisive was the trade boycott imposed on the Loyalist traders throughout the county. In April and May of 1920 northern units of the Volunteers attacked and burnt tax offices and police barracks in Belfast and several towns throughout the six Counties. In July of that year armed Orangemen retaliated by driving Catholic workers out of the shipyards, building-firms and engineering works of Belfast. In the sectarian rioting Catholic houses, businesses, churches, convents and monasteries in Belfast and the neighbouring towns were looted and burned with con-siderable loss of life. Seán MacEntee, Dail member for South Monaghan— later a prominent minister in many Fianna Fáil governments—proposed in the House on 6 August 1920 a boycott of goods from Belfast and a withdrawal of money from banks with headquarters in that city. When this boycott was enforced throughout Monaghan it exacerbated an already tense situation. Tension was increased when trains bearing Northern supplies were raided, derailed and in one instance, set on fire. It is remarkable that this climate of relentless sectarian strife left such little lasting effect on the sensibility of the young Kavanagh. His future prose is not without its visible, mostly rueful, religious prejudices; even less is he attracted to the desperate glories of nationalism.

The Irish Civil War, which began in April 1922 and raged on until April 1923, divided the country's population into the factions which were eventually to shape the present parliamentary parties. The 'Republicans', who refused to accept the compromises involved in the twenty-six-county Ireland, evolved into the present Fianna Fáil. The more constitutional 'Free Staters' who had negotiated that treaty eventually became Fine Gael.

James Kavanagh, with his hard-won, frugal sufficiency, was by circumstance as well as natural bent, a man of constitutional tendency—in as far as he let his politics show at all. Certainly he had his hands full keeping his wayward, romantic son out of trouble during that anarchic period of Irish history:

While I was being initiated into the secret guild of the Cobblers the Treaty was signed. Father read it from the paper. I was upstairs putting on my trousers at the time. I was mad, I was disappointed.

'It's betrayal,' I shouted down. 'Ireland has been let down by Griffith.'

And so it was betrayal of the rising generation that hadn't had a fight. I wanted a fight. I had missed the Black and Tans scrap and now it seemed we were in for the monotony of peace.[37]

Celia Kavanagh's memoir of her brother in *Lapped Furrows* begins by recording how his father 'guarded him most jealously fearing he might get into the wrong company' during those five years or so which came to be known as the 'Troubles'. She recalls that his companions would come to the house in the winter evenings, whistling for him to come out and join them:

Most times he managed to get going with them but on some occasions he had to go out and tell them he couldn't go—not too easy a task to face the jeers of his less disciplined companions. On one occasion when he did get to the village there was a raid on the Post Office with general looting. Patrick arrived home with a flashlamp, but he had to return it the following morning after getting an unmerciful walloping with an old umbrella, the while my mother cried, 'oh James, oh James you'll hurt him.' By the time the beating ended Patrick was only too glad to get out of the house to return the flashlamp.[38]

The raid in question was clearly part of no political programme, more a symptom of the current breakdown of law and order—at least in those areas of the parish beyond the sway of James Kavanagh's umbrella.

In a chapter of *The Green Fool* significantly entitled 'The Outlaws', Patrick describes without apparent remorse a series of similar escapades, beginning on the night of 8 December 1922—the Feast of the Immaculate Conception—when 'my career as a young gangster touched the high spot, fused and went out.'[39]

In the first of these adventures he and his companions tour the parish as 'Mummers'—a word and concept that will attain metaphorical force in his later poetry. Mumming is a form of folk drama, introduced to Ireland from England in the seventeenth century, flourishing largely along the east coast from Wexford to Antrim. Its form seems identical with the mumming rituals performed in Thomas Hardy's *Return of the Native,* involving a cast of characters drawn from history and folk myth. In Monaghan the characters might include St Patrick, Oliver Cromwell, Robert Emmet, together with Beelzebub, the Strawman, Johnny Funny who collected the money and Doctor Brown, who usually carried a medicine bottle. In the Louth-Monaghan area the Mummers tended to call upon the more prosperous houses during the winter months, on the nights of religious festivals, at Christmastide or at wedding celebrations. The characters had speaking parts in rude dramas which would usually climax in a mock battle with Cromwell being thrown out of the house.

On the night of the adventure Kavanagh plays the part of the Doctor. The youths move from house to house repaying the hospitality of their hosts with insolence, mayhem and eventually the theft of a side of bacon from a farmer's kitchen. They quarrel over the money collected, splitting it eventually on political lines, after which the 'Free Staters turned for home, the Republicans continued ahead.'[40] Kavanagh, still of the Republican persuasion, goes on with his cronies towards the main object of the night, a raid on King's—in real life Kelly's—public house.

The raiders force the pub door with a coulter wrenched from a neighbour's plough, rifle the till and make off with a number of whiskey bottles. The three coins snatched by Patrick turn out to be duds, the bottom of a pub's till being, as he discovers, 'the home of bad money'.[41] The 'whiskey' proves equally spurious—coloured water kept on shelves above the bar for display. The raiders manage a shambling getaway and Patrick arrives home just before the household rises. Though everyone in the townland seems to have known the culprits Patrick was not incriminated, and his father seems to have been kept in happy ignorance of his eldest son's night-time delinquency. Patrick rounds out his account of the escapade with these significant glosses:

That was the only 'stunt' of that nature in which I was a participant. I should have mentioned earlier that 'stunt' was the word for doings like this.[42]

The public house is still in the ownership of the Kelly family who recall the 'stunt' and Kavanagh's part in it as an amusing item of oral tradition. The episode, now as then, is ascribed to wildness and high spirits rather than to any political or criminal intent. Its ignominious failure, the irony of the empty bottles and false coins, viewed in tranquil retrospect, lend an endearing innocence to the felony.

It seems that in later years Kavanagh continued as their customer at Kelly's. He was noted for his assiduous reading of newspapers at the bar—dropping each page on the floor when he had exhausted its contents, for the general hauteur of his disposition, and for his tendency to converse largely in dogmatic pronouncements to which he seldom invited either opposition or assent. This in time was to become part of his style and posture in Dublin and London.

His few sporadic forays as a republican guerilla, Kavanagh does not include under the heading of 'stunts', though the anarchic spirit in which he undertook them seems little different. He claims to have 'got a kick' out of cutting the telegraph wires along the railway line. He is not present, however, when three of his colleagues 'commandeer' a car and are 'put up against the wall of the Dundalk Gaol and shot'. A sceptical side of his nature—together with his father's powerful influence—withheld him from total commitment to that, or any political cause. That same, ironical, side of his nature permitted him to pose as a republican policeman and intimidate a crooked roulette-player into slipping him a bribe in Carrickmacross; and to relish the momentary glamour of being mistaken for a desperado when 'four gunmen' visited him at the Carrickmacross Fever Hospital where he was a patient in 1923—'The stage was set for a hero and the worshippers were all ready to kneel.'[43] Like O'Casey's Davoren he enjoyed being 'the shadow of a gunman'. Like O'Casey he never got seriously embroiled in the patriot game. Unlike O'Casey, however, he was never drawn towards it as a theme. That is part of his strange individuality among the writers of his generation.

Most of Patrick's time, especially in the winter, was spent at home with his father who had apprenticed him to the cobbler's trade at the end of his schooling. Though he had no marked aptitude for the craft, he acquired enough skill to make a passable pair of shoes and to carry out every kind of reasonable repair. Between them father and son made a steady income especially during the years of the Great War when new shoes were expensive and hard to come by. Working so close together forged a strong bond between the two men and generated in the son a respect and affection closer even than that which he felt for his mother. Their most passionate theme was the world to come, so that they made a pact by which the first to die would return from the undiscovered country with information for the survivor.

James Kavanagh was fiery, acerbic and impatient, but never moody. His physical attacks on Patrick were therefore forgiven at the time, though sometimes resented and deplored in long-term retrospect. His powerful intelligence, well-stocked mind and artistic temperament—he played the melodeon superbly—were a source of continual fascination and a perfect foil for the son's vivid, wayward curiosity. In Celia's opinion their relationship 'went beyond the ordinary relationship of father and son. They were spirits alike'.[44] The father's influence, while he retained his faculties, was more than a match for the night-time distractions of the outside world, and a guarantee that only the more worthy distractions were entertained with any visible regularity.

Among these were the Gaelic League classes which Patrick attended around 1918 at Inniskeen village, and later at Drumlusty school. He seems to have achieved some competence in the Irish language, though he was always sceptical about its possible revival and kept a healthy distance from its more rabid enthusiasts. Peter Kavanagh may be right when he suggests that his brother went to these classes more for the girls he might meet there than for the language. In 1918 Patrick joined the newly formed Inniskeen Pipers Band and, under the instruction of one Dick Keelan, became, at least according to Peter, a 'tolerable piper'.[45] His less reverent younger sister Lucy, however, confides to the family's commonplace book at the time that Patrick

received private tuition from Mr Dick Keelan of Corduff in the art of music and proved to be a man of much brains. But Paddy, as he was called, was not to be a musician. He soon discarded the pipes and took to the art of cobbling.[46]

The poet himself recalled in later life that the band mastered only a single tune, 'The Dawning of the Day', whose melody he was to choose in 1946 for his most celebrated love song, 'On Raglan Road'.

One has to have lived in these rural parishes to realize the dramatic difference between the world of summer and of winter. In the days before rural electrification these little winding roads could be deeply and mysteriously dark before the moon was out. Lamps were lit in the cottages and farm-houses as early as four o'clock in the afternoon and doors were closed against the cold and darkness. While the country kitchens with their turf or coal fires were havens of cosiness and animation, a passion for ghost stories made the journey home, or even up the stairs to bed—as in the case of Celia Kavanagh—a nerve-testing ordeal. This was the time of year for 'stunts', when the more isolated houses felt especially vulnerable, and when the wilder or more delinquent young males could function with impunity.

Some houses were frequented by visiting neighbours, these were known as *céilí* [visiting] houses and Kavanagh's, the cobbler's, was one of them. The Kavanagh parents, by custom and perhaps inclination, except for one night of the year, never went céilíing. The mother, according to Peter, would go out once a year and 'collogue for half the day'[47] with the wife of Peter Hamill of nearby Dromore. James was always delighted when she came home having enjoyed her annual day out. It was to these Hamills that Patrick went to work in the summer months when neighbouring farmers swapped labour. Another neighbour with whom the Kavanaghs had a similar arrangement was Paddy Meegan. The character of the landscape and the activities of the people in the summer season contrasted so sharply with the winter that it might have been another country.

'The Great Hunger', Kavanagh's poem of sterility, enclosure and frustration, begins with a wintry potato-picking scene where 'crows gabble over worms and frogs',[48] and ends with the defeated hero, Patrick Maguire, standing in his doorway 'A ragged sculpture of the wind' while 'October creaks the rotted mattress,/The bedposts fall'.[49] *Tarry Flynn,* on the other hand, Kavanagh's novel of youth, passion and optimism, begins in summer and ends in a magical, autumnal countryside aglow with life, colour and promise. The lyric with which the novel closes reflects the young hero's mood as he sets out to work on a friendly neighbouring farm:

> On an apple-ripe September morning
> Through the mist-chill fields I went
> With a pitch-fork on my shoulder
> Less for use than for devilment.
>
> The threshing mill was set-up, I knew,
> In Cassidy's haggard last night,
> And we owed them a day at the threshing
> Since last year. O it was delight
>
> To be paying bills of laughter
> And chaffy gossip in kind
> With work thrown in to ballast
> The fantasy-soaring mind. . . .[50]

He remained an unambitious farmer, dreamy to the point of laziness, with schoolbooks hidden in every nook and cranny of the farm to solace the intervals of his work. The farm continued to prosper. That it did so was largely through the work of the mother—who tended to indulge her son, notwithstanding her continuous invective against the 'curse-o'-god books'—and the exertions of the long-suffering daughters who regarded Patrick's literary pretensions as an excuse for idleness.

# NOTES

First published in *Irish University Review*, Volume 22, Number 1, Special Issue: Essays and Poems in Honour of Maurice Harmon, edited by Christopher Murray (Spring/Summer 1992).

 1  Patrick Kavanagh, *The Green Fool* (1938; London: Martin Brian and O'Keefe, 1971), p. 31.
 2  *Ibid.*, p. 32.
 3  Kavanagh Papers, University College Dublin: Kav/B/160.
 4  Patrick Kavanagh, *The Green Fool*, p. 31.
 5  *Ibid.*, p. 36.
 6  *Ibid.*, p. 31.
 7  *Ibid.*, p. 33.
 8  I am indebted for this, as for much other information on Kavanagh's education, to Dr Una Agnew's brilliant pioneering research in her PhD thesis, 'The Word Made Flesh: Christian Mysticism in the Works of Patrick Kavanagh', 1991, for the Department of Anglo-Irish Literature and Drama, University College Dublin.
 9  Kavanagh Papers, UCD:Kav/B/162.
10  Patrick Kavanagh, *The Green Fool*, p. 107.
11  *Ibid.*, p. 110.
12  *Ibid.*, p. 38.
13  *Ibid.*, p. 35.
14  *Ibid.*, p. 108.
15  Patrick Kavanagh, *Tarry Flynn* (1948; London: Martin Brian and O'Keefe, 1972), p. 7.
16  *Ibid.*, p. 213.
17  *Ibid.*, p. 223.
18  Anthony Cronin, *Dead as Doornails* (Dublin: Dolmen Press, 1976), p. 92.
19  *Patrick Kavanagh: The Complete Poems*, edited by Peter Kavanagh (New York: Peter Kavanagh Hand Press, 1972; Newbridge: The Goldsmith Press, 1984), p. 214.
20  *Ibid.*, p. 70.
21  Eamon Grennan, 'A Piecemeal Meditation on Kavanagh's Poetry', *Patrick Kavanagh: Man and Poet*, edited by Peter Kavanagh (Orono: University of Maine, 1987; Newbridge: The Goldsmith Press, 1987), p. 34.
22  Patrick Kavanagh, *The Green Fool*, p. 64.
23  *Ibid.*, p. 67.
24  *Ibid.*, p. 68.
25  *Ibid.*, p. 70.
26  *Ibid.*, p. 235.
27  See Chapter Seven, Patrick Kavanagh, *The Green Fool*, pp. 190–222.
28  Patrick Kavanagh, *Collected Pruse* (London: MacGibbon and Kee, 1967), p. 258.
29  Patrick Kavanagh, *The Green Fool*, pp. 44–5.
30  *Ibid.*, p. 79.
31  Ann Carville, 'The Impact of Partition: A Case Study of County Monaghan, 1910–1926', an unpublished MA thesis for the Department of History, University College Galway, 1990, is a valuable source of information on political activity in County Monaghan at that time.
32  Patrick Kavanagh, *The Green Fool*, p. 138.
33  *Ibid.*, p. 139.
34  *Ibid.*, p. 138.
35  *Ibid.*, p. 137.
36  *Ibid.*, p. 143.
37  *Ibid.*, p. 168.
38  Celia Kavanagh, 'Patrick Kavanagh: A Memoir', *Lapped Furrows*, edited by Peter Kavanagh (New York: Peter Kavanagh Hand Press, 1969), p. 13.
39  Patrick Kavanagh, *The Green Fool*, p. 186.

40  *Ibid.*, p. 188.
41  *Ibid.*, p. 190.
42  *Ibid.*, p. 191.
43  *Ibid.*, p. 198.
44  *Lapped Furrows*, p. 3.
45  Peter Kavanagh, *Patrick Kavanagh Country* (The Curragh: The Goldsmith Press, no date), p. 43.
46  Kavanagh papers, UCD: Kav/B/160.
47  Personal conversation.
48  *Patrick Kavanagh: The Complete Poems*, p. 80.
49  *Ibid.*, p. 104.
50  Patrick Kavanagh, *Tarry Flynn*, pp. 255–6.

# 15

# Technique and Territory
# in Brendan Kennelly's
# Early Work

The first restless decade of Brendan Kennelly's work begins with a small book of verse, *Cast a Cold Eye* (1959) and ends with his edition of *The Penguin Book of Irish Verse* (1970). My survey stops just short of *Bread* (1971) where I feel he had definitively found his poetic voice. There are eleven volumes of original poetry between these dates as well as two novels. I read most and reviewed some of these volumes as they appeared, but didn't, as far as I can recall, meet the poet. My witness therefore is that of a contemporary looking back, and trying to recapture that decade when a generation of poets succeeding Clarke and Kavanagh explored their options

An initial assertion may be risked: that Kennelly was recklessly prolific during those early years; and that his publishers' faith in his precocious talent together with the user-friendly popularity of the poetry itself may have constituted a mixed blessing for his reputation, if not indeed for that talent itself. Now that his place is secure in the first rank of contemporary Irish poets, it may be forgivable to rehearse his sallies and retires during those formative ten years.

It will help if we glance at the field into which Kennelly first advances his standard. In 1959 Kavanagh's *A Soul for Sale* (1947), highly prized but out of print, could not be had in the bookshops for love or money. Kavanagh's iconoclastic personality still enlivened the Dublin scene, but few expected from him that poetic impact which *Come Dance with Kitty Stobling* was to deliver in 1960. Clarke's literary personality was muffled by his bumbling book reviews in *The Irish Times* every Saturday and his cosy, if highly professional, weekly poetry talks on Radio Éireann. In 1955 he broke a long silence with *Ancient Lights*—a slow fuse leading to the detonation of *Flight to Africa* (1963). I recall the late fifties as a dead time. Apart from the sporadic appearances of *Irish Writing* there were no literary magazines to speak of; the Abbey was in its Babylonian exile at the old Queen's Theatre, cranking out popular comedies; nothing much was happening, or so it seemed.

Then Liam Miller's Dolmen Press began to engender what we sensed might be a new stirring of imaginative life. Thomas Kinsella, six years Kennelly's senior, after a careful apprenticeship in translation from the Irish, produced his first substantial volume, *Another September* (1958). It struck a note of such authority that no young contemporary could look on it without dismay. John Montague, five years Kennelly's senior, published *Forms of Exile* (1958), a sophisticated book, quite free from the embarrassment of juvenilia.

Kennelly's first two volumes were also published by Dolmen, *Cast a Cold Eye* (1959) and *The Rain, The Moon* (1961), both collaborations with Rudi Holzapfel. They did not look like Dolmen publications, and they still don't. Kennelly made two more joint volumes with Holzapfel— a poet still publishing regularly who deserves more critical attention than he receives. Kennelly then proceeded alone, with the Dublin firm of Allen Figgis as his chief publisher. By 1963 Kinsella had produced his magisterial *Downstream*, Montague his formidable and original *Poisoned Lands*. Both writers, while maintaining their link with Dolmen, were taken up by British and American publishing houses. Richard Murphy— Kennelly's senior by nine years—whose first booklet, *The Last Galway Hooker* (1961), had appeared from Dolmen, now published, with Faber, *Sailing to an Island* (1963). The movement was under way.

Kennelly, loyal to his Dublin publisher and producing at a rate of knots, was still floundering gallantly among false starts: three books of verse— *Green Townlands, The Dark about Our Loves, Let Fall No Burning Leaf*—and a novel, *The Crooked Cross*, appeared in the years 1962–63. When Seamus Heaney, three years his junior, arrived on the scene with *Death of a Naturalist* (Faber, 1966), Kennelly had at last published a slender volume of poems, *My Dark Fathers* (1964), which could hold up its head in that rigorous company. It was the sixth of his poetry volumes. His first 'collected' was already in press, *Collection One: Getting up Early* (1966). Everyone was saying that Brendan Kennelly was publishing too much, and from where I now sit it looks as if everyone was right. But these things are not simple.

Kennelly has always had more gifts than were good for him. He was cursed from the start with a ready eloquence, a natural sense of rhythm, a mercurial range of sympathies and interests, a generous susceptibility to influence, inexhaustible energy and a Kerryman's conviction that there is nothing he cannot do. His original master, as the title of his first volume attests, was Yeats. He could pull a Yeatsian stroke—with a touch of Pearsean top-spin—without sweating. This is how 'The Mother' opens:

I have sent them out beyond the gaunt ridge
Of black stones above the thorny glen;
I have watched them go, my sons
Walking with the terrible strength of men
Who hated what they did.[1]

The control of rhythm in these lines is impressive. The poet is using the sonnet form and refusing its ready iambics. The movement of the thought is paced with admirable deliberation. But tone, idiom and image are incorrigibly derivative. Kennelly has not yet sensed the immense struggle with technical difficulties in which Yeats had engaged to achieve the rhythmic life of his poetry—the initial prose versions, the oral incantations, the slow curbing of easy eloquence in the successive drafts. Kennelly seems still to feel that a poet can write in 1961 of gaunt ridges, black stones, thorny glens and mothers sending sons out to break their terrible strength, and hope for the traditional poetic dividends. It is the strenuous conquest of that illusion over these early years that makes his development so fascinating.

But his virtuosity is endless. With a down-turn of the wrist he could produce another type of sonnet, energised apparently by the challenge of new subject and speech rhythm:

The negro smiled. His teeth showed white as snow,
His eyes stirred like the depths of muddy wine.
He said, 'Back in Jamaica, I use' go
Pick coconut every mawnin'. Sun shine
Early, five, six o'clock maybe, an' we
Spend all day hackin'. Jus' hackin', man. Fine
Time we have, though. Sometimes, under a tree,
I sleep during day, always watch for sign
Of sun. Man, it was warm. At night, I lie
On sand with girl. Toss her hair. Laugh. And we
Sing a li'l. Now, she have ten chil'ren. I
Know she ugly now, like my mother.' He
Paused and smiled again. 'My mother fine. But
Man, she think whole world made of coconut.'[2]

Few writers then or now could manage such a *tour de force*—Holzapfel maybe, but that's another story. Take the playful impudence of the rhymes throughout, and especially the rhymes of the sestet, lie/we, I/He—this is a sonnet!—and the delicious thump of the couplet. With the brisk ebb and flow of the negro's speech, the achieved presence of his personality, the reader is scarcely aware that the sonnet's formal demands are being nonchalantly fulfilled to the letter. We can only marvel at the versatility of the talent that produced this one-off prototype of a line immediately to be abandoned. The sonnet form, however, he never abandons. It remains one of the staples of Kennelly's mature art, coming on with magnum force ten years later in *Love Cry* (1972).

Among the many possible modes open to Kennelly in the late fifties was that of the *poète, doctus* or university wit. The campuses of the English-speaking world were swarming with clever young dons producing well-turned ambiguities in the manner of William Empson or W.H. Auden. He tried his hand at it and produced poems for the reader and lessons for himself which were to stand him in good stead when he came finally upon his own special mode and idiom. I often regret, for instance, that he has dropped 'Marlowe' from his later selections:

> There was a quarrel about the bill
> Of reckoning, not paid until
> Kit Marlowe, knifed above the eye
> By Ingram Frazier, finally
> Settled everything with his blood.
> The whole account was closed for good.[3]

Many of the later virtues are deployed here, as two registers of language are deftly counterpointed: the cool implications of bill, reckoning, settled, and account, nicely played off against the hotter importunities of knife and blood; the well-judged tension between syntax and metre as the single sentence moves to its routine yet appalled conclusion. In the third stanza there is a moment of sententiousness when Marlowe's spilt blood becomes 'the rich flux, preserved in art'. But it steadies itself and ends as a formidable poem. If Kennelly had gone on writing poems like 'Marlowe', picking his subjects coolly from the furniture of his academic day, he would have certainly achieved a respectable fame and a modest place in the anthologies. But he was playing for bigger stakes, and beginning to sense what they might be. But to distinguish purposeful beginning from energetic dawdling is very difficult in the early Kennelly. What, for instance, made him write in 1963 what I myself dismissed then as a 'sour little fable'[4] of his native Kerry, *The Crooked Cross*?

A tentative answer is not far to seek. He wanted to compose an allegorical tale on the state of Ireland, characterizing the country as a spiritual desert, enervated by unemployment, drained by emigration, sick with futility and self-hatred. So he invented a Kerry village called Deevna, shaped like a crooked cross—suitably recognizable as his home place, Ballylongford—where the people are crucified with a summer-long drought. After many failed stratagems they call in a sort of saviour figure called the Pope, Larry the Lad O'Gilligan. He has a passion for bottled stout and a gift for water-divining. He finds water, a shaft is drilled, the water spurts, and hope returns to Deevna—'they marvelled at it, as a thinking sinner would marvel at the prospect of finding his soul drenched in the grace of God'.[5]

The allegorical intention is easy to understand. The 'flight of earls' theme with its various threnody on the decay of rural Irish life in song, ballad, play and fiction was everywhere in the early sixties—from Bridie Gallagher's 'Goodbye, Johnny Dear' to John B. Keane's *Many Young Men of Twenty* and Brian Friel's *Philadelphia, Here I Come!* I wonder, however, if there wasn't a deeper personal exigency at the back of Kennelly's move, what might be termed the territorial interdiction. Harold Bloom has accustomed us to think of young poets struggling with giant predecessors in their genre in an attempt to get from out of their shadow and win personal space for their own developing art.[6] Yeats was, and still is, the commanding precursor for every modern Irish poet and we've seen a little of his impact on Kennelly.

But precursors can be even more troublesome when it comes to land-scape and territory. When, for instance, will a young English poet venture again into the Lake District after Wordsworth? a novelist into Wessex, after Hardy? an Irish poet into the drumlins of Monaghan, after Kavanagh? or into the boglands of County Derry, after Heaney? For how many centuries are Ben Bulben and Knocknarea to be no-go areas? And isn't it significant that Padraic Fallon could only reinter Loughrea and Gort in order to challenge the poetic expropriations of Yeats?

It is here we have to reckon with the figure of Bryan MacMahon. A decade before *The Crooked Cross*, MacMahon had published an idyllic account of a Kerry village entitled *Children of the Rainbow* (1952), a novel which may well have been in turn a rebuttal, in terms of cultural nationalism, of Brinsley MacNamara's fierce indictment of the Irish rural parish in *The Valley of the Squinting Windows* (1918) a generation before.

With hindsight we can trace in Kennelly's early work a homing back towards Kerry, the landscape of his birth, the real home of his imagination, only to find the place crowded with characters from Maurice Walsh, George Fitzmaurice, Eamon Kelly the seanchaí, but above all, the totemic figure of Bryan MacMahon with his plays, novels, short stories and ballads. MacMahon had written the priests, the tinkers, the fishermen, the publicans, the mountainy men and the townies of Friary Lane. I suspect that Kennelly was in near despair of securing a firm foothold on this territory when he thought of *The Crooked Cross*, a counter-truth showing the gangrenous underbelly of *Children of the Rainbow*.

As in MacMahon there is a cast of rural humours in *The Crooked Cross* with weirdly exotic names—Sheila Dark, Mickey Free, Goddy O'Girl, Naked Cully, Paddyo, All-or-nothin', the Dwarf and the One-eyed Palestine. As with MacMahon's Cloone the community is bound together with ties of kinship, avocation and trade. Like Cloone it even has an eccentric—Naked Cully—who never leaves his house. And like MacMahon, Kennelly provides a good deal of mating, drinking and brawling. There the resemblances end.

With MacMahon's characters there is an inner nobility, a romantic energy which is sensed to derive from a continuity with the past. This past at times assumes the status of a golden age, symbolized by song, dance, story, love of place, nature, religious faith, the poetry of an ancestral language. Under that ancestral pressure the present is characterized by neighbourliness, respect for the aged, a communal affection which embraces the crippled, the eccentric, the illegitimate, the retarded. In Kennelly's counter-truth the calamity of drought calls forth the anti-monial voices in full cry. Here's the womaniser, All-or-nothin', brooding on his illegitimate offspring:

Everybody in the village knew who they were, knew they would grow up known to all and sundry as "the three livin' bastards of All-or-nothin'." That would be hard on them. And, as surely as he stood there, All-or-nothin' knew what would happen to them. They would grow up dressed in shame; as children playing with other children they would hear their names bandied about as bastards. . . . (43)

And MacMahon's noble peasants suffer strange transmogrification in Kennelly. The drunken Dwarf walking down the street stumbles over an old mange-eaten sheepdog: 'The Dwarf kicked viciously at the creature's head, swore explosively and stumbled on, mumbling' (67). In the pub he finds himself in a trial of strength with the one-eyed Palestine:

They presented an odd, frightening sight as they sat facing each other on the floor of the public-house, the sweating Dwarf with his long yellow fangs and red face, and Palestine, eyes shut as he strained with all his drunken strength. A lacey ribbon of brown spittle lay on the Dwarf's chin as he heaved and struggled with body and soul. . . . (64–5)

There are admittedly more life-affirming spectacles in *The Crooked Cross* than these, but Kennelly's vision is closer to *Tobacco Row*—a contem-porary American best-seller banned from sale in Ireland—than to *Children of the Rainbow*. And the air is, of course, cleansed in the final chapters by the Pope's miraculous gift of water. But the author's creative exertion is barely redeemed by the book's merits. The heavy social and moral com-mentary at the end, leaning on a theme of emigration, is hardly justified by the novel's episodic central action:

Youth will never live long enough with total apathy, which is nothing less than a surly melancholy in the face of joy. The vital impulses of youth tend towards an exuberant robust gladness. . . . The tragic fact now was that nearly *all* the young people had left the village, turning their backs on their birthplace with a sigh of relief and a sense of hope. . . . The laws of nature sternly proclaim. . . . (134)

These are the gestures of a writer impatient to wrap up his fable and get back to something that really interests him. The blunt authorial intervention with its parade of verbal cliché and moral platitude does not bespeak a writer deeply interested in the craft of fiction. But *The Crooked Cross* has broken the territorial interdiction. It has planted the flag of his imagination in Kerry on his own terms.

MacMahon has a story, 'Chestnut and Jet', of a man and a stallion walking the streets of a Kerry town. It is a celebration of male power, of the stallion's 'chaotic blood', the 'treasured violence of his haunches'.[7] The people come out of their houses 'to see the grand man and the grand stallion'. A couple of years after writing *The Crooked Cross*, Kennelly writes one of his most assured poems, 'The Tamer', upon the same scenario, but curbing the inevitable machismo to the demands of a new emphasis, that of the power struggle between man and beast:

> The light rein links him to the brute;
> His head held high
> (As the stallion's is, the white
> Star splendid on the forehead),
> His hands stretch forth as though
> Supplicating the animal blood.[8]

But the man's supplication is his devious way to power and mastery. The poem as it proceeds subverts the romantic balance of MacMahon's 'grand man'/'grand stallion' to a ritual of taming and mastery:

> 'Hi, beast! Hi, beast!'—on many a road
> These words are said
> Gently to pacify the blood
> Unsubmissive still
> To the hand that soon bends power and pride
> To its own will.

In its nervous control of rhythm, its emotional restraint and its exactness of observation 'The Tamer' is, in its own right, a considerable poem. In a sonnet simply entitled 'The Stallion' the tone is pure Kennelly. Worshippers after Mass change from 'prayer to admiration' as they gaze on the splendour of 'the champing brute' outside the chapel gate; they then change to calculating the animal's worth, before shifting into a final, contemplative gear in which 'many a farmer there'

> Forgetting life and death and everything,
> Thinks of that stallion spraddled on a likely mare.[9]

Perhaps it was *The Crooked Cross* that enabled Kennelly's first great Kerry poem, 'My Dark Fathers', published in a volume of that name in the following year. There are Yeatsian echoes in the poem—of 'cold Clare rock and Galway rock and thorn'[10]—and its first line seems to recall the opening of Kavanagh's 'Shancoduff' in tone and rhythm—'My black hills have never seen the sun rising'.[11] This may indeed be, consciously or otherwise, part of the project. What matters is that the poem is unmistakably a Brendan Kennelly poem, as well as being a formal claim to ancestral territory.

I have suggested elsewhere[12] that while Joyce's hero, Stephen Dedalus, saw history as a nightmare from which he was trying to awake, the Kennelly persona habitually sees history as a nightmare which he must re-inhabit; as his Shelley does in Part VI of *Shelley in Dublin*:

> Who am I
> To have pity for these damned
> Who lurch and sway
> In the light and dark of nightmare?[13]

There is indeed a sense in which everything in his early work is leading towards *Cromwell* (1983) when the challenges of history, myth and identity are taken on in a sustained frontal assault. 'My Dark Fathers' is the first formal plotting of this historical retrospect.

> My dark fathers lived the intolerable day
> Committed always to the night of wrong,
> Stiffened at the hearthstone, the woman lay,
> Perished feet nailed to her husband's breastbone.
> Grim houses beckoned in the swelling gloom
> Of Munster fields where the Atlantic night
> Fettered the child within the pit of doom,
> And everywhere a going down of light.[14]

In a shrewd prosodic strategy the general, apocalyptic theme is consigned to the regular iambics; while the particularity of the old couple's death is rivetted in the powerful trochaic chords which open lines three and four. The event to which these lines apply are from Peadar Ó Laoghaire's autobiography *Mo Scéal Féin*: an old couple cannot bear the segregation of men from women in the famine workhouse; they escape to a country hovel so as to die together; and are found dead with the woman's feet clutched for warmth to her husband's breast. Thus the beckoning grim houses of line five is more specific than at first glance, referring to workhouses; the 'pit of doom' is the mass grave and the rotting potato-pit; the going down of light recalls that the sun rarely broke through the rainhaze during the worst famine years. Stanza two:

And yet upon the sandy Kerry shore
The woman once had danced at ebbing tide
Because she loved flute music—and still more
Because a lady wondered at the pride
Of one so humble. That was long before
The green plant withered by an evil chance;
When winds of hunger howled at every door
She heard the music dwindle and forgot the dance.

Again the reference is precise. The woman dancing on the shore, Kennelly notes in *New and Selected Poems* (1976), is recorded in the travel writings of Mrs Asenath Nicholson.[15] Kennelly is now at the centre of MacMahon country, confident in possession of his own magniloquence. The dying fall of 'withered', 'winds' and 'dwindle' prepares us for the tragic consequences for a culture when a people 'forgot the dance'. The apocalyptic horror of the famine—we think more of Mangan than of Yeats in this context—is registered in the third stanza as the woman with her 'innocent appalling cry' searches the sky for a sign. And in the fourth the poet's 'dark fathers' try to comprehend the 'giant grief that trampled night and day,/The awful absence moping through the land' while dance and music cease.

The third particular image in the poem, maybe more grievous than that of the dead pensioners or the girl by the sea, occurs in the final stanza. While asserting his kinship with the intolerable past, Kennelly invokes what used to be a common sight in rural Ireland within his own memory—that of a shy man facing the wall while he entertains the company with a song.

Since every moment of the clock
Accumulates to form a final name,
Since I am come from Kerry clay and rock,
I celebrate the darkness and the shame
That could compel a man to turn his face
Against the wall, withdrawn from light so strong
And undeceiving, spancelled in a place
Of unapplauding hands and broken song.

The image of the clock brings Kennelly's fable dramatically into the personal here and now, preparing us for his definitive poetic utterance. The symbolism of dark and light, which has carried his thought through the historical nightmare, returns in that remarkable cultural image of the singer who cannot face the reality of his liberation. The historical *via dolorosa* which begins with the nailed feet of the first stanza, through the 'thorny savage furze' of the third, accumulates in the traumatized, 'spancelled' immobility of the last lines.

Yet the poem is heroic in its ambitious sweep, as well as in the earned bravado of its stance, its declaration of artistic faith. I suspect that it is the poem he had been looking for through so many experiments with time and place, with character and landscape, with history, myth and geography. He can now be accounted one with Mangan, who is commemorated in another poem in the same volume, as 'Scrupulous poet of a people's loss'.[16]

Yet by no means is the ground gained, the energies released in 'My Dark Fathers', put to the most valuable account. *Up and At It* (1965), that celebration of footloose randiness, is to my mind a dubious departure, though the poet prizes it enough twenty years later to republish it as *Moloney Up and At It* (1984). Before considering it as a poetic sequence, a glance at his second, and less successful novel, *The Florentines* (1967) may help our perspective.

Re-reading *The Florentines* after a twenty-five year interval I find myself wondering why Kennelly took time off from his poetry to write it at all. Its model is Boccaccio's *Decameron* in which a group of worldly people spend a time telling tales, insulated, like Kennelly's postgraduates, from the world. Its hero is named Gulliver—so Kennelly gives notice that there is really no comparison that he is not willing to invite. Pitched in the convention of the picaresque, with the young hero setting out for his year's postgraduate study at the University of Barfield, the story is obviously based on a year the author spent in Leeds on graduate research. On the Liverpool boat Gulliver Stone encounters a boozy little Tipperaryman with a hurley-stick who sings rebel songs and shouts 'Up Tipp!', and a woman named Concepta McGillicuddy who gives his overtures the cold shoulder.

Gulliver's stay in Barfield is told in a deadpan prose which seldom rises to any sense of narrative excitement. The events are presented as a set of journalistic set-pieces: a street fight, a student booze-up, a student demonstration, an attempt at seduction aborted by the hero being drowned in the puke of the beloved, the sea-journey home. The characterizations are perfunctory and inconsequent. Above all, we don't get a single insight to the hero's heart or conscience. The one feature it shares with *The Crooked Cross* is its refusal to give anything away about its author. Swift's Gulliver is a character of subtlety and nuance by comparison with his lapidary successor in *The Florentines*.

There is significance, however, of a negative character in the events described in Gulliver's return to Ireland on the same Liverpool Boat. The little Tipperaryman is present again, this time singing nationalist songs in competition with an Ulsterman singing Orange ballads. He notes that the years had 'modified ancient bitterness', and that the boat had only one destination, Ireland:

Two little islands in a world of trouble, and they were best who travelled from one to the other with a song on their lips. . . . Gulliver thought of the island behind him. Busy, turbulent, frequently unhappy, and the island ahead, gay, mocking, secretive. He looked about him at the men, women and children, who were kin of the island waiting for them in the darkness. What could one do but drink their health?[17]

With these thoughts Gulliver, who still retains his virginity, goes to his bunk below, only to find the hitherto untouchable Concepta MacGillicuddy waiting for him there:

'Do you mind?' she said, more in hope than in anger.
  In answer, he laid his last bottle of Guinness reverently on the floor and sprang forward, echoing the little hurler's tribal battle cry. . . 'Up Tipp!'

The author—for it is his, not Gulliver's, voice we hear in the narrative—is not to be blamed for his optimism about Northern Ireland; we all shared that complacency in 1967. But even allowing for the fact that Kennelly is rounding off a story of temporary exile, there's no forgiveness for that sentimental reverie on 'Ireland-the-smile-and-the-tear-in-her-eye'. And the randy swagger of the final trope is not to be excused by the need for a romantic flourish and a happy ending. It's the self-conscious Kerryman at work, 'the likes of Owen Rua O'Sullivan and the poets of the Dingle Bay' as Pegeen Mike envisaged them in Synge's *Playboy*.

  Kennelly approves of Patrick Kavanagh when the elder poet condemns what he calls 'buck-lepping' and 'gallivanting' in Irish poetry. The latter word was used by Kavanagh to indict the rollicking poetic gestures of F.R. Higgins in an essay he entitled 'The Gallivanting Poet'.[18] The danger of such writing, Kavanagh asserts, is two-fold: it tempts the writer towards faking an energy he does not feel; and it prevents him from looking sincerely into his own condition. It is a besetting temptation in the early Kennelly, and it finds its most sustained outlet in the Moloney persona whom he seems to have created for the purpose in *Up and At It* (1965).

  These poems are widely, and perhaps justly, admired, for their rhythmic energy, their amoral extravagance, their *joie de vivre*. I am also aware that these tales of wandering rakes, and drunken hallucinations, of wakes where the corpse comes to life and wild men find themselves copulating on the graves of their mothers, have an honourable history in Irish folk tradition. What I distrust in the Moloney narratives is that they bespeak a sort of extrovert recklessness that is the opposite of what Kennelly feels most inwardly—an apprehension of existential terror, not unmixed with a sense of self-loathing, at the human condition.

  This quality begins to come through with thrilling authenticity in the nightmare title poem of *Dream of a Black Fox* (1968) which opens

> The black fox loped out of the hills
> And circled for several hours,
> Eyes bright with menace, teeth
> White in the light, tail dragging the ground.
> The woman in my arms cringed with fear,
> Collapsed crying, her head hurting my neck.
> She became dumb fear.[19]

The beloved, I take it, does not see the black fox. She sees its menace reflected in the poet's terror; hers is a fear of fear. The ease with which the irregular lines register the loping motion of the inscrutable monster is only matched by the pathos of the human lovers, reduced and vulnerable before its menace. In the last stanza the poet acknowledges that he had not just seen and felt fear, but 'Fear dispelled by what makes fear'. That is something permanent and central in his experience of living. Something that will re-appear with more dreadful particularity in 'The Black Fox, Again'.

The innocents in a poem of that name 'suffer martyrdoms,/Bleed invisible before/Our judges and centurions'.[20] The tone is too close to confession not to communicate a shudder of sympathy, evoke an impulse to absolution:

> They create, but mostly hell
> For others and themselves;
> It can't be otherwise until
>
> We see that suffering remains,
> Consumes itself, devours its neighbours
> Always causes pain . . .

In 'Nightmare' there is a marvellous, desperate play on the juxtaposed values of love and fear:

> And on your face was terror, love,
> The terror of knowing
> That the demon held our destiny
> And played with it. . . .[21]

It would be comforting to think that 'love' was merely appositional, but we know it's mostly vocative. These poems of terror are rather like those of Mangan in a poem like 'Shapes and Signs'. The ubiquity of the demon figure suggests that they may be about alcohol. What is certain is that they are about fear—which means that the poet is finding his true courage. This theme finds its most intense expression in such late lyrics as 'The Pig', 'The Joke', 'The Black Fox, Again', and in *The Book of Judas* where they are given veritable orchestration.

I've been cutting a sort of single-minded furrow through this first decade of Brendan Kennelly's prose and poetry, concentrating on swerves, side-steps, false starts and blind alleys as much as on the achievement itself which is of course the main event. One might even adopt another phrase from Stephen Dedalus and declare that these are not false starts at all, merely potholes of discovery. It is in the nature of things, as James Stephens observed, that pens are such as write too little or too much.

Before concluding, I must confess to having neglected a number of brilliant critical opportunities offered by Brendan Kennelly's work over this first decade of his creative life in the work of that decade. In pursuing the adventure of the poet's development in time and space I have virtually ignored the question of artifact, the poem itself, as manifest in the remarkable number of achieved lyrics created by the way.

Had I chosen another approach and emphasis I would have lingered, for instance, over 'The Gift' with its tentative delicacy of movement, echoed by a sort of sister poem 'Girl on a Rope'. 'Johnny Gobless', 'The Hunchback', 'The Dummies', 'The Blind Man', might have been explored as poems of empathy and inscape that James Stephens would not have disowned, troubling in the suggestion that they may be oblique self-portraits. There is the haunting city atmosphere of 'Light Dying', his moving elegy for a cardinal presence in his life, Frank O'Connor.

Then there are those curt, seminal images of rural life, 'A Farmer Thinks of His Daft Son', 'The Thatcher', The Tippler', 'The Pig-Killer', balanced against such an exquisite suburban genre-piece as 'At the Party'. One might have reflected on theme and technique in his declaration of personal faith, 'The Good', or on the powerful narrative thrust of 'Night-Drive' where his poetry of terror may have had its first promptings—or on 'Ghosts', which comes immediately after it in *Selected Poems* (1969), and in which he defines his vocation:

> Respecting the definition of death
> And the sea's untiring style,
> Desiring the precision of birds
> That flash from black to white,
>
> I look within, without,
> And write.[22]

Taken all in all, the sixties were for Brendan Kennelly a decade of astonishing productivity, of tireless experiment and genuine, various achievement. He keeps attacking on several fronts, apparently willing to take casualties with the same cheerfulness as when winning bridge-heads. Unlike Louis MacNeice's exasperated Mrs Carmichael in 'Bagpipe Music' he shows no sign whatever of being 'through with over-production'.[23]

And the direction of this ten years can now be seen as leading inexorably to the ambitious consolidations of *Cromwell* and *The Book of Judas*. There his great obsessions, historical, territorial, and personal have been elaborately rehearsed in a performance that shows no sign of closing.

## NOTES

First published in *Dark Fathers into Light: Brendan Kennelly*, edited by Richard Pine (Newcastle upon Tyne: Bloodaxe Books Ltd., 1994). Bloodaxe Critical Anthologies 2.

1   Rudi Holzapfel and Brendan Kennelly, *The Rain, the Moon* (Dublin: Dolmen Press, 1961), p. 39.
2   'Sonnet', *ibid.*, p. 57.
3   Brendan Kennelly, *Collection One, Getting up Early* (Dublin: Allen Figgis, 1966), p. 38.
4   See 'Inherited Dissent: The Dilemma of the Irish Writer', p. 96 in this volume.
5   Brendan Kennelly, *The Crooked Cross* (Dublin: Allen Figgis, 1963; Dublin: Moytura Press, 1989), p. 137. All future references to this novel will be incorporated within the text.
6   Harold Bloom, *The Anxiety of Influence* (New York: Oxford University Press, 1973).
7   Bryan MacMahon, *The Lion-Tamer* (London: Macmillan, 1948), p. 134.
8   Brendan Kennelly, *Good Souls to Survive* (Dublin: Allen Figgis, 1967), p. 22.
9   Brendan Kennelly, *Selected Poems* (Dublin: Allen Figgis, 1969), p. 33.
10  'In Memory of Major Robert Gregory', *The Variorum Edition of the Poems of W.B. Yeats*, edited by Peter Allt and Russell K. Alspach (New York: Macmillan, 1957), p. 326.
11  *Patrick Kavanagh: The Complete Poems*, edited by Peter Kavanagh (New York: Peter Kavanagh Hand Press, 1972; Newbridge: The Goldsmith Press, 1984), p. 13.
12  Augustine Martin, 'Very Tragical Mirth: The Poetry of Brendan Kennelly', *Ireland Today* (September/October 1987).
13  Brendan Kennelly, *Shelley in Dublin* (rev. ed., Dublin: Beaver Row Press, 1982), p. 18.
14  Brendan Kennelly, *A Time for Voices: Selected Poems 1960–1990* (Newcastle upon Tyne: Bloodaxe Books Ltd., 1990), pp. 18–19.
15  Brendan Kennelly, *New and Selected Poems*, edited by Peter Fallon (Dublin: Gallery Press, 1976), p. 62.
16  Brendan Kennelly, *My Dark Fathers* (Dublin: New Square Publications, 1964), p. 13.
17  Brendan Kennelly, *The Florentines* (Dublin: Allen Figgis, 1967), pp. 108–9.
18  Patrick Kavanagh, 'The Gallivanting Poet', *Irish Writing*, No. 3 (1947).
19  Brendan Kennelly, *A Time for Voices: Selected Poems 1960–1900*, pp. 63–4.
20  'The Innocents', Brendan Kennelly, *Dream of a Black Fox* (Dublin: Allen Figgis, 1968), pp. 53–4.
21  *Ibid.*, p. 60.
22  Brendan Kennelly, *Selected Poems*, p. 73.
23  *The Collected Poems of Louis MacNeice*, edited by E.R. Dodds (London: Faber, 1966), p. 97.

# 16

# Quest and Vision:
# *Eavan Boland's* The Journey

Eavan Boland at the age of twenty-two published her first volume of poems, *New Territory* in 1967. High Modernism in its Anglo-American panoply of classicism and impersonality was the dominating norm of poetic practice, the New Criticism of I.A. Richards, William Empson and Cleanth Brooks was its academic enforcer. An elegant child of its time, *New Territory* opened with a poem entitled 'The Poets', propounding an aesthetic which the poet has spent most of her subsequent career trying to reverse. Poets in this lyric are envisaged as heroic explorers, alchemists, lions, warriors who

> Ransacked their perishable minds and found
> Pattern and form
> And with their own hands quarried from hard words
> A figure in which secret things confide.[1]

Hound voices were they all, but not a woman among them, while they hunted 'without respite among fixed stars'. Solar and imperial, they permitted the 'tenant moon' a mere night's lodging in the sky until the 'absentee landlord of the dark' returned to assert his dominion. In the title poem of the same volume man is seen as heroic mariner and conquistador—'the ambitious wit/Of poets and exploring ships have been his eyes'.[2] Twenty-two years later Eavan Boland places these cautionary lyrics at the opening of her *Selected Poems* (1989) as signs and landmarks of what has now become the old territory.[3]

There is, however, a more intriguing and far more accomplished poem in *New Territory* entitled 'From the Painting *Back from Market* by Chardin'. It is, like 'Degas's Laundresses', 'On Renoir's *The Grape-Pickers*', 'Canaletto in the National Gallery of Ireland' and 'Growing Up', a shrewd piece of art criticism, but its real significance is in the way it looks forward, across an eight years' silence, towards the suburban poems of her second volume, *The War Horse* (1975), and finally to 'Self-Portrait on a Summer Evening' which revisits the Chardin picture with a revised agenda.

The first poem on 'Chardin's peasant woman' marvels at the picture's domestic detail:

> empty flagons of wine
> At her feet, bread under her arm. He has fixed
> Her limbs in colour, and her heart in line.[4]

The poet thus charges this least aggressive of artists with the death and petrifaction of his female subject, rather as Degas's artist is seen to be consigning his laundress to a 'winding sheet' of paint. A further startling ambiguity—of the kind New Critics used to revel in—follows in stanza two:

> I think of what great art removes:
> Hazard and death, the future and the past,
> This woman's secret history and her loves—

Then the woman, helpless object of the painter's art, transfixed as she is immortalized, beggared as she is endowed, is suddenly given back her motion and autonomy by the poet as the freeze-frame shifts into movement:

> And even the dawn market, from whose bargaining
> She has just come back, where men and women
> Congregate and go
> Among the produce, learning to live from morning
> To next day, linked
> By a common impulse to survive, although
> In surging light they are single and distinct,
> Like birds in the accumulating snow.

The woman writing the poem has momentarily liberated the woman in the painting—with what deliberateness must remain a fascinating mystery—only to return her finally to the cold immortality of artifact in the last two lines. We are forced to wonder how a woman, so long the object of the artist's attention, can become herself a subject acting in her own right, as an artist, upon the world. That is Eavan Boland's theme. It provides much of the drama in *The Journey*, and it is explored at length in the poet's pamphlet, *A Kind of Scar* (1989), which by self-denying ordinance I refrained from re-reading until I had written at least the first draft of the present article.

'Self-Portrait on a Summer Evening' in *The Journey*, which predates *A Kind of Scar* by two years, returns to the same picture, this time with a diminished reverence, a more muscular intent. Whereas in the earlier poem art was assuredly a matter of privilege—even male privilege—while life, especially female life, was a matter of necessity, in the later poem Chardin's art is seen as a sort of effrontery:

> All summer long
> he has been slighting her
> in botched blues, tints,
> half-tones, rinsed neutrals.[5]

Even nature is hurt and pillaged by the artist's creative greed with 'light unlearning itself, /an infinite unfrocking of the prism.' The vocatives become insistent, as if seeking some more active apology or intervention:

> Can't you feel it?
> Aren't you chilled by it?
> The way the late afternoon
> is reduced to detail—

The tone is now perilously close to the unreasonable. While the woman may have some right to protest at a great painter's methodology, the poet can hardly deny Chardin the privileges she herself claims and exercises. When it seems that she has literally painted herself into a corner the poem turns. As the grammar slips from second to first person, from vocative to nominative, the speaker slips in and out of the picture:

> before your eyes
> in my ankle-length
> summer skirt
>
> crossing between
> the garden and the house,
> under the whitebeam trees,
> keeping an eye on
> the length of the grass,
> the height of the hedge,
> the distance of the children
>
> I am Chardin's woman
>
> edged in reflected light,
> hardened by
> the need to be ordinary. (13)

The speaker thus lays claim to both worlds, art and life, privilege and necessity. And while the rhetorical performance is dazzling in its apparent ease, the exercise in self-definition is by far the more crucial part of the poem's achievement. Its priority becomes more evident if we reflect on Chardin, his subject and his period, the French Rococo.

Often mistaken for products of the earlier Dutch school, his pictures of ordinary life were undervalued by comparison with the fleshly mode of his contemporary Boucher whose women were emphatically sex objects. Chardin's woman, surrounded by the accoutrements and utensils of her trade, is just as emphatically a doer—one of the painter's titles to the piece is *La Pourvoyeuse*, the Provider. Hence her fascination for poet and woman, and her challenge. Boland enters that woman's world when she makes her poetry a register of the suburban routine and responsibility. She enters it as a housewife, masters and transcends it as an artist, a process in some sense analogous to Robert Frost's dilemma and resolution in 'Two Tramps in Mud-Time':

> My object in living is to unite
> My avocation and my vocation
> As my two eyes make one in sight.[6]

In one sense, however, it is quite distinct from Frost's complacent, if seductive, capitalism. His dilemma rests after all on his freedom to reject or employ a couple of needy fellow-humans to do a job he is enjoying himself. His world, notwithstanding its bluff frontier swagger, is all choice and privilege. Boland's two poems—the early one no less than the later— are in their quiet way implacably feminist. They are poems of necessity in which the woman-poet struggles for space, autonomy, identity, virtually for her life; and prevails.

Out of that conflict comes her remarkable body of 'suburban' poems in *The War Horse* and *Night Feed*. These poems are often read two-dimensionally, as merely bodying forth the small anxieties and cosmic angst of modern female experience—which would of course be achievement enough. More significantly, however, they are fables of hard-won spiritual freedom which must be daily renewed among the conditions which, in the official version of things, might be seen to stifle it. The prevalent mood in *The Journey* is buoyant, strenuous, vigilant and ultimately heroic. Furthermore the rituals of domesticity which occupy the foreground of these dramatic lyrics become vehicles for the poet's other thematic preoccupations—the elisions of memory, the strange commerce of self with former self, the role of nation, race, family, gender and environment in fixing certain moments of apprehended identity.

She maps out a territory, a family and a suburb snug against the Dublin Mountains, and wrests from that condition an answerable style, at once rational and passionate, secular and confessional, local in its referents, learned and universal in its allusions. This is of course a region of the imagination, as much a fictional construct as Clarke's Celtic-Romanesque or Kavanagh's childhood country of Ballyrush and Gortin—though less haunted with history as the one, or with topography as the other, and quite without the savage nostalgias that alternately energize and disable their sense of experience.

The marvellous genre-piece which opens *The Journey* epitomizes
Eavan Boland's dialogue with a former self:

> I remember the way the big windows washed
> out the room and the winter darks tinted
> it and how, in the brute quiet and aftermath,
> an eyebrow waited helplessly to be composed
>
> from the palette with its scarabs of oil
> colours gleaming through a dusk leaking from
> the iron railings and the ruined evenings of
> bombed-out, post-war London. . . . (9)

Her mother[7] has suspended work on a portrait of a sitter who has left until
the next session. Time and art have left the subject trapped and mutilated
amid the paint. The poet's childhood self, the 'interloper who knows both
love and fear', is perplexed between mother and easel, life and art. A
daughter of the embassy she has registered, without understanding it, a
rage for identity and permanence which art tries to satisfy but which life
seems to deny:

> a nine-year-old in high, fawn socks—
> the room had been shocked into a glacier
> of cotton sheets thrown over the almond
> and vanilla silk of the French Empire chairs.

Man shifts about. . . . These epiphanies of Wordsworthian spots of time
are retrievals, tributaries to a larger argument about what constitutes
identity. The mysterious imperatives of art already glanced at are an
element in the argument. But the more atavistic imperatives of race,
language and nation are more insistent in *The Journey*. The enabling
condition of this debate is the consolidated territory, the secure vantage-
point of the suburban experience. 'An Irish Childhood in England: 1951',
virtually continuous with 'I Remember', summons up in its first stanza a
London of confused accents, 'bickering of vowels on the buses', 'navy-
skirted ticket collectors', 'ration-book pudding' and the school pianist
playing *Iolanthe* and 'John Peel'. In the second it enacts the dilemma:

> I didn't know what to hold, to keep.
> At night, filled with some malaise
> of love for what I'd never known I had,
> I fell asleep and let the moment pass.
> The passing moment has become a night
> of clipped shadows, freshly painted houses,
> the garden eddying in dark and heat,
> my children half-awake, half-asleep. (50)

So many of the great definitive human words are there—night, hold, keep, love, moment, sleep, house, garden, children. The wrench of allegiances situates itself within that bridgehead on the quotidian that Boland has so resolutely constructed. If this is her territory then, on the 'national question' what is her choice? Memory, it seems, gives her, and her sleepy children, little choice:

> I came . . . in nineteen-fifty-one:
> barely-gelled, a freckled six-year-old,
> overdressed and sick on the plane
> when all of England to an Irish child
> was nothing more than what you'd lost and how:
> was the teacher in the London convent who
> when I produced 'I amn't' in the classroom
> turned and said—'you're not in Ireland now'. (51)

My hunch is that there is a long, painful journey between this poem, with its measured capitulation to the concept of 'race' and 'nation'—an honorific word is hard to find in these times of political correctness—and the culturally neutral stance of the young Trinity graduate who wrote *New Territory*. In that volume even her 'After the Irish of Egan O'Rahilly', rendered with no knowledge of Irish, seemed—and still seems—a gesture of distant respect to a culture and tradition for which she had as yet developed no real empathy. Yet when time and process brings her round, whether through the route of politics or atavism, to such considerations, she finds herself confronting the same dark, intimate dilemmas as Kinsella confronts formally in *An Duanaire*, Montague in his introduction to *The Faber Book of Irish Verse*, and Kennelly, less explicitly, in 'My Dark Fathers'. I exclude those endless flirtations with the theme which are perhaps best exemplified in a Field Day pamphlet by Tom Paulin. But I suspect that an encounter with an Achill woman while Ms Boland was still a student, recounted in *A Kind of Scar*—which I can no longer keep out of the argument—, may have been her causeway into that crucial *terra incognita* where ancestry and feminism could be discovered and possessed.

'Mise Eire', the second poem in *The Journey*, gives its name to *A Kind of Scar*. At the risk of exposing the obvious I must gloss the title. Patrick Pearse wrote a famous poem in which Ireland speaks, identifying itself with the *Cailleach Beara*, the Hag of Beare, a legendary Irish heroine who had once been the toast of chieftains, but who, under pressure from the Church, settled without enthusiasm for Christian service in her old age. Pearse's poem images Ireland as the Hag, old, betrayed, lonely, despite its distinguished, chequered history. The poet's problem with Chardin's woman is here infinitely complicated. For centuries Ireland has been imagined as a woman awaiting the sacrifice of patriot men, the adulation of male poets. She has been Cathleen ni Houlihan, Banba, Fodhla, Dark Rosaleen of whom Mangan has written:

> 'Tis you you shall have the golden throne,
> 'Tis you shall reign, and reign alone,
> My Dark Rosaleen![8]

How this iconography becomes a problem for a liberated woman poet in negotiating with her national identity is a fascinating concern. In *A Kind of Scar* the problem is vigorously rehearsed in discursive prose. In the poem it is dramatized in a rhetoric analogous to the second Chardin lyric. Boland's poem begins in a tone of truculent recoil, of refusal to enter upon the beckoning nightmare of history: 'I wont' go back to it' (10) The tone of rejection invites comparison with Kavanagh's 'Memory of Brother Michael' in which Ireland's past is denounced as a 'nettle-wild grave' and emblematized by 'Skull of bard, thigh of chief,/Depth of dried-up river.'[9] Or with Montague's 'Like Dolmens round My Childhood, the Old People':

> Ancient Ireland, indeed! I was reared by her bedside,
> The rune and the chant, evil eye and averted head,
> Fomorian fierceness of family and local feud.[10]

The rhetoric of these two countrymen—despite Montague's New York childhood—is that of escape. Boland's, on the other hand, is a sort of terror at the entry to the cave, a cosmopolitan sensibility recoiling from an ordeal which is as distasteful as it is ineluctable: 'No. I won't go back./My roots are brutal'. To go back she must cross a generation of middle-class civility, there to join not the druids or the warriors of tradition, but the women who had borne the real pains and humiliations:

> I am the woman—
> a sloven's mix
> of silk at the wrists,
> a sort of dove-strut
> in the precincts of the garrison. . . .
>
> I am the woman
> in the gansy-coat
> on board the 'Mary Belle',
> in the huddling cold,
>
> holding her half-dead baby to her
> as the wind shifts East (10–11)

Obeying a rhetoric analogous to the second Chardin poem—which follows in the volume by a mysterious but logical sequence—the speaker has yielded, though with considerably less triumph and buoyancy, to history's imperative. These famine women, according to the old woman who brings her water on Achill in *A Kind of Scar,* were 'great people',[11] a remark which seems to have been seminal in Boland's subsequent and arduous engagement with nationality and feminism. The question of class does not arise in the argument—or at all prominently in the poems—though it was the first thing to strike me on reading the pamphlet.

The phrase 'hewers of wood and drawers of water' is a phrase graven into the post-colonial memory of every child of Boland's generation educated in Ireland, to symbolize the dispossession of his or her ancestors. Yet the poet, who elsewhere in the pamphlet invokes with great point the character of the milkwoman in the first chapter of *Ulysses*—where the old woman is actually patronized by another Trinity student, Buck Mulligan—seems oblivious to the figure she herself must cut in the eyes of that old country-woman who serves her. The unforced respect in which the poet holds the old woman is cause enough for the aporia. But her eyes are upon what must seem the larger theme.

It seems that recent history is to blame. The rise of violence in Northern Ireland, and the coincident rise of post-colonialist theory around the globe, exploded the question of identity into the world of High Modernism which Eavan Boland had inherited as a student and junior academic in Dublin of the early sixties. It was a slow burn, and I suspect that the problems of identity which it raised for her were all the more formidable because of her cosmopolitan upbringing. Athwart these concerns came the further complications of feminism. The question of class was largely consumed in the friction and heat of these allied challenges. It never arises—and this must be unique—as a tension in her narratives of suburban existence. Thus Chardin's woman is embraced as a self-portrait, class is transcended in function, the kitchen-maid becomes invisible in the provider.

It all begins around 1975 when that war horse stumbles among suburban gardens making the fragility of domestic peace so apparent,[12] bringing together the two themes that have come to absorb the poet's imaginative cosmos. Throughout *The Journey,* history, threatening and prehensile, invades the existential world where love, solicitude and art—'whose end is peace'—had lived an illusion of security. 'Fever' recalls with a sort of helpless anger the death of the poet's grandmother in a fever ward—emblematical of the Famine and its miseries—leaving her with 'shadows, visitations, hints/ and a half-sense of half-lives' which challenge her to

> re-construct the soaked-through midnights;
> vigils; the histories I never learned
> to predict the lyric of; and re-construct
> risk; as if silence could become rage. . . . (17)

'The Oral Tradition' permits the poet, after a reading in some rural venue, to eavesdrop on a conversation between two women. They are using words like 'summer', 'birth' and 'great-grandmother' as they rehearse an incident where some woman had endured child-birth on her own in an open meadow. Such narratives are commonplace in Irish rural experience, but to Boland it is one of 'the histories I never learned' and carries the composite theme of feminist history, of woman as bearer of life and unofficial chronicler of events so recurrent and momentous that they never get written:

> the oral song
> avid as superstition,
> layered like an amber in
> the wreck of language
> and the remnants of a nation. (16)

The official, male-borne histories and middle-class education keep yielding to older, female narratives. The flashes of recognition issue in the drama of these related lyrics. Thus 'The Oral Tradition' enacts a radical reversal of values, class values included. The poet is sent forth, probably by the Arts Council, in Kavanagh's terms to 'spread in Naas and Clonakilty/ News of Gigli and R.M. Rilke.'[13] At the end of her work-shop, with her improving mission honourably accomplished, such pretensions are humbled by the half-heard narratives of her pupils. A fascinated eavesdropper, she hears them resume the rhythms of their own quotidian with its immemorial freight of memories.

There is progressively no house-space for the poetry of manners or of class. These concerns are only raised to be discarded or consumed in the aboriginal

> flame
> of hearth not history.
> And still no page
> scores the low music
> of our outrage. ('It's a Woman's World')[14]

Through a variety of orchestrations this theme pervades 'On Holiday', 'Listen. This is the Noise of Myth', 'Fond Memory' and 'The Emigrant Irish'.

The long poem from which *The Journey* takes its title is, beneath its wry exploitation of the Virgilian myth, perhaps the wittiest as well as the most compassionate poem in the book. Alone among her works it formally raises and lets fall the issue of class. It begins with the wry if obvious proposition that there has never been a poem about an antibiotic. Poets have, with accelerating frequency, owed their lives and those of their loved ones to pharmaceutical medicine, yet none has acknowledged, except by indirection, their debts to its preparations: 'emblem instead of the real thing./ Instead of sulpha we shall have hyssop. . . .' (39)

In her suburban sanctuary—'my room was a mess'—she falls asleep reading the Greek poet Sappho. In a dream, that proto-feminist comes and takes her to the underworld. They come to a river and perceive, across it, multitudes of afflicted women whose children had died in plagues and pestilences. Then, drawing to consciousness the theme that has so long been dormant, implicit or merely tentative, Sappho warns the poet not to 'define these women by their work' (41) as washerwomen, court ladies or laundresses:

> 'But these are women who went out like you
> when dusk became a dark sweet with leaves,
> recovering the day, stooping, picking up
> teddy bears and rag dolls and tricycles and buckets—'

Sappho, rather in the manner of a Christian annunciation, claims the poet as her 'own daughter', enjoins silence upon her and departs, the window clasp opening as the poet wakes from her dream. It has been a dream of women, a vision in which all the accidents and incidentals are burned off. It is a concentration of all her concerns, searing, witty and ferociously partisan. The vision gains force and dimension in being framed by the quotidian. She awakes to find the 'poetry books stacked higgledy piggledy'. (42) But the archetypal nightmare of womanhood has struck deep:

> nothing was changed; nothing was more clear
> but it was wet and the year was late.
> The rain was grief in arrears; my children
> slept the last dark out safely and I wept.

This great fable enfolds the central essence of *The Journey*. Its mythic structure of quest and vision, its didactic centre within the nonchalant verisimilitude of its setting, epitomize the thematic intensity and technical equilibrium with which Eavan Boland negotiates the circumstances of her art. The most abiding sense of *The Journey* is its energy, the constant sense of straining and testing beneath the urbane, stanzaic surfaces. Though the volume aims at, and consistently achieves, the rounded poem, its sense of process is stronger than its sense of artifice. A turbulent set of emotions involving race, nation, gender, history, class—as well as that neglected factor, personality—are still struggling for expression, manoeuvring for balance, within the creative ferment. The sense of energy is enormous both in its achievement and its promise. *The Journey is* a monument of formidable weight and graceful proportion. But the stone from which it is carven has not abandoned its volcanic origin, its metamorphic potentiality.

# NOTES

First published in *Irish University Review*, Volume 23, Number I, Eavan Boland Special Issue, guest-edited by Anthony Roche with Jody Allen-Randolph, Spring/Summer 1993.

1  Eavan Boland, *New Territory* (Dublin: Allen Figgis, 1967), p. 7.
2  *Ibid.*, p. 10.
3  See Eavan Boland, *Selected Poems* (Manchester: Carcanet, 1989). p. 9.
4  Eavan Boland, *New Territory*, p. 19.
5  Eavan Boland, *The Journey and Other Poems* (Dublin: Arlen House, 1986; Manchester: Carcanet, 1987), p. 12. All subsequent quotations from this book will be given parenthetically in the text.
6  *The Poetry of Robert Frost*, edited by Edward Connery Lathem (New York: Holt, Rinehart and Winston, 1969). p. 277.
7  [Editor's note. Boland's mother is the artist, Frances Kelly. Her father, Frederick Boland, was then Irish ambassador in London.]
8  James Clarence Mangan, 'Dark Rosaleen', *The Penguin Book of Irish Verse*, edited by Brendan Kennelly (2nd ed., Harmondsworth: Penguin, 1981), p. 150.
9  *Patrick Kavanagh: The Complete Poems*, edited by Peter Kavanagh (New York: Peter Kavanagh Hand Press, 1972; Newbridge: Goldsmith Press, 1984), p. 148.
10 John Montague, *Poisoned Lands and Other Poems* (London: MacGibbon and Kee, 1961), p. 19.
11 Eavan Boland, *A Kind of Scar: The Woman Poet in a National Tradition* (Dublin: Attic Press pamphlet, 1989), p. 5.
12 Eavan Boland, *The War House* (London: Victor Gollancz, 1975), pp. 9–10.
13 'Irish Stew', *Patrick Kavanagh: The Complete Poems*, p. 266.
14 Eavan Boland, *Night Feed* (Dublin: Arlen House, 1980; London and Boston: Marion Boyars, 1980), p. 42.

# Augustine Martin:
# A Checklist of Publications

The intention in compiling the following bibliography of Augustine Martin's publications has been to include every book, edition and article in scholarly journal and collection. The editor would welcome notice of any omissions.

## 1959

'A Note on J.D. Salinger', *Studies* 48 (Autumn 1959), pp. 336–45.

## 1960

'James Stephens: Lyric Poet', *Studies* 49 (Summer 1960), pp. 173–82.

## 1961

'James Stephens: *Reincarnations* and remaining works', *Studies* 50 (Spring 1961), pp. 74–87.

## 1962

'The Poet and the Policeman: A Note on *The Charwoman's Daughter* [by James Stephens]', *University Review* 3.2 (1962), pp. 54–63.

## 1963

'A Skeleton Key to the Stories of Mary Lavin', *Studies* 52 (Winter 1963), pp. 393–406.
'Brendan Behan', *Threshold* 18 (1963), pp. 22–8.
'James Stephens and the Irish Wonderworld', *The Kilkenny Magazine* 9 (Spring 1963), pp. 52–62.
'The Short Stories of James Stephens', *Colby Library Quarterly* 6.8 (December 1963), pp. 343–53.

## 1965

'Inherited Dissent: The Dilemma of the Irish Writer', *Studies* 54 (Spring 1965), pp. 1–20.

'James Stephens's *Reincarnations*', *The Capuchin Annual* (1965), pp. 163–77.
'The Rediscovery of Austin Clarke', *Studies* 54 (Winter 1965), pp. 408–34.
'Report from Ireland', *Chicago Review* 18.1 (1965), pp. 87–94.
'[James] Stephens's *Deirdre*', *University Review* 3.7 (1965), pp. 25–38.

## 1966

'Teaching the Irish Short Story', *Secondary Teacher* 2 (1966).
'To Make a Right Rose Tree: Reflections on the Poetry of 1916', *Studies* 55 (Spring 1966), pp. 38–50.

## 1967

*Exploring English 1: An Anthology of Short Stories for Intermediate Certificate*, edited by Martin, Dublin: Gill and Macmillan.
*Exploring English 3: An Anthology of Poetry for Intermediate Certificate*, edited by Martin [with J.J. Carey], Dublin: Gill and Macmillan.

## 1969

'Literature and Society', in Kevin B. Nowlan and T. Desmond Willams, ed., *Ireland in the War Years and After* (Thomas Davis Lectures), Dublin: Gill and Macmillan.
*Soundings: Leaving Certificate Poetry Interim Anthology*, edited by Martin, Dublin: Gill and Macmillan.

## 1970

'Anglo-Irish Literature', in Michael Hurley SJ, ed., *Irish Anglicanism 1869–1969*, Dublin: Allen Figgis Limited, pp. 120–32. [Reprinted in this volume as 'Anglo-Irish Literature: The Protestant Legacy'.]
'The First Year Arts Student', *ATE Journal of the Association of Teachers of English* 1 (Easter 1970).
'The Future of University Autonomy (Comment)', *Studies* 59 (Autumn 1970), pp. 248–51.
*Introducing English: An Anthology of Prose and Poems*, edited by Martin, Dublin: Gill and Macmillan.

## 1971

*Winter's Tales from Ireland*, edited by Martin, Dublin: Gill and Macmillan; London: Macmillan.

## 1972

'*The Playboy of the Western World*: Christy Mahon and the Apotheosis of Loneliness', in S.B. Bushrui, ed., *A Centenary Tribute to John Millington Synge 1871–1909: Sunshine and the Moon's Delight*, Gerrards Cross: Colin Smythe, pp. 61–73.

'"The Secret Rose" and Yeats's Dialogue with History', *Ariel* 3.3. (Fall 1972), pp. 91–103.

James Stephens, *The Charwoman's Daughter*, edited with introduction by Martin, Dublin: Gill and Macmillan; London: Macmillan.

## 1973

'Explications of the Irish Short Story', *English for Seniors*, Schulfunk, Westdeutscher Rundfunk.

'Metaphysical Poetry', *ATE Journal of the Association of Teachers of English* 4 (Easter 1973).

*Study Guide Series* (General Editor), Dublin: Gill and Macmillan. Booklets on Dickens's *Hard Times* (1974), James Stephens's *The Charwoman's Daughter* (1974), Edgeworth's *Castle Rackrent* (1979).

## 1975

'Apocalyptic Structure in Yeats's *Secret Rose*', *Studies* 64 (Spring 1975), pp. 24–34.

## 1976

'Priest and Artist in Joyce's Early Fiction', in P.J. Drudy, ed., *Anglo-Irish Studies* 2, Chalfont St Giles, Bucks: Alpha Academic. pp. 69–81.

## 1977

*James Stephens: A Critical Study.* Dublin: Gill and Macmillan.

## 1978

'What Stalked Through the Post Office? (Reply to Seamus Deane)', *The Crane Bag* 2. 1 and 2 (1978), pp. 164–77.

## 1980

*Anglo-Irish Literature*. Dublin: Department of Foreign Affairs.

'Hound Voices Were They All: An Experiment in Yeats Criticism', in A. Norman Jeffares, ed., *Yeats, Sligo and Ireland: Essays to mark the 21st Yeats International Summer School,* Gerrards Cross: Colin Smythe, pp. 139–52.

James Stephens, *Desire, and Other Stories*, selected and with introduction by Martin, Dublin: Poolbeg Press.

## 1982

'Sin and Secrecy in Joyce's Fiction', in Suheil Badi Bushrui and Bernard Benstock, eds., *James Joyce: An International Perspective,* Gerrards Cross: Colin Smythe; Totowa, New Jersey: Barnes and Noble Books, pp. 143–55.

**1983**

'Donald Davie and Ireland', in George Dekker, ed., *Donald Davie and the Responsibilities of Literature*, Manchester: Carcanet, pp. 49–63.

'Joyce's Narrative Strategies in the Central Stories of *Dubliners*', in Karl-Heinz Westarp, ed., *Joyce Centenary Offshoots: James Joyce, 1882–1982*, Aarhus, Denmark: Seklos, Department of English, University of Aarhus; *The Dolphin* 8 (October 1983), pp. 27–46.

*W.B. Yeats*. Gill's Irish Lives, Dublin: Gill and Macmillan; revised and reissued in 1990 by Colin Smythe, Gerrards Cross, Bucks.

**1984**

'Kinesis, Stasis, and Revolution in Yeats's Plays', *Gaeliana* 6 (1984), pp. 155–62; reprinted in Okifumi Komesu and Masaru Sekine, eds., *Irish Writers and Politics*, Gerrards Cross: Colin Smythe, 1990, pp. 176–85.

'Novelist and City: The Technical Challenge.' in Maurice Harmon, ed., *The Irish Writer and the City*, Gerrards Cross, Bucks: Colin Smythe; Totowa, New Jersey: Barnes and Noble Books, pp. 37–51.

'Yeats's Revolutionary Drama', *Yeats Society of Japan Bulletin* 15 (October 1984).

**1985**

*The Genius of Irish Prose*, edited and with introduction by Martin, Dublin and Cork: The Mercier Press in assoc. with RTÉ.

'Fable and Fantasy', in *The Genius of Irish Prose*, pp. 110–20.

'Prose Fiction in the Irish Literary Renaissance', in Masaru Sekine, ed., *Irish Writers and Society at Large*, Gerrards Cross, Bucks: Colin Smythe; Totowa, New Jersey: Barnes and Noble Books, pp. 139–62.

**1986**

'Anglo-Irish Poetry: Moore to Ferguson', in Cyril J. Byrne and Margaret Harry, eds., *Talamh an Éisc: Canadian and Irish Essays*, Halifax, Nova Scotia: Nimbus Publishing, pp. 84–104; reprinted in *Canadian Journal of Irish Studies* 12.2 (June 1986), pp. 84–104.

'Apocalypse Then: Pastorini, Ferguson, Mangan, Yeats', *Gaeliana* 8, Caen: Centre de Publications de l'Université de Caen, pp. 55–62.

'Time and Place in *The Wild Swans at Coole*', *The Yeats Society of Japan Bulletin* 17 (October 1986), pp. 87–93.

**1987**

'The Apocalypse of Clay: Technique and Vision in *The Great Hunger*', in Peter Kavanagh, ed., *Patrick Kavanagh: Man and Poet*, Newbridge: The Goldsmith Press; Orono: University of Maine, pp. 285–93.

Mary Lavin, *The House in Clewe Street*, edited with critical afterword by Martin, London: Virago Press.

Mary Lavin, *Mary O'Grady*, edited with critical afterword by Martin, London: Virago Press.

## 1988

'Desmond Egan: Universal Midlander', *Etudes Irlandaises* 13.2, pp. 81–4.

'A House for the Irish Psyche: The Abbey Theatre from Yeats to Modern Times', *India International Centre Quarterly* 15.2 (Summer 1988), pp. 99–115.

'Technique and Passion in Clarke's *Mnemosyne Lay In Dust*', in Austin Clarke Supplement, *Poetry Ireland* 22/23 (Summer 1988), pp. 97–104.

'Julia Cahill, Father McTurnan, and the Geography of Nowhere [on George Moore's *The Untilled Field*]', in Robert Welch and Suheil Badi Bushrui, eds., *Literature and the Art of Creation: Essays and Poems in Honour of A. Norman Jeffares*, Gerrards Cross, Bucks: Colin Smythe; Totowa, New Jersey: Barnes and Noble Books, pp. 98–111.

## 1989

*Forgiveness: Ireland's Best Contemporary Short Stories*, edited with introduction by Martin, London: Ryan Publishing.

*Friendship: Twelve Masterpieces of Short Fiction*, edited with introduction by Martin, London: Ryan Publishing.

'The Yeatsean Apocalypse', in Jacqueline Genet, ed., *Studies on W.B. Yeats*, Caen: Groupe de Recherches d'Etudes anglo-irlandaises du C.N.R.S., pp. 223–37; revised and reprinted as 'Politics and the Yeatsian Apocalypse', in Peter Liebregts and Peter van de Kamp, ed., *Tumult of Images: Essays on W.B. Yeats and Politics; The Literature of Politics, The Politics of Literature* (Proceedings of the Leiden IASAIL Conference: 3), Amsterdam; Atlanta, Ga: Rodopi,1995, pp. 27–41.

## 1990

*James Joyce: The Artist and the Labyrinth,* edited with introduction by Martin, London: Ryan Publishing.

'The Artist and the Labyrinth', in *James Joyce: The Artist and the Labyrinth*, pp. 11–24.

W.B. Yeats, *Collected Poems*, edited with introduction and notes by Martin, London: Arrow Books, 544 pp.

'Yeats's Noh: The Dancer and the Dance', introduction to Masaru Sekine and Christopher Murray, eds., *Yeats and the Noh: A Comparative Study*, Gerrards Cross: Colin Smythe, pp. xiii–xviii.

## 1991

'Prose Fiction 1880–1945', edited and introduced by Martin, in Seamus Deane, ed., *The Field Day Anthology of Irish Writing* 2, Derry: Field Day Publications, pp. 1021–223.

## 1992

'Heart Mysteries There', *Yeats: An Annual of Critical and Textual Studies* 10 (1992), pp. 187–9.

'That Childhood Country: Extracts from a Biography of Patrick Kavanagh', *Irish University Review* 22.1 (Spring/Summer 1992), pp. 107–26.

## 1993

'Quest and Vision: [Eavan Boland's] *The Journey*', *Irish University Review* 23.1 (Spring/Summer 1993), pp. 75–85.

## 1994

'The Fabulous Realism of Bryan MacMahon', in Gabriel Fitzmaurice, ed., *The Listowel Literary Phenomenon: North Kerry Writers — A Critical Introduction*, Conamara: Cló Iar–Chonnachta, pp. 83–95.

'Technique and Territory in Brendan Kennelly's Early Work', in Richard Pine, ed., *Dark Fathers into Light: Brendan Kennelly*, Newcastle-upon-Tyne: Bloodaxe, pp. 36–49.

## 1996

'Kavanagh and After: An Ambiguous Legacy', in Theo Dorgan, ed., *Irish Poetry Since Kavanagh*, Dublin: Four Courts Press, pp. 21–31.

'Clarke — A Life' and 'Clarke — His Literary Legacy', in R. Dardis Clarke, ed., *Austin Clarke Remembered*, Dublin: The Bridge Press, pp. 66–82.

*The Works of James Clarence Mangan* (six volumes), General Editor, Dublin: Irish Academic Press.

*The Collected Prose of James Clarence Mangan* (Volume V of the Works), edited by Martin, Peter van de Kamp and Jacques Chuto, Dublin: Irish Academic Press.

'John Montague: Passionate Contemplative', in Jacqueline Genet and Wynne Hellegouarc'h, eds., *Irish Writers and Their Creative Process*, Gerrards Cross: Colin Smythe, pp. 37–51.

'The Past and the Peasant in the Stories of Seamus O'Kelly', in Jacqueline Genet, ed., *Rural Ireland, Real Ireland?*, Gerrards Cross: Colin Smythe, pp. 185–200

# Index